# Team Leadership and Management

# Team Leadership and Management

Thomas Husher

RANDOM PUBLICATIONS
NEW DELHI - 110 002 (INDIA)

**Team Leadership and Management**

---

ISBN 978-93-51113-05-8


Published in 2014 in India by

**RANDOM PUBLICATIONS**

4376-A/4B, Gali Murari Lal, Ansari Road
New Delhi-110 002
Phone: +9111-43580356, 23289044
E-mail: randomexports@gmail.com; sales@randompublications.com;
info@randompublications.com

Reprinted 2021

*Type Setting by:* Friends Media, Delhi-110089
*Digitally Printed at:* Replika Press Pvt. Ltd.

# Preface

There are many elements that create and are essential to be an effective leader that has the power to motivate a team and drive success. There is often a balancing act that the leader must manage between being a leader and a member while ensuring the goal is clear and obtainable. There are six leadership competencies that are the building blocks to becoming an effective leader; focus on the goal, ensure a collaborative climate, build confidence, demonstrate sufficient technical know-how, set priorities, and manage performance as described *When Teams Work Best* by LaFasto and Larson. Therefore, the question arises, "Does an effective team leader both merge into the group as a member of the team and also maintain a leadership role? And if so, how?" A leader is the key player in the game that is comprised of challenge and risk. Therefore, an effective team leader must be both a component to the team and also a leader to manage the team's progress. The leader cannot possibly be competent in every area without being engaged in the team. The leader must know each member and the team as a whole in order to bring them all together and create a process that is open, productive, and promotes confidence. An effective leader uses each member's contributions and energy to focus on a common goal. Essentially, a leader's job is to add importance to the team's effort, which cannot be done without being a member.

It is very common for a team leader to be in the dark about their team and the everyday operations. This is a consequence of a leader's disengagement and lack of membership with the team. Moreover, the team's contention usually gives birth at this point and lends itself to decreased productivity and satisfaction. An effective leader needs to be able to pinpoint problems and praise excellence within the group, which cannot be done from the sideline. The leader is a part of the overall process; therefore, a relationship naturally exists. However, it is up to the leader whether to nurture that relationship or minimize its importance. The team leader must understand the team's vision and clearly define the goal to guarantee success and member loyalty. One cannot lead a team without knowing the purpose and goal of the team. Furthermore, a team leader must create a collaborative climate to ensure that the best thinking and ideas of the team are represented. Again, a wholesome climate cannot be established without knowing the members and becoming engaged in the team. The foundation of a highly motivated and successful team is the member's understanding and relevance of their goal. An effective leader's trust in the team goal is vital to the member's commitment. The members become isolated and discouraged when the leader's investment is minimal. Team members want the opportunity to prove their value and worth to the goal and the leader. The leader must be involved and a member of the team to effectively influence the member's productivity and function in the grand scheme of things. There has been a gradual progression and contemporary focus on the leader's mutual relationship with the members as opposed to the authority position in the modern day. This leader-member relationship breeds trust, confidence, stimulation, responsiveness, and problem solving which are the keys for success and satisfaction. As demonstrated, an effective leader should be a part and merge with the team and simultaneously lead and encourage it's constituents toward the goal. The leader can bring inspiring growth or demise to a team and company; therefore, it is essential for a leader to be effective and powerful.

The present book has been planned in such a way to given an overall view of this subject.

I thank all members of my team who have helped in the preparation of the book. My special thanks go to "Random Publications" who have published the book.

*—Thomas Husher*

# Contents

# 1

# Leadership Theories

Leadership has been described as the "process of social influence in which one person can enlist the aid and support of others in the accomplishment of a common task". Definitions inclusive of nature of leadership have also emerged. Alan Keith of Genentech states that, "Leadership is ultimately about creating a way for people to contribute to making something extraordinary happen." According to Ken "SKC" Ogbonnia, "effective leadership is the ability to successfully integrate and maximize available resources within the internal and external environment for the attainment of organizational or societal goals."

## Theories

Leadership is "organizing a group of people to achieve a common goal." The leader may or may not have any formal authority. Students of leadership have produced theories involving traits, situational interaction, function, behaviour, power, vision and values, charisma, and intelligence among others.

### *Rise of Alternative Theories*

In the late 1940s and early 1950s, however, a series of qualitative reviews of these studies prompted researchers to take a drastically different view of the driving forces behind leadership. In reviewing the extant literature, Stogdill and Mann found that while some traits were common across a number of studies, the overall evidence suggested that persons who are leaders in one situation may not necessarily be leaders in other situations.

Subsequently, leadership was no longer characterized as an enduring individual trait, as situational approaches posited that individuals can be effective in certain situations, but not others. This approach dominated much of the leadership theory and research for the next few decades.

### Reemergence of Trait Theory

New methods and measurements were developed after these influential reviews that would ultimately reestablish the trait theory as a viable approach to the study of leadership. For example, improvements in researchers' use of the round robin research design methodology allowed researchers to see that individuals can and do emerge as leaders across a variety of situations and tasks. Additionally, during the 1980s statistical advances allowed researchers to conduct meta-analyses, in which they could quantitatively analyse and summarize the findings from a wide array of studies.

This advent allowed trait theorists to create a comprehensive and parsimonious picture of previous leadership research rather than rely on the qualitative reviews of the past. Equipped with new methods, leadership researchers revealed the following:

- Individuals can and do emerge as leaders across a variety of situations and tasks
- Significant relationships exist between leadership and such individual traits as:
- intelligence
- adjustment
- extraversion
- conscientiousness
- openness to experience
- general self-efficacy.

While the trait theory of leadership has certainly regained popularity, its reemergence has not been accompanied by a corresponding increase in sophisticated conceptual frameworks.

Specifically, Zaccaro (2007) noted that trait theories still:

1. Focus on a small set of individual attributes such as Big Five personality traits, to the neglect of cognitive abilities, motives, values, social skills, expertise, and problem-solving skills
2. Fail to consider patterns or integrations of multiple attributes
3. Do not distinguish between those leader attributes that are generally not malleable over time and those that are shaped by, and bound to, situational influences

4. Do not consider how stable leader attributes account for the behavioural diversity necessary for effective leadership

### *Attribute Pattern Approach*

Considering the criticisms of the trait theory outlined above, several researchers have begun to adopt a different perspective of leader individual differences-the leader attribute pattern approach. In contrast to the traditional approach, the leader attribute pattern approach is based on theorists' arguments that the influence of individual characteristics on outcomes is best understood by considering the person as an integrated totality rather than a summation of individual variables. In other words, the leader attribute pattern approach argues that integrated constellations or combinations of individual differences may explain substantial variance in both leader emergence and leader effectiveness beyond that explained by single attributes, or by additive combinations of multiple attributes.

### *Behavioural and Style Theories*

In response to the early criticisms of the trait approach, theorists began to research leadership as a set of behaviours, evaluating the behaviour of 'successful' leaders, determining a behaviour taxonomy and identifying broad leadership styles. David McClelland, for example, Leadership takes a strong personality with a well-developed positive ego. Not so much as a pattern of motives, but a set of traits is crucial. To lead; self-confidence and a high self-esteem is useful, perhaps even essential. [Kevin Mick]

Kurt Lewin, Ronald Lipitt, and Ralph White developed in 1939 the seminal work on the influence of leadership styles and performance. The researchers evaluated the performance of groups of eleven-year-old boys under different types of work climate. In each, the leader exercised his influence regarding the type of group decision making, praise and criticism (feedback), and the management of the group tasks (project management) according to three styles: authoritarian, democratic and laissez-faire.

The managerial grid model is also based on a behavioural theory. The model was developed by Robert Blake and Jane Mouton in 1964 and suggests five different leadership styles, based on the leaders' concern for people and their concern for goal achievement.

### *Positive Reinforcement*

B.F. Skinner is the father of behaviour modification and developed the concept of positive reinforcement. Positive reinforcement occurs when a positive stimulus is presented in response to a behaviour, increasing the likelihood of that behaviour in the future. The following is an example of how positive reinforcement can be used in a business setting. Assume praise is a positive reinforcer for a particular employee. This employee does not show up to work on time every day. The manager of this employee decides to praise the employee for showing up on time every day the employee actually shows up to work on time. As a result, the employee comes to work on time more often because the employee likes to be praised. In this example, praise (i.e. stimulus) is a positive reinforcer for this employee because the employee arrives (i.e. behaviour) to work on time more frequently after being praised for showing up to work on time.

The use of positive reinforcement is a successful and growing technique used by leaders to motivate and attain desired behaviours from subordinates. Organizations such as Frito-Lay, 3M, Goodrich, Michigan Bell, and Emery Air Freight have all used reinforcement to increase productivity. Empirical research covering the last 20 years suggests that reinforcement theory has a 17 percent increase in performance. Additionally, many reinforcement techniques such as the use of praise are inexpensive, providing higher performance for lower costs.

### Situational and Contingency Theories

Situational theory also appeared as a reaction to the trait theory of leadership. Social scientists argued that history was more than the result of intervention of great men as Carlyle suggested. Herbert Spencer (1884) said that the times produce the person and not the other way around. This theory assumes that different situations call for different characteristics; according to this group of theories, no single optimal psychographic profile of a leader exists. According to the theory, "what an individual actually does when acting as a leader is in large part dependent upon characteristics of the situation in which he functions."

Some theorists started to synthesize the trait and situational approaches. Building upon the research of Lewin et al., academics began to normatize the descriptive models of leadership climates, defining three leadership styles and identifying which situations each style works better in. The *authoritarian leadership style*, for example, is approved in periods of crisis but fails to win the "hearts and minds" of their followers in the day-to-day management; the *democratic leadership style* is more adequate in situations that require consensus building; finally, the *laissez faire leadership style* is appreciated by the degree of freedom it provides, but as the leader does not "take charge", he can be perceived as a failure in protracted or thorny organizational problems. Thus, theorists defined the style of leadership as contingent to the situation, which is sometimes classified as contingency theory. Four contingency leadership theories appear more prominently in the recent years: Fiedler contingency model, Vroom-Yetton decision model, the path-goal theory, and the Hersey-Blanchard situational theory.

The Fiedler contingency model bases the leader's effectiveness on what Fred Fiedler called *situational contingency*. This results from the interaction of leadership style and situational favorableness (later called "situational control"). The theory defined two types of leader: those who tend to accomplish the task by developing good-relationships with the group (*relationship-oriented*), and those who have as their prime concern carrying out the task itself (*task-oriented*). According to Fiedler, there is no ideal leader. Both task-oriented and relationship-oriented leaders can be effective if their leadership orientation fits the situation. When there is a good leader-member relation, a highly structured task, and high leader position power, the situation is considered a "favorable situation". Fiedler found that task-oriented leaders are more effective in extremely favourable or unfavourable situations, whereas relationship-oriented leaders perform best in situations with intermediate favourability.

Victor Vroom, in collaboration with Phillip Yetton (1973) and later with Arthur Jago (1988), developed a taxonomy for describing leadership situations, taxonomy that was used in a normative decision model where leadership styles were connected to situational variables, defining which approach was more suitable to which situation. This approach was novel because it supported the idea that the same manager could rely on different group decision making approaches depending on the attributes of each situation. This model was later referred as situational contingency theory.

The path-goal theory of leadership was developed by Robert House (1971) and was based on the expectancy theory of Victor Vroom. According to House, the essence of the theory is "the meta proposition that leaders, to be effective, engage in behaviours that complement subordinates' environments and abilities in a manner that compensates for deficiencies and is instrumental to subordinate satisfaction and individual and work unit performance. The theory identifies four leader behaviours, *achievement-oriented, directive, participative,* and *supportive*, that are contingent to the environment factors and follower characteristics. In contrast to the Fiedler contingency model, the path-goal model states that the four leadership behaviours are fluid, and that leaders can adopt any of the four depending on what the situation demands. The path-goal model can be classified both as a contingency theory, as it depends on the circumstances, but also as a transactional leadership theory, as the theory emphasizes the reciprocity behaviour between the leader and the followers.

The situational leadership model proposed by Hersey and Blanchard suggests four leadership-styles and four levels of follower-development. For effectiveness, the model posits that the leadership-style must match the appropriate level of followership-development. In this model, leadership behaviour becomes a function not only of the characteristics of the leader, but of the characteristics of followers as well.

### Functional Theory

Functional leadership theory is a particularly useful theory for addressing specific leader behaviours expected to contribute to organizational or unit effectiveness. This theory argues that the leader's main job is to see that whatever is necessary to group needs is taken care of; thus, a leader can be said to have done their job well when they have contributed to group effectiveness and cohesion While functional leadership theory has most often been applied to team leadership. It has also been effectively applied to broader organizational leadership as well (Zaccaro, 2001). In summarizing literature on functional leadership observed five broad functions a leader performs when promoting organization's effectiveness. These functions include: (1) environmental monitoring, (2) organizing subordinate activities, (3) teaching and coaching subordinates, (4) motivating others, and (5) intervening actively in the group's work.

A variety of leadership behaviours are expected to facilitate these functions. In initial work identifying leader behaviour, Fleishman (1953) observed that subordinates perceived their supervisors' behaviour in terms of two broad categories referred to as consideration and initiating structure.

Consideration includes behaviour involved in fostering effective relationships. Examples of such behaviour would include showing concern for a subordinate or acting in a supportive manner towards others. Initiating structure involves the actions of the leader focused specifically on task accomplishment. This could include role clarification, setting performance standards, and holding subordinates accountable to those standards.

### *Transactional and Transformational Theories*

Eric Berne first analysed the relations between a group and its leadership in terms of Transactional Analysis.

The transactional leader (Burns, 1978) is given power to perform certain tasks and reward or punish for the team's performance.

It gives the opportunity to the manager to lead the group and the group agrees to follow his lead to accomplish a predetermined goal in exchange for something else. Power is given to the leader to evaluate, correct and train subordinates when productivity is not up to the desired level and reward effectiveness when expected outcome is reached.

The transformational leader (Burns, 1978) motivates its team to be effective and efficient. Communication is the base for goal achievement focusing the group on the final desired outcome or goal attainment. This leader is highly visible and uses chain of command to get the job done. Transformational leaders focus on the big picture, needing to be surrounded by people who take care of the details. The leader is always looking for ideas that move the organization to reach the company's vision.

### *Emotions*

Leadership can be perceived as a particularly emotion-laden process, with emotions entwined with the social influence process. In an organization, the leader's mood has some effects on his/her group. These effects can be described in 3 levels:

1. The mood of individual group members. Group members with leaders in a positive mood experience more positive mood than do group members with leaders in a negative mood. The leaders transmit their moods to other group members through the mechanism of emotional contagion. Mood contagion may be one of the psychological mechanisms by which charismatic leaders influence followers.
2. The affective tone of the group. Group affective tone represents the consistent or homogeneous affective reactions within a group. Group affective tone is an aggregate of the moods of the individual members of the group and refers to mood at the group level of analysis. Groups with leaders in a positive mood

have a more positive affective tone than do groups with leaders in a negative mood.

3. Group processes like coordination, effort expenditure, and task strategy. Public expressions of mood impact how group members think and act. When people experience and express mood, they send signals to others. Leaders signal their goals, intentions, and attitudes through their expressions of moods. For example, expressions of positive moods by leaders signal that leaders deem progress toward goals to be good. The group members respond to those signals cognitively and behaviorally in ways that are reflected in the group processes.

In research about client service, it was found that expressions of positive mood by the leader improve the performance of the group, although in other sectors there were other findings.

Beyond the leader's mood, her/his behaviour is a source for employee positive and negative emotions at work. The leader creates situations and events that lead to emotional response. Certain leader behaviours displayed during interactions with their employees are the sources of these affective events. Leaders shape workplace affective events. Examples – feedback giving, allocating tasks, resource distribution. Since employee behaviour and productivity are directly affected by their emotional states, it is imperative to consider employee emotional responses to organizational leaders. Emotional intelligence, the ability to understand and manage moods and emotions in the self and others, contributes to effective leadership in organizations.

### *Neo-emergent Theory*

The Neo-emergent leadership theory (from the Oxford school of leadership) espouses that leadership is created through the emergence of information by the leader or other stakeholders, not through the true actions of the leader himself. In other words, the reproduction of information or stories form the basis of the perception of leadership by the majority. It is well known that the great naval hero Lord Nelson often wrote his own versions of battles he was involved in, so that when he arrived home in England he would receive a true hero's welcome. In modern society, the press, blogs and other sources report their own views of a leader, which may be based on reality, but may also be based on a political command, a payment, or an inherent interest of the author, media or leader. Therefore, it can be contended that the perception of all leaders is created and in fact does not reflect their true leadership qualities at all.

### Styles

Leadership style refers to a leader's behaviour. It is the result of the philosophy, personality and experience of the leader.

### Autocratic or Authoritarian Style

Under the autocratic leadership style, all decision-making powers are centralized in the leader, as with dictator leaders.

They do not entertain any suggestions or initiatives from subordinates. The autocratic management has been successful as it provides strong motivation to the manager. It permits quick decision-making, as only one person decides for the whole group and keeps each decision to himself until he feels it is needed to be shared with the rest of the group.

### Participative or Democratic Style

The democratic leadership style favours decision-making by the group as shown, such as leader gives instruction after consulting the group. They can win the co-operation of their group and can motivate them effectively and positively. The decisions of the democratic leader are not unilateral as with the autocrat because they arise from consultation with the group members and participation by them.

### Laissez-faire or Free Rein Style

A free-rein leader does not lead, but leaves the group entirely to itself as shown; such a leader allows maximum freedom to subordinates, i.e., they are given a free hand in deciding their own policies and methods.

Different situations call for different leadership styles. In an emergency when there is little time to converge on an agreement and where a designated authority has significantly more experience or expertise than the rest of the team, an autocratic leadership style may be most effective; however, in a highly motivated and aligned team with a homogeneous level of expertise, a more democratic or laissez-faire style may be more effective. The style adopted should be the one that most effectively achieves the objectives of the group while balancing the interests of its individual members.

### Narcissistic Leadership

Various academics such as Kets de Vries, Maccoby and Thomas have identified narcissistic leadership as an important and common leadership style.

### Toxic Leadership

A toxic leader is someone who has responsibility over a group of people or an organization, and who abuses the leader-follower relationship by leaving the group or organization in a worse-off condition than when s/he first found them.

## Performance

In the past, some researchers have argued that the actual influence of leaders on organizational outcomes is overrated and romanticized as a result of biased attributions about leaders. Despite these assertions however, it is largely recognized and accepted by practitioners and researchers that leadership is important, and research supports the notion that leaders do contribute to key organizational outcomes . To facilitate successful performance it is important to understand and accurately measure leadership performance.

Job performance generally refers to behaviour that is expected to contribute to organizational success (Campbell, 1990). Campbell identified a number of specific types of performance dimensions; leadership was one of the dimensions that he identified. There is no consistent, overall definition of leadership performance (Yukl, 2006). Many distinct conceptualizations are often lumped together under the umbrella of leadership performance, including outcomes such as leader effectiveness, leader advancement, and leader emergence (Kaiser et al., 2008). For instance, leadership performance may be used to refer to the career success of the individual leader, performance of the group or organization, or even leader emergence. Each of these measures can be considered conceptually distinct. While these aspects may be related, they are different outcomes and their inclusion should depend on the applied/research focus.

## Contexts

### Organizations

An organization that is established as an instrument or means for achieving defined objectives has been referred to as a formal organization. Its design specifies how goals are subdivided and reflected in subdivisions of the organization. Divisions, departments, sections, positions, jobs, and tasks make up this work structure. Thus, the formal organization is expected to behave impersonally in regard to relationships with clients or with its members. According to Weber's definition, entry and subsequent advancement is by merit or seniority.

Each employee receives a salary and enjoys a degree of tenure that safeguards her/him from the arbitrary influence of superiors or of powerful clients. The higher his position in the hierarchy, the greater his presumed expertise in adjudicating problems that may arise in the course of the work carried out at lower levels of the organization. It is this bureaucratic structure that forms the basis for the appointment of heads or chiefs of administrative subdivisions in the organization and endows them with the authority attached to their position.

In contrast to the appointed head or chief of an administrative unit, a leader emerges within the context of the informal organization that underlies the formal structure. The informal organization expresses the personal objectives and goals of the individual membership. Their objectives and goals may or may not coincide with those of the formal organization. The informal organization represents an extension of the social structures that generally characterize human life — the spontaneous emergence of groups and organizations as ends in themselves.

In prehistoric times, humanity was preoccupied with personal security, maintenance, protection, and survival. Now humanity spends a major portion of waking hours working for organizations. Her/His need to identify with a community that provides security, protection, maintenance, and a feeling of belonging continues unchanged from prehistoric times. This need is met by the informal organization and its emergent, or unofficial, leaders.

Leaders emerge from within the structure of the informal organization. Their personal qualities, the demands of the situation, or a combination of these and other factors attract followers who accept their leadership within one or several overlay structures. Instead of the authority of position held by an appointed head or chief, the emergent leader wields influence or power. Influence is the ability of a person to gain co-operation from others by means of persuasion or control over rewards. Power is a stronger form of influence because it reflects a person's ability to enforce action through the control of a means of punishment.

A leader is a person who influences a group of people towards a specific result. It is not dependent on title or formal authority. (elevos, paraphrased from Leaders, Bennis, and Leadership Presence, Halpern & Lubar). Ogbonnia (2007) defines an effective leader "as an individual with the capacity to consistently succeed in a given condition and be viewed as meeting the expectations of an organization or society." Leaders are recognized by their capacity for caring for others, clear communication, and a commitment to persist. An individual who is appointed to a managerial position has the right to command and enforce obedience by virtue of the authority of his position. However, she or he must possess adequate personal attributes to match his authority, because authority is only potentially available to him.

In the absence of sufficient personal competence, a manager may be confronted by an emergent leader who can challenge her/his role in the organization and reduce it to that of a figurehead. However, only authority of position has the backing of formal sanctions. It follows that whoever wields personal influence and power can legitimize this only by gaining a formal position in the hierarchy, with commensurate authority. Leadership can be defined as one's ability to get others to willingly follow. Every organization needs leaders at every level.

### Management

Over the years the philosophical terminology of "management" and "leadership" have, in the organisational context, been used both as synonyms and with clearly differentiated meanings. Debate is fairly common about whether the use of these terms should be restricted, and generally reflects an awareness of the distinction made by Burns (1978) between "transactional" leadership (characterised by e.g. emphasis on procedures, contingent reward, management by exception) and "transformational" leadership (characterised by e.g. charisma, personal relationships, creativity).

### Group Leadership

In contrast to individual leadership, some organizations have adopted group leadership. In this situation, more than one person provides direction to the group as a whole. Some organizations have taken this approach in hopes of increasing creativity, reducing costs, or downsizing. Others may see the traditional leadership of a boss as costing too much in team performance. In some situations, the main the team member(s) best able to handle any given phase of the project become(s) the temporary leader(s). Additionally, as each team member has the opportunity to experience the elevated level of empowerment, it energizes staff and feeds the cycle of success. Leaders who demonstrate persistence, tenacity, determination and synergistic communication skills will bring out the same qualities in their groups. Good leaders use their own inner mentors to energize their team and organizations and lead a team to achieve success.

*According to the National School Boards Association (USA)*

These Group Leadership or Leadership Teams have specific characteristics:

Characteristics of a Team:

- There must be an awareness of unity on the part of all its members.
- There must be interpersonal relationship. Members must have a chance to contribute, learn from and work with others.
- The member must have the ability to act together toward a common goal.

Ten characteristics of well-functioning teams:

- Purpose: Members proudly share a sense of why the team exists and are invested in accomplishing its mission and goals.
- Priorities: Members know what needs to be done next, by whom, and by when to achieve team goals.
- Roles: Members know their roles in getting tasks done and when to allow a more skillful member to do a certain task.
- Decisions: Authority and decision-making lines are clearly understood.
- Conflict: Conflict is dealt with openly and is considered important to decision-making and personal growth.
- Personal traits: members feel their unique personalities are appreciated and well utilized.
- Norms: Group norms for working together are set and seen as standards for every one in the groups.
- Effectiveness: Members find team meetings efficient and productive and look forward to this time together.
- Success: Members know clearly when the team has met with success and share in this equally and proudly.
- Training: Opportunities for feedback and updating skills are provided and taken advantage of by team members.

## Primates

Mark van Vugt and Anjana Ahuja in Naturally Selected: The Evolutionary Science of Leadership present evidence of leadership in nonhuman animals, from leadership in ants and bees to baboons and chimpanzees. They suggest that leadership has a long evolutionary history and that the same mechanisms underpinning leadership in humans can be found in other social species too. Richard Wrangham and Dale Peterson, in *Demonic Males: Apes and the Origins of Human Violence* present evidence that only humans and chimpanzees, among all the animals living on earth, share a similar tendency for a cluster of behaviours: violence, territoriality, and competition for uniting behind the one chief male of the land. This position is contentious. Many animals beyond apes are territorial, compete, exhibit violence, and have a social structure controlled by a dominant male (lions, wolves, etc.), suggesting Wrangham and Peterson's evidence is not empirical. However, we must examine other species as well, including elephants (which are matriarchal and follow an alpha female), meerkats (who are likewise matriarchal), and many others.

It would be beneficial, to examine that most accounts of leadership over the past few millennia (since the creation of Christian religions) are through the perspective of a patriarchal society, founded on Christian literature. If one looks before these times, it is noticed that Pagan and Earth-based tribes in fact had female leaders. It is important also to note that the peculiarities of one tribe cannot necessarily be ascribed to another, as even our modern-day customs differ.

The current day patrilineal custom is only a recent invention in human history and our original method of familial practices were matrilineal. The fundamental assumption that has been built into 90% of the world's countries is that patriarchy is the 'natural' biological predisposition of homo sapiens. Unfortunately, this belief has led to the widespread oppression of women in all of those countries, but in varying degrees. The Iroquoian First Nations tribes are an example of a matrilineal tribe, along with Mayan tribes, and also the society of Meghalaya, India.

By comparison, bonobos, the second-closest species-relatives of man, do *not* unite behind the chief male of the land. The bonobos show deference to an alpha or top-ranking female that, with the support of her coalition of other females, can prove as strong as the strongest male in the land. Thus, if leadership amounts to getting the greatest number of followers, then among the bonobos, a female almost always exerts the strongest and most effective leadership. However, not all scientists agree on the allegedly "peaceful" nature of the bonobo or its reputation as a "hippie chimp".

## Historical Views

Sanskrit literature identifies ten types of leaders. Defining characteristics of the ten types of leaders are explained with examples from history and mythology. Aristocratic thinkers have postulated that leadership depends on one's blue blood or genes: monarchy takes an extreme view of the same idea, and may prop up its assertions against the claims of mere aristocrats by invoking divine sanction: see the divine right of kings. Contrariwise, more democratically-inclined theorists have pointed to examples of meritocratic leaders, such as the Napoleonic marshals profiting from careers open to talent.

In the autocratic/paternalistic strain of thought, traditionalists recall the role of leadership of the Roman *pater familias*. Feminist thinking, on the other hand, may object to such models as patriarchal and posit against them emotionally-attuned, responsive, and consensual empathetic guidance, which is sometimes associated with matriarchies.

Comparable to the Roman tradition, the views of Confucianism on "right living" relate very much to the ideal of the (male) scholar-leader and his benevolent rule, buttressed by a tradition of filial piety.

Leadership is a matter of intelligence, trustworthiness, humaneness, courage, and discipline... Reliance on intelligence alone results in rebelliousness. Exercise of humaneness alone results in weakness. Fixation on trust results in folly. Dependence on the strength of courage results in violence. Excessive discipline and sternness in command result in cruelty. When one has all five virtues together, each appropriate to its function, then one can be a leader. — Sun Tzu

In the 19th century, the elaboration of anarchist thought called the whole concept of leadership into question. (Note that the *Oxford English Dictionary* traces the word "leadership" in English only as far back as the 19th century.) One response to this denial of élitism came with Leninism, which demanded an élite group of disciplined cadres to act as the vanguard of a socialist revolution, bringing into existence the dictatorship of the proletariat.

Other historical views of leadership have addressed the seeming contrasts between secular and religious leadership. The doctrines of Caesaro-papism have recurred and had their detractors over several centuries. Christian thinking on leadership has often emphasized stewardship of divinely-provided resources-human and material-and their deployment in accordance with a Divine plan. Compare servant leadership. For a more general take on leadership in politics, compare the concept of the statesman.

## Action Oriented Environments

This is a unique approach to team leadership that is aimed at action oriented environments where effective functional leadership is required to achieve critical or reactive tasks by small teams deployed into the field. In other words leadership of small groups often created to respond to a situation or critical incident.

In most cases these teams are tasked to operate in remote and changeable environments with limited support or backup (action environments). Leadership of people in these environments requires a different set of skills to that of front line management. These leaders must effectively operate remotely and negotiate both the needs of the individual, team and task within a changeable environment.

This has been termed Action Oriented Leadership. Some example action oriented leadership is demonstrated in the following ways: extinguishing a rural fire, locating a missing person, leading a team on an outdoor expedition or rescuing a person from a potentially hazardous environment.

## Titles Emphasizing Authority

At certain stages in their development, the hierarchies of social ranks implied different degrees or ranks of leadership in society. Thus a knight led fewer men in general than did a duke; a baronet might in theory control less land than an earl.

In the course of the 18th and 20th centuries, several political operators took non-traditional paths to become dominant in their societies. They or their systems often expressed a belief in strong individual leadership, but existing titles and labels ("King", "Emperor", "President" and so on) often seemed inappropriate, insufficient or downright inaccurate in some circumstances. The formal or informal titles or descriptions they or their flunkies employ express and foster a general veneration for leadership of the inspired and autocratic variety. The definite article when used as part of the title (in languages that use definite articles) emphasizes the existence of a sole "true" leader.

### *Varieties of Individual Power*

According to Patrick J. Montana and Bruce H. Charnov, the ability to attain these unique powers is what enables leadership to influence subordinates and peers by controlling organizational resources. The successful leader effectively uses these power(s) to influence employees, and it is important for the leader to understand the uses of power to strengthen the leadership functioning.

The authors distinguish the following types of organizational power:

- Legitimate Power refers to the different types of professional positions within an organization structure that inherit such power (e.g. Manager, Vice President, Director, Supervisor, etc.). These levels of power correspond to the hierarchical executive levels within the organization itself. The higher position such as President of the company has a higher power than the rest of professional positions in the hierarchical executive levels.
- Reward Power is the power given to managers that attain administrative power over a range of rewards. Employees who work for managers desire the reward from the manager and will be influenced by receiving it as a result of work performance. The rewards may be pay raisse or promotions.
- Coercive Power is the manager's ability to punish an employee. Punishment can be a mild punishment such as a suspension or a serious punishment such as termination.
- Expert Power is attained by the manager due to his or her own talents such as skills, knowledge, abilities, or previous experience. A manager which has this power within the organization may be a very valuable and important manager in the company.
- Charisma Power A manager who has charisma will have a positive influence on workers, and create the opportunity for interpersonal influence. A person has charisma, and this will confer great power as a manager.
- Referent Power a power that is gained by association. A person who has power by association is often referred to assistant or deputy.
- Information Power a person who has possession of important information at an important time when such information is needed to organizational functioning. Someone who has this information knowledge has genuine power. For example, a manager's secretary would be in a powerful position if the secretary has information power.

Corporations are the most common form of business organization, and one which is chartered by a state and given many legal rights as an entity separate from its owners. This form of business is characterized by the limited liability of its owners, the issuance of shares of easily transferable stock, and existence as a going concern.

The process of becoming a corporation, called incorporation, gives the company separate legal standing from its owners and protects those owners from being personally liable in the event that the company is sued (a condition known as limited liability). Incorporation also provides companies with a more flexible way to manage their ownership structure. In addition, there are different tax implications for corporations, although these can be both advantageous and disadvantageous. In these respects, corporations differ from sole proprietorships and limited partnership.

## Corporate Leadership

Probably the biggest challenge corporations or organizations face today is balancing the need for increasing shareholder value while simultaneously providing a work environment that truly engages the passion and commitment of its' employees. Increasingly, corporate growth and profitability depend upon an organization's ability to mentally engage and retain its workforce. Workforce demographics and attitudes are shifting at a rapid pace. Boomers, who make up the bulk of management and leadership with most large organizations today, traditionally worked in an environment characterized by the exchange of labour for the promise of lasting employment and financial reward. This is no longer a concept that works within our society. There is an undeniable need for a different social contract within our workplace. Employees, whether they be GenXers or Boomers, are not willing to trade in their intellectual capital, passion, and life energy in exchange for the "opportunity" to work within a corporate environment where they are shunned from employing initiative, taking risks, and being innovative and creative. Today's employees demand personal growth and learning that will engage and stimulate them. They want to be challenged, and they need to be trusted and held accountable.

Every year at The Banff Centre for Management, we work with over 3,000 executives, middle, and senior level managers from over 1,000 organizations in Canada and the U.S. on our leadership development programs. Although these individuals are focused on improving upon existing leadership skills and developing new ones, one common theme that they all share is a thirst for effective, impactful corporate or organizational leadership. Our experience in increasing leadership effectiveness at both the corporate and individual level is that enduring, impactful leadership within corporations must start at the top and become part of an organization's culture.

The best leadership development initiatives at the individual level will not benefit the organization long-term, if the organization cannot provide the supporting organizational culture, including structures, process, and systems necessary for individual leadership to develop within a corporation. Effective leadership, at both the individual and corporate level, is the key to long-term organizational results in our ever-changing business landscape. Now, more than ever before, there is a need for corporate leadership. The crucial role of corporate culture

Over the long-term, an organization's culture alone probably does more to influence corporate leadership than anything else does. It determines how individuals and organizations as a whole react and perform on a daily basis. An organization's culture is comprised of years and years of history, which includes successes and failures, good and bad decisions, and individual and collective stories.

All of these create a set of values, explicit and implicit, for the corporation that underpins the corporation's leadership culture. Organizational culture is synonymous with leadership culture and determines how leadership is or isn't manifested in an organization. And just as individuals demonstrate good and bad leadership, so do corporations!

What we see...

So often, we see organizations investing in leadership development at the individual level while the corporation's values and leadership culture remain unchanged. At the individual level this disconnect typically results in individuals returning to the workplace where they try to implement some of these new behaviours. At the individual and team level these new behaviours are very often successful; however, at a corporate level they often are not. If employees are persistent then they may be able to continue to demonstrate these new behaviours even though they are not supported or encouraged by the organization. However, this is usually stressful for individuals and often they will abandon these new behaviours – despite the fact that they have been somewhat successful – in order to conform to the organization's values, or they will leave the organization in search of another organization that is aligned with their values, or perhaps do both. The organization then often attributes blame for the departure to the individual, or to "turnover," rather than attributing it to the organization.

The greatest two single corporate leadership issues we see in organizations today are lack of trust and poor communication –

specifically communication regarding corporate values, vision, mission, and critical success factors. Combined, these two elements seem to be at the root of leadership duress within organizations. Trust is a heady, multifaceted, and elusive concept that pervades and manifests itself in everything we do. It comprises such weighty ideals such as accountability, integrity, truth, and honesty. As with individual leaders, nothing erodes or destroys corporate leadership more than not being trusted by its employees.

Sure distrustful leaders might achieve mediocre results, but they will never be able to truly harness people's passion and generate the energy truly required to achieve outstanding business results. Continuously, we hear middle and senior level managers citing the inability or failure of senior management and the organization as a whole to "walk the talk" as a critical dissatisfier and prime indicator of lack of leadership. Poor communication (and this includes listening) is probably the greatest weakness of many of the organizations that we have worked with. Poorly communicated, misunderstood, and unclear corporate goals, vision, direction, corporate values, and critical success factors are a leading cause of poor organizational performance, poor morale, and internal confusion.

Frequently, we speak with senior VP's who are adamant that their organization's values and goals are absolutely clear and understood throughout the organization, yet when we speak with individuals at levels ranging from senior to junior managers this is clearly not the case. Organizational goals, objectives, values, and critical success factors need to be communicated and reinforced on a continuous basis. As things change, individuals within organizations need to be able to contextualize this change with their organization's values, vision, direction, etc., and be able to assess the impact of change and take the necessary actions.

Debra Amidon, faculty at The Banff Centre for Management, and also one of North America's leading thinkers on Innovation and Knowledge Management uses the following matrix to describe five levels of generational management and where each level focuses to create value in the marketplace. Noteworthy here is that most organizations are striving to operate at the third, fourth, and fifth levels for Core Strategy, Processes, and Technology, and has accepted that Change Factors are at the fourth level and beyond. However, many organizations are still operating at the first and second level for Organizational Structure and People. Until organizations begin to recognize this disconnect and begin to align these levels they will find it increasingly difficult and frustrating to achieve the economic rewards these higher levels of operation offer.

More information on Debra's research can be found at *So where does an organization start?* Truly successful organizations recognize that longer-term business success and employee well being and fulfilment are linked. Employee well-being and engagement requires effective corporate leadership. Clearly, if an organization is looking to increase its capabilities then addressing its leadership culture is perhaps the best place to start. This traditionally means starting at the top of the organization with those who can most greatly influence and shape culture. Leadership culture can be developed from the bottom up, but it is a costly and unhealthy process for any organization. Effective corporate leadership is very similar to effective individual leadership. An organization might consider starting with a snapshot or initial assessment of what the leadership culture is by conducting a survey of individuals across different levels of the company.

The Organizational Cultural Inventory, produced by Human Synergistics of Ingersoll, Ontario assesses culture across a number of categories including tendencies toward power, achievement, avoidance, competitiveness, and self-actualizing. From this basis point, the organization can then look at what the leadership culture needs to be. However, it is essential that this assessment is done within the context of the longer-term strategic plan of the organization, market place dynamics, how the corporation creates value, and how it plans on continuing to create value in the marketplace. From this exercise should flow a list of corporate values and competencies that speak to a new or perhaps more refined sense of what the corporation needs to be doing and how it can get there. More specifically, it needs to define what type of internal operating environment and culture it must create for its employees in order for it to be successful.

The next challenge would then be to develop the skills and competencies within the corporation that would help create and define this new leadership culture-again starting at the top. Our experience has been that 70% of organizational competencies are common, with the remaining 30% being specific to the organization and its industry sector. Common skills and competencies themes that corporations would very likely pursue include the following:

- Develop organizational values that not only speak to profit generation but also to the growth, development, and well being of employees.

- Create and implement corporate wide business metrics that provides a clear sense of what needs to be done.
- Provide clear and constant two-way communication of corporate values, vision, mission, and critical success factors for the purposes of understanding and context. The corporation must also listen to employees and take appropriate action. Effective corporate leadership is open to criticism, seeks feedback, and is accountable for its actions.
- Embrace and foster creativity, innovation and learning. An organization's ability to learn in today's marketplace is perhaps its greatest strategic advantage.
- Create an environment of trust and respect.
- Remove redundant corporate bureaucracy.
- Create and implement a succession/career progression planning program that clearly articulates corporate expectations and charts a course for employee development.
- Create space for leadership to grow.

Today, longer-term (can anything be long-term today?) corporate sustainability requires a powerful corporate leadership culture where employee energy, passion, and intellectual capital can flourish in support of an organization's objectives. Based upon our experience we believe creating this environment should be the number one priority within organizations. This is the gas that fuels the organizational engine. Is it possible for organizations to change their leadership culture? We believe it is but it is no easy task. It requires significant commitment throughout the organization and leadership...especially from the top!

Corporate leadership is comprised of the executives and managers who run a company. It occurs when a company foresees ultimate success from the strong leaders that run its daily operations. Leaders themselves are responsible for effectively managing the company's resources, working with advertising teams and inspiring others to do their best work. They also envision ways to improve the company from the perspective of overall involvement. Ultimately, the actions and decisions of executives are what is referred to as corporate leadership.

It takes both training and talent to be able to take on a role as a leader of a company, whether it's in a major international firm or a smaller company that deals only at the local level. It also takes certain character or personality traits to be able to thrive in such a high pressure, often cutthroat environment. Adapting to change is one of the most important traits when leading a company. One must be good at talking with people if not precisely charismatic, and public speaking skills are needed for some roles within a company's leadership. Corporate leaders know that a customer may leave the company even if they're content if another company is out there offering a better deal, even on a slightly lesser service. It's the job of those in a position of leadership to scout the competition. They need to brainstorm and think of ways to make the company constantly better or consistently successful.

As businesses around the world change and adapt to an international market in a way that's never been done before, leaders of all backgrounds and cultures often come together for meetings and decisions. Those in corporate power are often expected to do a lot of travel and research. While one cannot be expected to pick up a language overnight, knowing other languages now can help a manager rise within a company, a skill that would have simply been a nice resume anecdote in the more localized corporate world of the past.

Corporate leadership has changed a lot over the years. Company leaders of the past thrived by running operations by the book as they were instructed by the owner. Now, the success of the company is often met by allowing those in charge to use a variety of personal talents and skills to help keep the company on the path to a planned vision. The old style gave the business owner what he asked for, but the new system gives the owner what he needs to have his company become or remain successful.

There are organizations around the world that exist to help companies excel the effectiveness of those in charge. This can ultimately benefit everyone involved in the company. A company that is run efficiently is often a more successful one. In fact, the Corporate Leadership Centre was founded in the US as a business-academic forum to assist, encourage and instruct others in the art and science of corporate leadership. Its program Leading Women Executives gives recognition and support to women, aiming to help qualified women rise to top in positions of leadership.

# 2

# Leadership Styles

There are a number of different approaches, or 'styles' to leadership and management that are based on different assumptions and theories. The style that individuals use will be based on a combination of their beliefs, values and preferences, as well as the organizational culture and norms which will encourage some styles and discourage others.

## Charismatic Leadership

### *Assumptions*

Charm and grace are all that is needed to create followers.

Self-belief is a fundamental need of leaders.

People follow others that they personally admire.

### *Style*

The Charismatic Leader gathers followers through dint of personality and charm, rather than any form of external power or authority.

### *The Searchlight of Attention*

It is interesting to watch a Charismatic Leader 'working the room' as they move from person to person. They pay much attention to the person they are talking to at any one moment, making that person feel like they are, for that time, the most important person in the world.

Charismatic Leaders pay a great deal of attention in scanning and reading their environment, and are good at picking up the moods and concerns of both individuals and larger audiences. They then will hone their actions and words to suit the situation.

### *Pulling all of the Strings*

Charismatic Leaders use a wide range of methods to manage their image and, if they are not naturally charismatic, may practice assiduously at developing their skills. They may engender trust through visible self-sacrifice and taking personal risks in the name of their beliefs. They will show great confidence in their followers. They are very persuasive and make very effective use of body language as well as verbal language.

Deliberate charisma is played out in a theatrical sense, where the leader is 'playing to the house' to create a desired effect. They also make effective use of storytelling, including the use of symbolism and metaphor.

Many politicians use a charismatic style, as they need to gather a large number of followers. If you want to increase your charisma, studying videos of their speeches and the way they interact with others is a great source of learning. Religious leaders, too, may well use charisma, as do cult leaders.

### *Leading the Team*

Charismatic Leaders who are building a group, whether it is a political party, a cult or a business team, will often focus strongly on making the group very clear and distinct, separating it from other groups. They will then build the image of the group, in particular in the minds of their followers, as being far superior to all others.

The Charismatic Leader will typically attach themselves firmly to the identify of the group, such that to join the group is to become one with the leader. In doing so, they create an unchallengeable position for themselves.

### *Alternative Views*

The description above is purely based on charisma and takes into account varying moral positions. Other descriptions tend to assume a more benevolent approach.

Conger & Kanungo (1998) describe five behavioural attributes of Charismatic Leaders that indicate a more transformational viewpoint:

- Vision and articulation;
- Sensitivity to the environment;
- Sensitivity to member needs;
- Personal risk taking;
- Performing unconventional behaviour.

Musser (1987) notes that charismatic leaders seek to instil both commitment to ideological goals and also devotion to themselves. The extent to which either of these two goals is dominant depends on the underlying motivations and needs of the leader.

### *Discussion*

The Charismatic Leader and the Transformational Leader can have many similarities, in that the Transformational Leader may well be charismatic. Their main difference is in their basic focus. Whereas the Transformational Leader has a basic focus of transforming the organization and, quite possibly, their followers, the Charismatic Leader may not want to change anything.

Despite their charm and apparent concern, the Charismatic Leader may well be somewhat more concerned with themselves than anyone else. A typical experience with them is that whilst you are talking with them, it is like being bathed in a warm and pleasant glow, in which they are very convincing. Yet afterwards, ask the sunbeam of their attention is moved elsewhere, you may begin to question what they said (or even whether they said anything of significance at all).

The values of the Charismatic Leader are highly significant. If they are well-intentioned towards others, they can elevate and transform an entire company. If they are selfish and Machiavellian, they can create cults and effectively rape the minds (and potentially the bodies) of the followers.

Their self-belief is so high, they can easily believe that they are infallible, and hence lead their followers into an abyss, even when they have received adequate warning from others. The self-belief can also lead them into psychotic narcissism, where their self-absorption or need for admiration and worship can lead to their followers questioning their leadership. They may also be intolerant of challengers and their irreplaceability (intentional or otherwise) can mean that there are no successors when they leave.

## Participative Leadership

### *Assumptions*

Involvement in decision-making improves the understanding of the issues involved by those who must carry out the decisions.

People are more committed to actions where they have involved in the relevant decision-making. People are less competitive and more collaborative when they are working on joint goals.

When people make decisions together, the social commitment to one another is greater and thus increases their commitment to the decision. Several people deciding together make better decisions than one person alone.

### *Style*

A Participative Leader, rather than taking autocratic decisions, seeks to involve other people in the process, possibly including subordinates, peers, superiors and other stakeholders. Often, however, as it is within the managers' whim to give or deny control to his or her subordinates, most participative activity is within the immediate team.

There are many varieties on this spectrum, including stages where the leader sells the idea to the team. Another variant is for the leader to describe the 'what' of objectives or goals and let the team or individuals decide the 'how' of the process by which the 'how' will be achieved (this is often called 'Management by Objectives').

The level of participation may also depend on the type of decision being made. Decisions on how to implement goals may be highly participative, whilst decisions during subordinate performance evaluations are more likely to be taken by the manager.

### *Discussion*

There are many potential benefits of participative leadership, as indicated in the assumptions, above.

This approach is also known as consultation, empowerment, joint decision-making, democratic leadership, Management By Objective (MBO) and power-sharing.

Participative Leadership can be a sham when managers ask for opinions and then ignore them. This is likely to lead to cynicism and feelings of betrayal.

## Situational Leadership

### *Assumptions*

The best action of the leader depends on a range of situational factors.

### *Style*

When a decision is needed, an effective leader does not just fall into a single preferred style, such as using transactional or transformational methods. In practice, as they say, things are not that simple.

Factors that affect situational decisions include motivation and capability of followers. This, in turn, is affected by factors within the particular situation. The relationship between followers and the leader may be another factor that affects leader behaviour as much as it does follower behaviour.

The leaders' perception of the follower and the situation will affect what they do rather than the truth of the situation. The leader's perception of themselves and other factors such as stress and mood will also modify the leaders' behaviour.

Yukl (1989) seeks to combine other approaches and identifies six variables:

- *Subordinate effort*: the motivation and actual effort expended.
- *Subordinate ability* and *role clarity*: followers knowing what to do and how to do it.
- *Organization of the work*: the structure of the work and utilization of resources.
- *Cooperation and cohesiveness*: of the group in working together.
- *Resources and support*: the availability of tools, materials, people, etc.
- *External coordination*: the need to collaborate with other groups.

Leaders here work on such factors as external relationships, acquisition of resources, managing demands on the group and managing the structures and culture of the group.

### Discussion

Tannenbaum and Schmidt (1958) identified three forces that led to the leader's action: the forces in the situation, the forces in then follower and also forces in the leader.

This recognizes that the leader's style is highly variable, and even such distant events as a family argument can lead to the displacement activity of a more aggressive stance in an argument than usual.

Maier (1963) noted that leaders not only consider the likelihood of a follower accepting a suggestion, but also the overall importance of getting things done. Thus in critical situations, a leader is more likely to be directive in style simply because of the implications of failure.

## Transactional Leadership

### *Assumptions*

People are motivated by reward and punishment.

Social systems work best with a clear chain of command.

When people have agreed to do a job, a part of the deal is that they cede all authority to their manager.

The prime purpose of a subordinate is to do what their manager tells them to do.

### *Style*

The transactional leader works through creating clear structures whereby it is clear what is required of their subordinates, and the rewards that they get for following orders. Punishments are not always mentioned, but they are also well-understood and formal systems of discipline are usually in place.

The early stage of Transactional Leadership is in negotiating the contract whereby the subordinate is given a salary and other benefits, and the company (and by implication the subordinate's manager) gets authority over the subordinate.

When the Transactional Leader allocates work to a subordinate, they are considered to be fully responsible for it, whether or not they have the resources or capability to carry it out. When things go wrong, then the subordinate is considered to be personally at fault, and is punished for their failure (just as they are rewarded for succeeding).

The transactional leader often uses *management by exception*, working on the principle that if something is operating to defined (and hence expected) performance then it does not need attention. Exceptions to expectation require praise and reward for exceeding expectation, whilst some kind of corrective action is applied for performance below expectation.

Whereas Transformational Leadership has more of a 'selling' style, Transactional Leadership, once the contract is in place, takes a 'telling' style.

### *Discussion*

Transactional leadership is based in *contingency*, in that reward or punishment is contingent upon performance.

Despite much research that highlights its limitations, Transactional Leadership is still a popular approach with many managers. Indeed, in the Leadership vs. Management spectrum, it is very much towards the management end of the scale.

The main limitation is the assumption of 'rational man', a person who is largely motivated by money and simple reward, and hence whose behaviour is predictable. The underlying psychology is Behaviorism, including the Classical Conditioning of Pavlov and Skinner's Operant Conditioning. These theories are largely based on controlled laboratory experiments (often with animals) and ignore complex emotional factors and social values. In practice, there is sufficient truth in Behaviorism to sustain Transactional approaches. This is reinforced by the supply-and-demand situation of much employment, coupled with the effects of deeper needs, as in Maslow's Hierarchy. When the demand for a skill outstrips the supply, then Transactional Leadership often is insufficient, and other approaches are more effective.

## Transformational Leadership

### *Assumptions*

People will follow a person who inspires them.

A person with vision and passion can achieve great things.

The way to get things done is by injecting enthusiasm and energy.

### *Style*

Working for a Transformational Leader can be a wonderful and uplifting experience. They put passion and energy into everything. They care about you and want you to succeed.

### *Developing the Vision*

Transformational Leadership starts with the development of a vision, a view of the future that will excite and convert potential followers. This vision may be developed by the leader, by the senior team or may emerge from a broad series of discussions. The important factor is the leader buys into it, hook, line and sinker.

### *Selling the Vision*

The next step, which in fact never stops, is to constantly sell the vision. This takes energy and commitment, as few people will immediately buy into a radical vision, and some will join the show much more slowly than others. The Transformational Leader thus takes every opportunity and will use whatever works to convince others to climb on board the bandwagon.

In order to create followers, the Transformational Leader has to be very careful in creating trust, and their personal integrity is a critical part of the package that they are selling. In effect, they are selling themselves as well as the vision.

### *Finding the way Forwards*

In parallel with the selling activity is seeking the way forward. Some Transformational Leaders know the way, and simply want others to follow them. Others do not have a ready strategy, but will happily lead the exploration of possible routes to the promised land. The route forwards may not be obvious and may not be plotted in details, but with a clear vision, the *direction* will always be known. Thus finding the way forward can be an ongoing process of course correction, and the Transformational Leader will accept that there will be failures and blind canyons along the way. As long as they feel progress is being made, they will be happy.

### *Leading the Charge*

The final stage is to remain up-front and central during the action. Transformational Leaders are always visible and will stand up to be counted rather than hide behind their troops. They show by their attitudes and actions how everyone else should behave. They also make continued efforts to motivate and rally their followers, constantly doing the rounds, listening, soothing and enthusing.

It is their unswerving commitment as much as anything else that keeps people going, particularly through the darker times when some may question whether the vision can ever be achieved. If the people do not believe that they can succeed, then their efforts will flag. The Transformational Leader seeks to infect and reinfect their followers with a high level of commitment to the vision.

One of the methods the Transformational Leader uses to sustain motivation is in the use of ceremonies, rituals and other cultural symbolism. Small changes get big hurrahs, pumping up their significance as indicators of real progress. Overall, they balance their attention between action that creates progress and the mental state of their followers. Perhaps more than other approaches, they are people-oriented and believe that success comes first and last through deep and sustained commitment.

### *Discussion*

Whilst the Transformational Leader seeks overtly to transform the organization, there is also a tacit promise to followers that they also will be transformed in some way, perhaps to be more like this amazing leader. In some respects, then, the followers are the *product* of the transformation.

Transformational Leaders are often charismatic, but are not as narcissistic as pure Charismatic Leaders, who succeed through a belief in themselves rather than a belief in others. One of the traps of Transformational Leadership is that passion and confidence can easily be mistaken for truth and reality. Whilst it is true that great things have been achieved through enthusiastic leadership, it is also true that many passionate people have led the charge right over the cliff and into a bottomless chasm. Just because someone *believes* they are right, it does not mean they *are* right.

Paradoxically, the energy that gets people going can also cause them to give up. Transformational Leaders often have large amounts of enthusiasm which, if relentlessly applied, can wear out their followers. Transformational Leaders also tend to see the big picture, but not the details, where the devil often lurks. If they do not have people to take care of this level of information, then they are usually doomed to fail.

Finally, Transformational Leaders, by definition, seek to transform. When the organization does not need transforming and people are happy as they are, then such a leader will be frustrated. Like wartime leaders, however, given the right situation they come into their own and can be personally responsible for saving entire companies.

## The Quiet Leader

### *Assumptions*

The actions of a leader speak louder than his or her words.

People are motivated when you give them credit rather than take it yourself.

Ego and aggression are neither necessary nor constructive.

### *Style*

The approach of quiet leaders is the antithesis of the classic charismatic (and often transformational) leaders in that they base their success not on ego and force of character but on their thoughts and actions. Although they are strongly task-focused, they are neither bullies nor unnecessarily unkind and may persuade people through rational argument and a form of benevolent Transactional Leadership.

### *The 'Level 5' Leader*

In his book *Good To Great*, Jim Collins, identified five levels of effectiveness people can take in organizations. At level four is the merely effective leader, whilst at level five the leader who combines professional will with personal humility. The 'professional will' indicates how they are far from being timid wilting flowers and will march against any advice if they believe it is the right thing to do. In 'personal humility' they put the well-being of others before their own personal needs, for example giving others credit after successes but taking personal responsibility for failures.

### *Taoist Writings*

The quiet leader is not a modern invention and Lao Tzu, who, in the classic Taoist text *Tao Te Ching,* was discussing the same characteristic around 500 BC:

The very highest is barely known by men,
Then comes that which they know and love,
Then that which is feared,
Then that which is despised.
He who does not trust enough will not be trusted.
When actions are performed
Without unnecessary speech,
People say "We did it!"

Here again, the highest level of leadership is virtually invisible.

### *Discussion*

To some extent, the emphasis on the quiet leader is a reaction against the lauding of charismatic leaders in the press. In particular during the heady days of the dot-com boom of the 1990s, some very verbal leaders got much coverage. Meanwhile, the quiet leaders were getting on with the job. Being quiet, of course, is not the secret of the universe, and leaders still need to see the way forwards. Their job can be harder when they are faced with people of a more external character.

For people accustomed to an extraverted charismatic style, a quiet style can be very confusing and they may downplay the person, which is usually a mistake. Successful quiet leaders often play the values card to persuade others, showing selfishness and lack of emotional control as being unworthy characteristics. Again there is a trap in this and leadership teams can fall into patterns of behaviour where peace and harmony are prized over any form of challenge and conflict.

## Servant Leadership

### *Assumptions*

The leader has responsibility for the followers.

Leaders have a responsibility towards society and those who are disadvantaged.

People who want to help others best do this by leading them.

### *Style*

The servant leader serves others, rather than others serving the leader. Serving others thus comes by helping them to achieve and improve.

There are two criteria of servant leadership:

- The people served grow as individuals, becoming 'healthier, wiser, more autonomous and more likely themselves to become servants' (Greenleaf, 1977).
- The extent to which the leadership benefits those who are least advantaged in society (or at least does not disadvantage them).

Principles of servant leadership defined by the Alliance for Servant Leadership are:

- *Transformation* as a vehicle for personal and institutional growth.
- *Personal growth* as a route to better serve others.
- *Enabling environments* that empower and encourage service.
- *Service* as a fundamental goals.
- *Trusting relationships* as a basic platform for collaboration and service.
- *Creating commitment* as a way to collaborative activity.
- *Community building* as a way to create environments in which people can trust each other and work together.
- *Nurturing the spirit* as a way to provide joy and fulfilment in meaningful work.

Spears (2002) lists: listening, empathy, healing, awareness, persuasion, conceptualization, foresight, stewardship, commitment to growth of people, and building community.

An excellent example of a servant leader is Ernest Shackleton, the early 20th century explorer who, after his ship became frozen in the Antarctic life, brought every one of his 27 crew home alive, including an 800 mile journey in open boats across the winter Antarctic seas. It took two years, but Shackleton's sense of responsibility towards his men never wavered.

### *Discussion*

Greenleaf says that true leadership "emerges from those whose primary motivation is a deep desire to help others." Servant leadership is a very moral position, putting the well-being of the followers before other goals. It is easy to dismiss servant leadership as soft and easy, though this is not necessarily so, as individual followers may be expected to make sacrifices for the good of the whole, in the way of the servant leader. The focus on the less privileged in society shows the servant leader as serving not just their followers but also the whole of society. Servant leadership is a natural model for working in the public sector. It requires more careful interpretation in the private sector lest the needs of the shareholders and customers and the rigors of market competition are lost. A challenge to servant leadership is in the assumption of the leader that the followers want to change. There is also the question of what 'better' is and who decides this. Servant leadership aligns closely with religious morals and has been adopted by several Christian organizations.

## Negative Styles

There are some relatively common styles of management that are anything but models of good leadership.

- Post-hoc Management: A poor, but common style.

Although not an 'official' management theory, what can be called 'Post-hoc management' is practiced widely on a daily basis around the world and most people will instantly recognize it. It is very common in small companies where there are few formal systems and where there is a general autocratic style. It also appears in larger organizations where results take precedence over rules or where politics leads to impression management being a primary activity.

### *Principle*

The basic principle of post-hoc management is that, as judge and jury, the manager is always right and never to blame. In this way they can remain secure in their job.

### Vague Objectives

The first sign of post-hoc management is a vague start to work, typically with unclear and general objectives. If the manager is asked for clarity, they will typically say something like 'you're the expert' or 'this is why we employ you', with the implication that not knowing what indicates a lack of competence on your part. This can be endemic in an organization where it happens all the way up the management tree. The edict 'Managers must manage' is a typical statement by a more senior person that essentially implies that you are on your own.

### Wise in Hindsight

Being right means judging others after the fact, where 20-20 hindsight allows them to conclude what *should* have been done. It places the manager as a wise expert who cannot be challenged. In fact the manager actually uses the respect required by their formal position as a substitute for the true respect engendered by expertise. Their seniority thus acts as a protective wall and any challenge to their expertise is reinterpreted as an attack on their rank, which they can repel with accusations of insubordination.

One way of recognizing the post-hoc manager is the phrase 'Why didn't you...' Their suggestions usually sound reasonable but do not take into account time limitations and the myriad of other things that could have been done. Most work planning includes decisions not to do a lot of things that would make sense if you had the time, but get prioritized out by the greater importance and urgency of other work.

If you are always right then others are always wrong and the post-hoc manager often bemoans how they are surrounded by fools. Yet this also makes the manager feel clever and superior, and they seldom seek to employ people who are better than them. This sometimes does happen by accident when a good person slips through the mediocre net, but the frustrations caused by post-hoc management often means that the best people quickly understand the problem and move on as soon as possible.

### Critical Benefits

The post-hoc manager also benefits from the 'critic effect', whereby people who criticize are seen as being more intelligent that those who propose creative solutions. The manager may be creative too, but does it in a way that protects them from blame. For example they may make various interesting suggestions as to what should be done, which puts the other person in the double bind that if they do not follow the manager's suggestions then, if things go less than perfectly the manager will blame them for not taking up the idea. If they implement the idea and it works then the manager can take most of the credit, whilst if it fails then the manager can blame them for a poor implementation or say 'It was only an idea, effectively suggesting that you are incapable of developing your own ideas.'

Whilst not an official management theory, Post-hoc management is sadly an all-too-frequent reality. It reflects the human condition and the need for control, safety and status that often take priority over values that require integrity and concern for others.

## Leadership vs. Management

What is the difference between management and leadership? It is a question that has been asked more than once and also answered in different ways. The biggest difference between managers and leaders is the way they motivate the people who work or follow them, and this sets the tone for most other aspects of what they do. Many people, by the way, are both. They have management jobs, but they realize that you cannot buy hearts, especially to follow them down a difficult path, and so act as leaders too.

### *Managers have Subordinates*

By definition, managers have subordinates-unless their title is honorary and given as a mark of seniority, in which case the title is a misnomer and their power over others is other than formal authority.

### *Authoritarian, Transactional Style*

Managers have a position of authority vested in them by the company, and their subordinates work for them and largely do as they are told. Management style is transactional, in that the manager tells the subordinate what to do, and the subordinate does this not because they are a blind robot, but because they have been promised a reward (at minimum their salary) for doing so.

### *Work Focus*

Managers are paid to get things done (they are subordinates too), often within tight constraints of time and money. They thus naturally pass on this work focus to their subordinates.

### *Seek Comfort*

An interesting research finding about managers is that they tend to come from stable home backgrounds and led relatively normal and comfortable lives. This leads them to be relatively risk-averse and they will seek to avoid conflict where possible. In terms of people, they generally like to run a 'happy ship'.

### Leaders have Followers

Leaders do not have subordinates-at least not when they are leading. Many organizational leaders do have subordinates, but only because they are also managers. But when they want to lead, they have to give up formal authoritarian control, because to lead is to have followers, and following is always a voluntary activity.

### Charismatic, Transformational Style

Telling people what to do does not inspire them to follow you. You have to appeal to them, showing how following them will lead to their hearts' desire. They must want to follow you enough to stop what they are doing and perhaps walk into danger and situations that they would not normally consider risking.

Leaders with a stronger charisma find it easier to attract people to their cause. As a part of their persuasion they typically promise transformational benefits, such that their followers will not just receive extrinsic rewards but will somehow become better people.

### People Focus

Although many leaders have a charismatic style to some extent, this does not require a loud personality. They are always good with people, and quiet styles that give credit to others (and takes blame on themselves) are very effective at creating the loyalty that great leaders engender. Although leaders are good with people, this does not mean they are friendly with them. In order to keep the mystique of leadership, they often retain a degree of separation and aloofness. This does not mean that leaders do not pay attention to tasks-in fact they are often very achievement-focused. What they do realize, however, is the importance of enthusing others to work towards their vision.

### Seek Risk

In the same study that showed managers as risk-averse, leaders appeared as risk-seeking, although they are not blind thrill-seekers. When pursuing their vision, they consider it natural to encounter problems and hurdles that must be overcome along the way. They are thus comfortable with risk and will see routes that others avoid as potential opportunities for advantage and will happily break rules in order to get things done.

A surprising number of these leaders had some form of handicap in their lives which they had to overcome. Some had traumatic childhoods, some had problems such as dyslexia, others were shorter than average. This perhaps taught them the independence of mind that is needed to go out on a limb and not worry about what others are thinking about you.

## In Summary

This table summarizes the above (and more) and gives a sense of the differences between being a leader and being a manager. This is, of course, an illustrative characterization, and there is a whole spectrum between either ends of these scales along which each role can range. And many people lead and manage at the same time, and so may display a combination of behaviours.

| *Subject* | *Leader* | *Manager* |
|---|---|---|
| Essence | Change | Stability |
| Focus | Leading people | Managing work |
| Have | Followers | Subordinates |
| Horizon | Long-term | Short-term |
| Seeks | Vision | Objectives |
| Approach | Sets direction | Plans detail |
| Decision | Facilitates | Makes |
| Power | Personal charisma | Formal authority |
| Appeal to | Heart | Head |
| Energy | Passion | Control |
| Culture | Shapes | Enacts |
| Dynamic | Proactive | Reactive |
| Persuasion | Sell | Tell |
| Style | Transformational | Transactional |
| Exchange | Excitement for work | Money for work |
| Likes | Striving | Action |
| Wants | Achievement | Results |
| Risk | Takes | Minimizes |
| Rules | Breaks | Makes |
| Conflict | Uses | Avoids |
| Direction | New roads | Existing roads |
| Truth | Seeks | Establishes |
| Concern | What is right | Being right |
| Credit | Gives | Takes |
| Blame | Takes | Blames |

## Power

Power is the ability to get what you want. As what you want is often constrained by other people, the use of power often includes changing or influencing what others think, believe and do. It is at the heart of all techniques of changing minds.

### *Formal Authority*

The simplest form of power is that vested in the position of 'manager'. A manager has subordinates who must do his or her bidding, only within legal and organizational rules. The basic employment transaction is 'we give you money, you do as your are told'.

Of course there are many more ways that power can be exerted, and in particular in motivating people more effectively such as is found in transformational leadership.

### *Control of Scarce Resources*

Other than directing employees, managers control budgets and the assets and other resources that the firm holds, from technology to people. A part of this control is the ability to allocate these resources to projects and other work.

It is not unsurprising that many of the political battles in organizations is over control of resources and 'empire-building' is a classic game, with a significant risk that organizational goals get forgotten in the cut and thrust of winning and losing control of resources.

### *Use of Organizational Structure, Rules and Regulations*

Organizations have hierarchies, departments, teams and other structures, often each with its own rules as well as the rules that govern the action within the organization as a whole. Many people do not know all of these rules, which makes them a source of power for those who care to take time to learn their detail.

Power can also be gained from quoting rules that do not exist or misquoting rules by overstating or understating their meaning.

## Control of Decision Processes

Work is selected and resources are allocated by decisions, many of which are decided in some form by groups of people. By managing how decisions are made, for example by requiring consensus or senior-manager signoff, the power of some people may be curtailed whilst others gain the ability to shape decisions. When decisions are made in committee or other meetings, the person who chairs the meeting or keeps the minutes may have notable power to control decisions.

### *Control of Knowledge and Information*

Knowledge is power, as they say, and how you gather and distribute it is a source of power, whether it is technical or social information.

Experts often work in this way, protecting their elevated status by hiding the sources of their knowledge and exacting high prices (whether financial or social) for their learned opinions.

### *Control of Boundaries*

The structures and groups of the organization are only so because they have boundaries which people cross in order to access resources and meet people. Thus, for example, an executive's Personal Assistant may have disproportionate power in the ability to allow access or not to the executive. Likewise security guards, though not paid very much can allow, bar or hassle people crossing their boundaries.

### *Ability to Cope with Uncertainty*

A quite different source of power is personal resilience, the ability to handle uncertainty and stress that might debilitate others. Such people can gain position by taking on work that others fear and is a common route for upwardly-mobile go-getters who seek early promotion.

### *Control of Technology*

Technology is (or should be) an enabler, providing data, analysis, information, access and other benefits. Those who control what technology is used by the organization or who gets the latest computers and software has significant power, and the person who used to be the 'IT Manager' may now be the 'Chief Information Officer'.

Having the latest technology can also be a status symbol, thereby giving the holder social power in the way they can show themselves to be influential and clever.

### *Interpersonal Alliances, Networks and Control of 'Informal Organization'*

Who you know makes a lot of difference. We naturally help our friends and those who have helped us in some way in the past. Social networks are the glue of organizations and those who build and work their informal associates can thereby gain significantly more power.

In the time when smoking was allowed but only in special 'smoking rooms', it was often said that this became a 'club' where the low and the high in the organization rubbed shoulders, which no doubt gave power to the lower people in the name-dropping they could use and and help they might get.

### *Control of Counter-organizations*

Not to every organization is there an equal and opposite counter-organization, but in the battlefield of businesses, whole ecologies spring up, include local opposition to factory expansion, trade unions seeking ever-increasing pay and benefits and so on. If you can infiltrate or otherwise hold some sway over the groups who might oppose you, you may at least be able to damp the danger they power and possibly neutralize them completely.

### *Symbolism and the Management of Meaning*

We live a lot, more than perhaps we realize, in the sway of the symbols and semiotics of the workplace. If you can recognize the subtlety and understand the workings of how meaning is created, then you have a surprisingly powerful tool for change and influence. Symbols and meaning-making is a particular pattern of culture, and those who would change the underlying culture of an organization can make use of these.

### *Gender and the Management of Gender Relations*

In a balanced workplace, around half the people are men and half are women. In practice, some women gravitate towards particular roles whilst men seek other work positions. The 'glass ceiling' still exists in many companies and, perhaps due to life breaks such as having children, fewer women make it to the higher echelons. This can lead to frustrations and energy that can be put to good and destructive use. If you can harness this, you have power. There is also the power of sexual attraction, and tall and shapely people continue to make good use of their physical assets.

### *Structural Factors that Define the Stage of Action*

The 'stage of action' in organizations is set up by the organizational purpose, vision, mission, strategy and other high-level shaping activities that lead to scenarios of activity, from driving into new markets to struggling with organizational change. If you can shape the direction of the organization, you have tremendous power to affect much of what it does and consequently the futures (and power) of others in the firm.

### *The Power one Already Has*

Last, but certainly not least, is the power of the individual. We can be charming, willing, obstinate and more. And we have feet we can use to leave the company at any time we choose.

### *So What?*

So take note! If you are feeling powerless in an organization, think again and review the above list. Everyone has the ability to acquire and use more power than they might reasonably expect to have.

## Risk Bias

Some people take all kinds of risks, whilst others focus more on safely steering clear of them.

### *Risk Attraction*

People who are attracted to risks may do so for one of two main reasons. First, the goal may be the risk itself. Risk creates the buzz of arousal. The actual risk taken to cause excitement depends on the person's arousal threshold.

For many, the apparent risk (yet known safety) of roller-coasters is more than enough. Others need the real risks of extreme sports. For those with a low arousal threshold, the vicarious excitement of movies is often sufficient.

Another reason that people seem attracted to risk is that it the shortest route to what lies beyond it. They desire a certain outcome more than they fear the risk. Thus a young man will dare to ask out a beautiful young woman. A thief will risk prison. A gambler will lay a high stake on a horse with only an outside chance of winning. There may still be a buzz in the risk, but it is not the real goal. Taking risks can also seem like cheating death or other down-sides, making the risk-taker feel invulnerable and all-powerful.

### *Risk Avoidance*

Those who tend more to avoiding risks are at the opposite end of the scale to the risk-seekers. They generally have somewhat lower arousal and stress levels. They are often driven more by fear and focus more on what they might lose than what they might gain.

Others who seem to avoid risk may do so purely because they are already contented and have neither unquenched desires nor need for further stimulation.

### *Variation*

Note that although they may have general tendencies, individuals can have different profiles for different types of risk, for example those that affect:

- Physical harm
- Financial gains or losses
- Social position
- Danger to family, friends or other people in general

Risk decisions are also balanced against potential gain, and individuals may treat this potential gain differently, for example:

- Financial gain
- Gain in social status
- Thrilling physical sensations
- Success at work

Perhaps the most 'dangerous' risk-takes are those that think little about the down-side of risks, seeking only the almost addictive physiological 'thrill' sensations (for example joy-riders who steal cars and then drive them recklessly, revelling in the danger).

So what?

Challenge *risk-seekers*. Show them thrills and excitement. Tell them how others have failed. Dare them to have a go.

With *risk-takers*, hold up a picture of a desirable future and either ignore or play down risks.

*Risk-avoiders* see the risks, and perhaps even see the risk as greater than it really is. Don't pretend the risk isn't there, but you can rescue them or otherwise offer help and advice. You can also strategically place risks to shepherd them in the right direction.

If faced with the passive *risk-ignorer*, either crank up the risk until they cannot avoid it or seek another way to move them.

## Self vs. Others Preference

One of the basic social dilemmas is the extent to which we put ourselves first or whether we put other people first.

### *Self*

People with a 'me' focus put themselves first in all decisions where they are interacting or otherwise considering other people. Their focus is often on their sense identity which may not be strong enough to stand up without constant reassurance. They may have a founding belief that all people are basically selfish and that the only way to succeed is to 'look after number one'.

Although they are self-centred, they may not necessarily selfish, for example they may appear moderately considerate but this is typically only done because they realize that they may be socially punished for appearing too selfish.

It is philosophically arguable that all we can do is to be self-centred because we are indeed at the 'Centre of the known universe'. We can thus point out that charitable acts are done because it makes us feel good. Nevertheless, there is still a difference in thinking and acting between those who focus mostly on themselves and those who focus mostly on others.

### *Others*

People who focus first on others believe that helping others is the best way to help themselves, although in full prosocial behaviour this self-benefit consideration may be hardly considered, if at all. Other-oriented people typically see the world as a basically good (or at least neutral) place, and that within a society and as social animals, it is our duty to help one another, and that selfishness is the root of most acts evil.

### *So What?*

With self-oriented people, frame persuasions in terms of the threats and benefits to them as individuals. Focus on the WIIFM factors (What's In It For Me). If they feel threatened by others, be conspiratorial and show how they can get things for themselves without others knowing.

With other-focused people, talk about threats or benefits to the group, the company or to society at large. Do not appear selfish yourself.

## Followership

The nature of leadership can perhaps be best understood by turning the coin over and studying followership. Why do people follow leaders? If we can understand this, then we will be a long way down the road to creating those followers and hence becoming an effective leader. People don't just follow anyone. You can't just say 'follow me' and expect people to follow out of the goodness of their hearts. You have to give them good reason for them to follow.

Key aspect of creating followers:

- The Leader-Follower loop: Leaders create followers create leaders.
- Five reasons to follow: From coercive push to the pull of inspirational vision.
- Followers and Respect: Both leader and solution are important.
- Followers and Trust: I will follow someone I trust.
- Followers and Liking: I will follow someone I like.
- Followers and Support: I will follow someone who supports me.
- Followers and Ideas: I will follow ideas, not objectives.
- Non-followership: Why people do not follow.

Also:

- Zaleznik's follower typology: Based on control and activity.
- Kelley's follower typology : Five different types.
- Kellerman's follower typology: Five different types.
- Chaleff's follower typology: Based on type of support.

The principle of followership was summed by the 19th century British Prime Minister Benjamin Disraeli, who said, 'I must follow the people. Am I not their leader?'

### Micromanagement: Controls Every Detail

There is a style of management with which many are familiar and which has acquired the name 'micromanagement'. The manager in question acts as if the subordinate is incapable of doing the job, giving close instruction and checking everything the person does. They seldom praise and often criticize. Whatever their subordinates do, nothing seems good enough. It is the opposite of leadership.

### The Micromanagement Experience

For the individual, this tends to be incredibly frustrating. They are being treated as if they are incapable and untrustworthy. We often see ourselves as others see us and, when treated as unworthy, we will soon feel unworthy.

In this way, people who are micromanaged can become dependent, unable to make the smallest decision without asking their manager. Alternatives to this total submission, which many take, include remaining frustrated or leaving. In any case, it is easy for one's confidence to be severely knocked.

### *Why Micromanage?*

Why do managers micromanage? There can be a number of reasons. First, they may reasonably not trust the person either because there is evidence to support this or because the newness of the relationship has not yet yielded evidence to support trust. There might also be a high-risk situation which merits extra management attention.

A more likely explanation is an internal need for the manager to manage closely. They may fear failure personally, transfer that risk to the person then take ownership of the person's work. The manager may also feel (or want to feel) superior to the person, effectively confusing authority with ability. The person thus seems incompetent and the manager looks for confirmation of this in the smallest details of the person's work. A minor error is thus taken as evidence of the person's total incompetence and the manager's obvious superiority. This can be a reversal of a childhood situation with a critical parent. Just as the abused become abusers, so also may the criticized become critical.

Micromanagement also plays to strong identity and control needs. Telling people what to do and not do is a strong controlling action, whilst the sense of superiority strokes the identity ego.

### *When it is Appropriate*

Sometimes, close management is a realistic option. When a person is working in a job where they do not have the knowledge or ability to do the job, and where mistakes are costly and highly undesirable, then they will need careful supervision and education until they are able to work by themselves.

Sometimes also a person may become destructive for some inner reason, such as disliking the company or its managers and they need careful watching in case they do something harmful.

### *How to Handle Micromanagers*

So what should you do when faced with a micromanager? The first thing is to recognize that it is their issue, not yours. However, this disability means they lack certain abilities and because of your situation, you are going to have to handle it.

The worst thing you can do is to get into a power struggle, as this is very likely to result in the micromanager using all the formal power at their disposal to beat you into submission, including threats of dismissal and negative references. The simplest approach is to listen patiently and attentively when they tell you what to do (they hate being ignored). If you really disagree with what they are saying, ask politely for their reasons or explain your concern and ask for their advice. Quietly and carefully ensure you cannot be blamed for the micromanager's decisions (it can be useful to keep notes and confirm directives in emails in case of later disagreement).

You can give them feedback (through a third party, if necessary) about how they are behaving and how this makes you feel. Some micromanagers do not intend to act this way and will make genuine attempts to improve. Many, however, will feel slighted and the result can be unhelpful. In consequence, think carefully before using this approach.

A reversal can be an interesting alternative, effectively, micromanaging them. Book their time to agree what you will be doing. Agree in detail what you will be doing. Let them make every decision. Then do exactly what they said and report back that you have completed each step. Go back often to check for new each decision. In the end they may tire of your constant attention and tell you to back off. You can also pre-empt and prompt this by occasionally asking if your approach to managing the detail through them is ok and whether they'd prefer you to decide more things yourself.

Another approach is to use their control and identity needs as levers. Use these as punishment and reward, carefully removing control and isolating them, or giving feedback that shows they are in control and are wonderful. For example when they over-control, avoid them, whilst when they give you more space, even a little, look at them and smile (identity stroking). Be very subtle in all this — if the micromanager feels micromanaged, they will react strongly.

In this way you will feel more in control yourself even as you give them a greater sense of control. Living with a micromanager need not be painful and it can be an interesting challenge

### *The Need for: Control*

No, this is not so much about how to control people as about their needs for control. The real secret is the deep, deep need that people have for a sense of control. By managing their sense of control, you can achieve far greater actual control. If you ignore this, you will soon fall into a power battle for control of the conversation and the agenda.

### *Control is a Deep, Deep Need*

Perhaps the deepest need people have is for control. When we feel out of control, we experience a powerful and uncomfortable tension between the need for control and the evidence of inadequate control. One of the most disturbing things about having a terminal illness, as those who unfortunately suffer from such afflictions will tell you, is the feeling of powerlessness, of being unable to do anything about it. Being unable to control the illness can be even more painful than impending death.

From an evolutionary standpoint, if we are in control of our environment, then we have a far better chance of survival. Our deep subconscious mind thus gives us strong biochemical prods when we face some kind of danger.

Other needs that lead to a sense of control include:

- A sense of certainty.
- Completion of outstanding things, so we don't have to worry about them..
- Understanding of how things work.
- Being able to predict what will happen.
- That people (including ourselves) and things are consistent.

### Maslow Revisited

Psychologist Abraham Maslow defined a hierarchy of needs, with the particular revelation that when lower level needs are not met, then higher-level needs will be abandoned in favour of shoring up the deeper needs.

### Not Control, Just the Sense

In fact, we don't actually need to be in control all of the time. What we really seek is a *sense* of control.

When our parents or our managers are controlling us, we can still be happy because we trust them to provide the control we seek in our lives. In fact many people actively seek parent-figures in all walks of their life who will provide this control. When seek the advice of experts and obey those in authority, we are depending on them for our sense of control.

### Control is Embedded in much of what we Do

Look around and watch what people do. A significant portion of our everyday activity is related to achieving our much-needed sense of control.

Rituals, for example, are everywhere. Why do we have them? They exist to reassure people everything is as it was and to provide a familiar framework for our daily lives. Social norms and values tell us what to do, what is right and wrong, what is good and bad. When everyone in the group follows the rules, we feel a sense of control.

### *Power and Trust*

The sense of control is closely related in opposite ways to power and trust. You can get a sense of control by taking control and acting, which is effectively using power. You can also get a sense of control by ceding it to others, which requires trust.

### *The Control Trap*

There is a trap into which many sales people and other would-be persuaders fall. This pitfall is to try to hold tightly to the reins of control throughout the whole process.

### *Grabbing Control Causes Resistance*

When I grab control of the conversation, talking past the point when you want to reply, you will get increasingly frustrated as you wait for a pause in which you can respond.

Sales people do this when they insist on going through the whole sales pitch even when the customer just wants to pay, take the product and leave.

Parents do it when they over-do the lectures to their children. A point which is initially accepted is later rejected at what gets seen as unfair punishment.

Taking direct control of a conversation or situation does not persuade. It is possible that you get temporary compliance, but you will not get true persuasion.

### *Fishing is a Delicate Game*

The control game is much like fly fishing. Pull to hard and the fish will slip the hook. Let it out too far and the line will snag or the fish will swim away.

It is only through a sometimes-long process of give and take, you steadily reel in your fish.

### *So What?*

So manage the other person's sense of control by changing those things that make them certain, able to understand and predict the things around them. This can be done by making things uncertain and inconsistent.

### *Giving Control to get Control*

Giving up control gets control in two ways. First, by choosing when, where and how you give control, you still have hold of the reins. You have defined the cage in which the other person can play. Secondly, having allowed them to exercise control, you can evoke the reciprocity principle, such that the other person will willingly give up control of the conversation to redress the social balance.

As someone said long ago, 'Give, in order that ye shall receive'.

### *Give them Choice*

When people exercise choice, they are controlling their environment. So give them a choice, ensuring that whatever they choose gives you an advantage.

One of the most common sales closes is the alternative close, where you assume the other person is ready to buy, and give them a simple choice ('Do you want the red one or the yellow one.').

Don't give them too much choice, because this makes the decision harder and can thus lead to a reduced sense of control. Because we make our easiest decisions by contrasting two things at one time, the best number of options to give is two.

### *Open Questions*

Closed questions do not give control. In fact they can seem very controlling. Open questions give people the floor, letting them talk. This can be a scary step and can indeed lose all control.

But you are the person who asked the question, so choose the question well to contain their response and possibly even give you information. Just having them talk is itself a great persuader. When people talk about something themselves, they are far more likely to believe in it than if they just sit back and listen to you.

### *Give them Something to Do*

The corollary of questioning is to give them something active to do. Just like when they are talking, actively doing something, especially when they have choice, gives a sense of control.

As with questioning, when you are directing the action, you are still in overall control.

### *Reflecting*

People often keep talking because they are not sure that you have really understood what they have said.

When you reflect back to people what they have told you, you show them that you have heard, that they have been successful, that they have controlled their environment. This will speed the point at which they will give you back the talking stick.

## Seagull Management

Flying in, pooping on you and flying off again.

### *Description*

'Seagull management' is a humorous term that is used to describe a style of management whereby the person 'flies in, poops on you and then flies away again'.

When they are there, they typically give criticism and direction in equal quantities, often without any real understanding of what the job entails. Then before you can object or ask what they really want, they have an 'important meeting' to go to.

The experience of having a seagull manager is not positive. Whilst they are there, they talk non-stop and actively discourage anyone else from saying anything. This can include avoiding eye contact and continuing to talk over you if you start to say anything.

You may typically feel under-valued and generally abuse. The best thing that can be said is that they are typically there not very often and you can largely get on with the job by yourself.

### *Why it Happens*

The Seagull Manager like to consider themselves as important. However they also know that they do not know that much and fear being exposed by questions or debate. They consequently grab the talking stick and do not stop until they can excuse themselves and leave.

It is possible that they really are busy, but what they miss is the importance of person-management. They are likely to be strongly task-based and consider the 'soft stuff' as fluffy and unnecessary. Their approach is thus highly transactional, based on the simple premise 'do as I say and you'll continue to get paid'.

### *What to do About It*

What you need to do about Seagull Managers depends largely on your job. If you can work independently, then the best approach is often to listen patiently then ignore them. As long as you are delivering value, they may not actually be too concerned about how you get there. Unlike the micromanager, they are not that interested in control over you.

If, however, their approach is damaging to your career and health, then you need to address the issue. Book a meeting with them (if you can) to discuss your work. Write down what your objectives are and what you are doing and give it to them. They may ignore it but this will give you tacit ammunition if you need it later. If things are particularly bad, this is a definite case for assertiveness (which is probably good anyway). Talk to them about what they are doing and the effect they are having. You may also need to talk with their manager or HR. Worst case, look for another position with a better manager who knows how to lead.

A novel approach is to deliberately 'chase' them with complex detail for which they have 'no time'. As they retreat or woffle at you, offer a simpler alternative that is easy for them to accept. You can also always reframe what they said, casting it into a more sensible light. Because the most important thing in the Seagull Manager's life is the Seagull Manager, if you can deliver results, then they may well leave you to your own devices or give moderate support. Deliver regular short messages that shows you are making good progress. Also work to make them look good to the rest of the organization (despite temptations to the contrary!). If they think you are acting contrary to their interests, they will just fly by more often and poop on you even more!

### *If you are a Manager*

If you are a manager, then seagull management is of course something to avoid. It is a trap that may seem easy but in practice it will alienate and demotivate your staff. If there are wiser people above you, then they also will find out what is happening and your advancement will halt or regress. The real lesson here is to sustain a good relationship with your people. Whilst you need not (and should not) be best mates with them, you should respect them and communicate regularly and with integrity. Listen too — this is a key skill and frequent activity of good leaders.

## Mushroom Management

Drop them in the poo and keep them in the dark.

### *Description*

In a common metaphor, the 'mushroom manager' plants you knee-deep (or worse) in the smelly stuff and keeps you in the dark.

In practice, this means you get to do all the work that they do not want. They do not communicate and generally ignore you, so you do not know their plans or what else might be going on in the organization.

### *Why it Happens*

Mushroom managers are often more concerned about their own career and image. Anyone who appears as a threat may well be deliberately held back as their ability may make the mushroom manager look bad.

Mushroom managers may also have their favorites on whom they lavish attention and the plum jobs. Others are swept away and given the dross.

Managers may take the mushroom route is that they just do not care about some or all of their people. Sometimes mushroom managers are just incompetent and know no better.

### *What to do About It*

If you are a quiet mouse who likes to keep your head down and avoid other people, then you may like a mushroom manager, just so long as they do not over-do it. Somebody has to handle the unpopular work which may make you feel safe and comfortable. Staying away from other work is fine as it lets you go home at a regular hour. Not everyone needs high ambition.

On the other hand, a mushroom manager may annoy you as they hold back your career and give you little opportunity to shine. Be assertive. Talk to them about what they are doing and the effect they are having. Do not lie down and be the doormat who says 'thank you' for any scraps they care to throw you. Remember that you always have more power than you think you have.

## Seagull Management

### *Description*

'Seagull management' is a humorous term that is used to describe a style of management whereby the person 'flies in, poops on you and then flies away again'.

When they are there, they typically give criticism and direction in equal quantities, often without any real understanding of what the job entails. Then before you can object or ask what they really want, they have an 'important meeting' to go to.

The experience of having a seagull manager is not positive. Whilst they are there, they talk non-stop and actively discourage anyone else from saying anything. This can include avoiding eye contact and continuing to talk over you if you start to say anything. You may typically feel under-valued and generally abuse. The best thing that can be said is that they are typically there not very often and you can largely get on with the job by yourself.

### Why it Happens

The Seagull Manager like to consider themselves as important. However they also know that they do not know that much and fear being exposed by questions or debate. They consequently grab the talking stick and do not stop until they can excuse themselves and leave.

It is possible that they really are busy, but what they miss is the importance of person-management. They are likely to be strongly task-based and consider the 'soft stuff' as fluffy and unnecessary. Their approach is thus highly transactional, based on the simple premise 'do as I say and you'll continue to get paid'.

### What to do About It

What you need to do about Seagull Managers depends largely on your job. If you can work independently, then the best approach is often to listen patiently then ignore them. As long as you are delivering value, they may not actually be too concerned about how you get there. Unlike the micromanager, they are not that interested in control over you.

If, however, their approach is damaging to your career and health, then you need to address the issue. Book a meeting with them (if you can) to discuss your work. Write down what your objectives are and what you are doing and give it to them. They may ignore it but this will give you tacit ammunition if you need it later.

If things are particularly bad, this is a definite case for assertiveness (which is probably good anyway). Talk to them about what they are doing and the effect they are having. You may also need to talk with their manager or HR. Worst case, look for another position with a better manager who knows how to lead.

A novel approach is to deliberately 'chase' them with complex detail for which they have 'no time'. As they retreat or woffle at you, offer a simpler alternative that is easy for them to accept. You can also always reframe what they said, casting it into a more sensible light.

Because the most important thing in the Seagull Manager's life is the Seagull Manager, if you can deliver results, then they may well leave you to your own devices or give moderate support. Deliver regular short messages that shows you are making good progress. Also work to make them look good to the rest of the organization (despite temptations to the contrary!). If they think you are acting contrary to their interests, they will just fly by more often and poop on you even more!

### *If you are a Manager*

If you are a manager, then seagull management is of course something to avoid. It is a trap that may seem easy but in practice it will alienate and demotivate your staff. If there are wiser people above you, then they also will find out what is happening and your advancement will halt or regress. The real lesson here is to sustain a good relationship with your people. Whilst you need not (and should not) be best mates with them, you should respect them and communicate regularly and with integrity. Listen too — this is a key skill and frequent activity of good leaders.

## Kipper Management: Two-faced Approach

### *Description*

Fish might unfairly be accused of being two-faced, as you only get to see one side at once. This principle is also applicable to the two-faced manager who has different faces and styles depending on the situation.

When they are with more senior managers they are typically model employees, putting business first and themselves last. Yet with their subordinates, the reverse is often true, with the individuals carrying the can for both pulling out the stops to get things done in time and then blame when things go wrong through no fault of their own.

The kipper will change with the wind as the need arises. They are chums when things need doing and backstabbers when there is glory or reward to be gained. The kipper's hero is probably Machiavelli.

### *Why it Happens*

The key reason why the kipper is so two-faced (or many-faced) is that their values with regard to integrity are largely non-existent.

They literally see nothing wrong in acting differently with different people and may even be proud of their ability to act differently in different situations, calling it something like 'style flexibility'.

Historically, the kipper may have been taught that 'this is how it works'. They may also have a deeper background where trust was low and abusive relationships common.

### *What to do About It*

Make sure you always have something that the kipper needs. This will keep their kinder face towards you.

If the kipper regularly turns their bad face on you, consider fighting fire with fire and standing up to them. Many kippers will turn a kinder face to those who are not easily cowed. Also consider taking the matter further, particularly if you can show the kipper is seriously breaking company values.

Kippers are natural cowards and admire power. They are hence susceptible to blackmail, although this is seldom a good approach. If, however, they know that you know something that they do not want others to know, no words may be necessary and they may treat you much better.

If you are a more senior manager and suspect you have a kipper in your ranks, get 360 degree views on them from different people. The kipper may also happily betray themselves in boasts of what and how they got people to do things for them.

## 8 Major Leadership Theories

Interest in leadership increased during the early part of the twentieth century. Early leadership theories focused on what qualities distinguished between leaders and followers, while subsequent theories looked at other variables such as situational factors and skill levels. While many different leadership theories have emerged, most can be classified as one of eight major types:

### *1. "Great Man" Theories*

Great man theories assume that the capacity for leadership is inherent – that great leaders are born, not made. These theories often portray great leaders as heroic, mythic and destined to rise to leadership when needed. The term "Great Man" was used because, at the time, leadership was thought of primarily as a male quality, especially in terms of military leadership. Learn more about the great man theory of leadership.

### 2. Trait Theories

Similar in some ways to "Great Man" theories, trait theories assume that people inherit certain qualities and traits that make them better suited to leadership. Trait theories often identify particular personality or behavioural characteristics shared by leaders. If particular traits are key features of leadership, then how do we explain people who possess those qualities but are not leaders? This question is one of the difficulties in using trait theories to explain leadership.

### 3. Contingency Theories

Contingency theories of leadership focus on particular variables related to the environment that might determine which particular style of leadership is best suited for the situation. According to this theory, no leadership style is best in all situations. Success depends upon a number of variables, including the leadership style, qualities of the followers and aspects of the situation.

### 4. Situational Theories

Situational theories propose that leaders choose the best course of action based upon situational variables. Different styles of leadership may be more appropriate for certain types of decision-making.

### 5. Behavioural Theories

Behavioural theories of leadership are based upon the belief that great leaders are made, not born. Rooted in behaviorism, this leadership theory focuses on the actions of leaders not on mental qualities or internal states. According to this theory, people can *learn* to become leaders through teaching and observation.

### 6. Participative Theories

Participative leadership theories suggest that the ideal leadership style is one that takes the input of others into account. These leaders encourage participation and contributions from group members and help group members feel more relevant and committed to the decision-making process. In participative theories, however, the leader retains the right to allow the input of others.

### 7. Management Theories

Management theories, also known as transactional theories, focus on the role of supervision, organization and group performance. These theories base leadership on a system of rewards and punishments.

Managerial theories are often used in business; when employees are successful, they are rewarded; when they fail, they are reprimanded or punished. Learn more about theories of transactional leadership.

### 8. Relationship Theories

Relationship theories, also known as transformational theories, focus upon the connections formed between leaders and followers. Transformational leaders motivate and inspire people by helping group members see the importance and higher good of the task. These leaders are focused on the performance of group members, but also want each person to fulfil his or her potential. Leaders with this style often have high ethical and moral standards.

# 3

# Leadership and Motivation

Leadership and motivational qualities are excellent to have not only among management in a business, but among employees as well. Many individuals tend to have a propensity to be leaders, while some learn successful leadership behaviours and go on to be effective leaders. Leading is the ability to influence others in a group. Being a good leader takes understanding of what motivates others. Leaders want to influence things to continue or create change. Either way it takes a person with certain skills to do the task.

In order to be a leader, it is important to understand what motivates the employees around you. It is necessary to discover the fundamental needs that employees, coworkers, and bosses have. All people have a need for a basic income and necessities. Additionally, they have a need for a deep social connection and friendships. People want to fit in somewhere and feel as if they belong. Another large category of human need is the need for growth and challenges. A worker lured to a job by high salary may find their job dissatisfying if they are unable to have friendships and connect with other people at work. It is much easier to lead and motivate if you understand what people's undeniable needs are.

There are a few qualities that seem to put people at the head of the pack as far as their ability to obtain leadership positions. Many leaders tend to be outgoing, brave, tall in stature, well-liked, articulate, and task oriented. By no means are these qualities always correct. Napoleon happened to be a very short man, and Abraham Lincoln has been described as being very introverted. There are countless factors that can make a person a good leader, but it depends on the group of people that they are leading. There is a common misconception that leaders are always outspoken, flamboyant people, and this just isn't the case. Less articulate individuals with other combinations of skills are quite successful as well.

Leading is used to channel motivation into practical use. There are many factors that play into keeping employees motivated. A common factor in motivation is the type of work that the employee is doing. You might think that if an employee has simple tasks that they would become more efficient at them over time. However, it is also important to look at the fact that doing a job that is the same day in and day out can become quite boring. When employees are given a job with varied tasks and ability to grow they tend to stay more motivated. Sadly, many workers are underutilized and do not get challenged or the ability to show their creativity to its fullest potential.

Many people are goal oriented once a leader shows where their efforts should be focused. They respond well to deadlines and planning. It is a good feeling to have a concrete goal to shoot for. Having the ability to achieve goals can be very personally satisfying. In organizations usually there may be specific planned goals. Attempts by many within an organization to achieve the same goal can also create stronger drive to be successful. As a manager, it is important to make sure that the goals are reasonable. The effect of having a goal that is impossible to attain has reverse effects and can cause discouragement rapidly.

When goals are eventually accomplished or milestones are reached, many people like to be able to get a reward or benefit. Some goals create personal satisfaction upon completion naturally such as learning, growth, and self-esteem. Additional rewards such as salary increases, bonuses, and celebrations are also good reminders that individuals are appreciated for what they are doing. Rewards work so well for some as motivating tools that workers will go out of their way to make sure they use and develop the kinds of things that are rewarded. This is also a double-edged sword because some rewarded activities will take effort away from non-reward areas. For example, if employees are paid based on the amount of output that they generate, the employees might try to increase their output. They might have more of what they were doing, but it may not be of as good of quality.

The work atmosphere in general has a lot to do with employee motivation. Typically managers that treat employees in a friendly manner are apt to get more of a positive response. You want to work at a business with individuals that enjoy their work and like their surroundings. Employees will compare themselves to others to make sure they are being treated in a way that they perceive as fair. If an employee feels that they are not being treated fair, they will lack the motivation to work hard.

Everyone likes to have a little independence and to be useful while they are working. Some control is always needed, but flexibility is appreciated. Employees and coworkers are also happy when they feel like they fit in and are able to be themselves. This goes back to the basis needs that humans strive to fulfil.

Unfortunately, the ability to lead and increase motivation in people is not always used properly. Leadership should not be based on lies, trickery, or manipulation. You can look back in history and see that there are people who have abused their power and used motivation in negative ways. When leading other individuals it is important they are getting a benefit out of their own actions. It is important to be ethical and considerate of others at all times.

In order to achieve leadership and promote motivation there are an assorted variety of skills that anyone in an organization can use. Remember the basic things that people have needs for, and look how individuals respond on a personal level.

Make sure that you do not require things from others that you would not want required of yourself. In fact, one of the best ways to be a leader is to be a good example for others to follow. Do not feel that you have to conform to what you think that a leader should be. People with different personalities and approaches are able to be terrific leaders. Concentrate on developing interpersonal skills and you will be able to lead others more effectively.

Motivation is a goal-oriented characteristic that helps a person achieve his objectives. It pushes an individual to work hard at achieving his or her goals. An executive must have the right leadership traits to influence motivation. However, there is no specific blueprint for motivation. As a leader, one should keep an open perspective on human nature. Knowing different needs of subordinates will certainly make the decision-making process easier.

Both an employee as well as manager must possess leadership and motivational traits. An effective leader must have a thorough knowledge of motivational factors for others. He must understand the basic needs of employees, peers and his superiors. Leadership is used as a means of motivating others.

Given below are important guidelines that outline the basic view of motivation:

- Harmonize and match the subordinate needs with the organizational needs. As a leader, the executive must ensure that the business has the same morals and ethics that he seeks in his employees. He should make sure that his subordinates are encouraged and trained in a manner that meets the needs of the business.
- Appreciation and rewards are key motivators that influence a person to achieve a desired goal. Rewarding good/exceptional behaviour with a small token of appreciation, certificate or letter can be a great motivator. If a certificate is awarded to a person, it should mention the particular act or the quality for which the individual is being rewarded.
- Being a role model is also a key motivator that influences people in reaching their goals. A leader should set a good example to ensure his people to grow and achieve their goals effectively.
- Encouraging individuals to get involved in planning and important issues resolution procedure not only motivates them, but also teaches the intricacies of these key decision-making factors. Moreover, it will help everyone to get better understanding of their role in the organization. The communication will be unambiguous and will certainly attract acknowledgement and appreciation from the leader.
- Developing moral and team spirit certainly has a key impact on the well-being of an organization. The metal or emotional state of a person constitutes his or her moral fabric. A leader's actions and decisions affect the morale of his subordinates. Hence, he should always be aware of his decisions and activities. Team spirit is the soul of the organization. The leader should always make sure his subordinates enjoy performing their duties as a team and make themselves a part of the organization's plans.
- A leader should step into the shoes of the subordinates and view things from subordinate's angle. He should empathize with them during difficult times. Empathizing with their personal problems makes them stronger-mentally and emotionally.

- A meaningful and challenging job accomplished inculcates a sense of achievement among employees. The executive must make their employees feel they are performing an important work that is necessary for the organization's well-being and success. This motivational aspect drives them to fulfil goals.

Remember, "To become an efficient leader, you must be self-motivated". You must know your identity, your needs and you must have a strong urge to do anything to achieve your goals. Once you are self-motivated, only then you can motivate others to achieve their goals and to harmonize their personal goals with the common goals of the organization.

## Reaction to Change

Command-and-control leadership is the primary style in our society. It is accepted because efficiency is created by repetitive action, teaching people to resist change. Once acquiring a skill, they do not want to learn another. The worker adapts to level three with an occasional trip to level two.

Worker responsibility is just the opposite, it motivates people to thrive on change by seeking challenges, finding ways to achieve goals. Level one is the leader of changing technology, finding ways to create efficiency.

### *Reaction to Efficiency*

The efficiency of advancing technology is forcing change. It is up to the individual or business to decide which side of change they want to be on, the leading edge or trailing edge. The leading edge is exciting while the trailing edge is a drag. Playing catch-up drains motivation while leaders of change inspire motivation.

With today's changing technology, an individual must be willing to abandoned old skills and learn new ones. The ability to adapt is achieved through self-development programs. Because level one thrives on change, they adapt to whatever methods gets things done with the least amount of effort. This brings us to work habits.

In level one, management and front line workers, together, are searching for ways to solve and prevent problems. Decisions are made on the front line where alternative methods are analysed. Being able to prevent problems is a motivating force. In level three management makes all decision, as a result, management must find ways to solve all problems and find alternative methods. Front line employees may be aware conflicts, but they don't have the authority to take action and have learned not to be concerned. Supervisors are only concerned with elements that management thinks are important.

Under command-and-control leadership, management considers the opinions or concerns of people on the front line to be trivial. As a result, management takes action only when problems become too big to ignore.

If workers have conflicts with their supervisors, they will find ways to increase the magnitude of problems, creating a combative environment. A downward spiral of management implementing more control and workers resisting control develop. Under worker responsibility, management and workers unite to prevent or solve problems.

### Reaction to Learning Habits

In level two, young workers are establishing work habits, developing attitudes and learning a professional skill. Out of training and on the job, motivation level will depend on the leadership style they work under. Under command-and-control leadership, ambitions will be associated with maintaining the status quo. Under worker responsibility, ambitions will be associated with opportunity. They will continually expand their skills as the need or as opportunity arises.

### Reaction to Goals

Self-motivated people are goal motivated. Once they conquer one goal, they establish another. Every goal is a learning process that requires all the elements in level one. Companies that attract and keep this type of person stay on the leading edge of technology. The CEO is a visionary in customer service and employee leadership. The employees' goals are the same as the CEO's. If the CEO desires control, then he will lead in such a way that trains subordinates to lead by control. As a result, the employees' goals are quitting time and payday.

### Reaction to Recognition

Recognition is important; it builds positive self-esteem. By itself, its benefits are short lived. Long-term benefits are achieved when the employee feels the job could not have been done without them. This means they were faced with a challenge, which means, they had the responsibility and authority to take action. This environment is found in level one.

### Self Motivated Projects

Self-motivated projects' is the ability to start and finish what one has started. Most people, working alone, do not finish what they start.

The ability to finish challenging projects is the secret to being a winner. First requirement is interest, then asking questions which inspires' the learning process. With information, a challenge is presented and a goal set. When action is taken, the barriers of persistence, risk, fear and failure become a challenge by itself. Self-motivated projects are difficult because no one cares if they succeed, which is another barrier. This is why most people quit before they get a good start. People, who find ways to overcome barriers and hang in there, are the winners. They develop skills and confidence, which are required steps to larger projects.

### Team Motivated Projects

Everyone can be inspired to achievement in a team-motivated environment. With a common goal, team members support each other until success is achieved. In this environment, others do care and team members are needed for achieving the goal. For this reason, team motivation is extremely powerful. The exchange of ideas, information and testing the results, adds to the motivating force. As a result, each member seeks to be a leader of quality input.

## Leadership Development

Leadership development refers to any activity that enhances the quality of leadership within an individual or organization. These activities have ranged from MBA style programs offered at university business schools to action learning, high-ropes courses and executive retreats.

### Developing Individual Leaders

Traditionally, leadership development has focused on developing the leadership abilities and attitudes of individuals.

Just like people aren't all born with the ability to, say, play football (soccer) like Zinedine Zidane or sing like Luciano Pavarotti, people aren't all born with the ability to lead. Different personal characteristics can help or hinder a person's leadership effectiveness and require formalized programs for developing leadership competencies Yet, everyone can develop their leadership effectiveness. Achieving such development takes focus, practice and persistence more akin to learning a musical instrument than reading a book.

Classroom-style training and associated reading is effective in helping leaders to know more about what is involved in leading well. However, knowing what to do and doing what you know are two very different outcomes; management expert Henry Mintzberg is one person to highlight this dilemma. It is estimated that as little as 15% of learning from traditional classroom style training results in sustained behavioural change within the workplace. The success of leadership development efforts has been linked to three variables :

- Individual learner characteristics
- The quality and nature of the leadership development program
- Genuine support for behavioural change from the leader's supervisor.

Military officer training academies, such as the Royal Military Academy Sandhurst, go to great lengths to only accept candidates who show the highest potential to lead well. Personal characteristics that associated with successful leadership development include leader motivation to learn, a high achievement drive and personality traits such as openness to experience, an internal focus of control, and self-monitoring. Development is also more likely to occur when the design of the development program:

- Integrates a range of developmental experiences over a set period of time (e.g. 6–12 months). These experiences may include 360 degree feedback, experiential classroom style programs, business school style coursework, executive coaching, reflective journaling, mentoring and more.
- Involve goal setting, following an assessment of key developmental needs and then evaluate the achievement of goals after a given time period.

Among key concepts in leadership development one may find:

- Experiential learning: positioning the individual in the focus of the learning process, going through the four stages of experiential learning as formulated by David A. Kolb: 1. concrete experience 2. observation and reflection 3. forming abstract concept 4. testing in new situations.
- Self efficacy: The right training and coaching should bring about 'Self efficacy' in the trainee, as Albert Bandura formulated: A person's belief about his capabilities to produce effects.

- Visioning: Developing the ability to formulate a clear image of the aspired future of an organization unit.

A good personal leadership development program should enable you to develop a plan that helps you gain essential leadership skills required for roles across a wide spectrum from a youth environment to the corporate world. These characteristics include:

- Taking responsibility
- Gaining focus
- Developing life purpose
- Starting action immediately
- Developing effective and achievable goals and dreams.

### Developing Leadership at a Collective Level

More recently, organizations have come to understand that leadership can also be developed by strengthening the connection between, and alignment of, the efforts of individual leaders and the systems through which they influence organizational operations. This has led to a differentiation between leader development and leadership development. Leader development focuses on the development of the leader, such as the personal attributes desired in a leader, desired ways of behaving, ways of thinking or feeling. In contrast, leadership development focuses on the development of leadership as a process. This will include the interpersonal relationships, social influence process, and the team dynamics between the leader and his/her team at the dyad level, the contextual factors surrounding the team such as the perception of the organizational climate and the social network linkages between the team and other groups in the organization.

One practical example of developing leadership specifically so as to influence an organization's safety culture is described by Burman & Evans. Both forms of development may mutually influence each other, as exemplified in the concept of "Deep Change" in Robert E. Quinn [1]'s 1996 book of the same title.

Leadership development can build on the development of individuals (including followers) to become leaders. In addition, it also needs to focus on the interpersonal linkages between the individuals in the team.

In the belief that the most important resource that an organization possesses is the people that comprise the organization, some organizations address the development of these resources (even including the leadership). In contrast, the concept of "Employeeship" recognizes that what it takes to be a good leader is not too dissimilar to what it takes to be a good employee. Therefore, bringing the notional leader together with the team to explore these similarities (rather than focusing on the differences) brings positive results. This approach has been particularly successful in Sweden where the power distance between manager and team is small.

### *Succession Planning*

The development of "high potentials" to effectively take over the current leadership when their time comes to exit their positions is known as succession planning. This type of leadership development usually requires the extensive transfer of an individual between departments. In many multinationals, it usually requires international transfer and experience to build a future leader. Succession planning requires a sharp focus on organization's future and vision, in order to align leadership development with the future the firm aspires to create. Thus successive leadership development is based not only on knowledge and history but also on a dream. For such a plan to be successful, a screening of future leadership should be based not only on "what we know and have" but also on "what we aspire to become". Persons involved in succession planning should be current leadership representing the vision and HR executives having to translate it all into a program. According to Meir Jacob and Amit Cohen (1995) three critical dimensions should be considered: 1. Skills and knowledge 2. Role perception and degree of acceptance of leading role 3. Self-efficacy (Albert Bandura). These three dimensions should be a basis of any leadership succession programme.

## Leadership Competencies

The leader is the central person who guides the group toward its goal. No single trait has been found which separates leaders from non-leaders; nonetheless, leaders usually have more drive and determination and probably a greater concentration of positive qualities than non-leaders.

Research over many years, some of which formed the basis for the original conceptualization of the White Stag program, has revealed that leaders commonly share a definite set of skills, or competencies. We do not believe in "born leaders;" we believe the leadership is a skill, ability, or competency that can be acquired. In White Stag, our functional definition of competence is: knowledge, understanding, way of thinking, skills and disposition. Our program is designed to affect all of these qualities.

The idea of born-leaders has become outdated. The founder of White Stag, Béla Bánáthy, in his research for his Master's thesis on leadership, compiled a list of over 80 behaviours that authorities in the field described as "leadership." The key notion here is that these behaviours are skills that can be learned.

For many years, leadership in traditional Boy Scout of America junior leader training programs was referred to only indirectly, by example and inference.

White Stag does not depend on happenstance or luck for leadership training to take place. This "indirect" way of training for leadership is what the White Stag method challenges and transforms into a "direct approach." The skills of leadership are specifically described.

### *Defining Leadership Objectively*

The direct approach is oriented toward a specific leadership behaviour which is clearly and objectively defined. The elements of leadership behaviour are isolated as specific learnings which are systematically programmed into a long-term developmental process.

The direct approach ensures that appropriate and sufficient time is given the development of leadership skills, to bring about the desired change in behaviour and to achieve leadership competence.

The SECOND concept is that, rather than being some nebulous characteristic which one has to be born with, leadership can be defined as a set of competencies which can be learned. Some eighty aspects of knowledge, skills, and attitudes have been taken into account in our research which have been clustered into competencies. To sum it up. an understanding of the concepts described here has helped us to bring into focus that the acquisition of leadership competencies should occur by plan and design, rather than by accident. Although leaders may emerge-as they do today-as by-products of group processes, this is neither an economical nor an effective way of developing leadership. Based on the concepts described above, in our experimental program:

Specific competencies of leadership—relevant to Scouting—have been identified...

### *The Leadership Curriculum*

Bánáthy condensed his 80 descriptors into eleven competencies that now comprise the curriculum of White Stag Leadership

Development. Much research has been done since then to supplement, amend, and above all, keep the knowledge base current.

The eleven competencies are part of the overall leadership development design. The framework of competencies provides a consistent reference base for all members as they gain increased knowledge. Instead of learning greater and greater numbers of competencies, members reach higher "plateaus" of knowledge within the existing schema. The objectives within each competency will eventually be so discrete that selective groups of objectives may be chosen by the manager of learning that reflect exactly the needs of the learners.

Knowledge of or the ability to manage the learning of any or several of these competencies does not a leader make. What makes a leader is the degree to which the competency is an integral characteristic of an individual and the degree to which it influences the individual's behaviour (and by inference, his values).

A competency of primary significance is communication, or "Getting and Giving Information." Nothing else can happen until communication, on one or more levels, has been established. Identification of and with group norms and group goals leads to the maintenance of group membership; the ability to call on group members' knowledge, skills and abilities insures that the task can be tackled. "Knowing the Needs and Characteristics of the Group," and "Knowing and Using Group Resources" are the next most important.

The need among program participants for them to learn more about these competencies is made plain to them in a number of ways. Specific learning activities are conceived and executed that draw their attention to the group dynamic and the role of leadership among them.

One of the most important talents a leader needs is empathy; that is, an appreciation for and understanding of others' needs. (Empathy includes both the ability to uncover needs and sensitivity to those needs.) The empathic leader is one with the group, is helpful; he is willing to face problems, and has at his disposal a variety of problem-solving tools.

Some other behaviours that indicate positive qualities of leadership are cheerfulness, enthusiasm, alertness, integrated character, deliberate will control, risk-taking, and absence of suspicious anxiety.

Leadership can be developed by acquiring the competencies described below.

## *Leadership Can be Learned*

Leadership competencies cannot be acquired in a few training sessions or in a single training course, but only as the result of a long-range development process over a number of years. Leadership development must begin during the formative years of youth, and is a life-long process that never ends.

The acquisition of leadership competencies occurs by plan and design.

[It is a] process with a purpose. It is a process of the learner moving from a state wherein he cannot yet perform as the described purpose of the training to a state where he can demonstrate such performance. This move is what training is about. Training is the making of specific arrangements in the environment of the learner which provide him with experiences by which he can confront and master the learning task, by which he can be transformed to the state where he can perform as desired.

Leadership development cannot be perceived as a single training course or as a one-shot event, but must be a continuous seqence of closely chained and systematically organized learning and experience-building opportunities.

Developmental psychologists postulate that each child passes through a series of specific stages; White Stag addresses each youth in terms appropriate to his particular stage of development and levels of need. The program is structured in three tiers, or "phases," each designed to meet the needs of developing adolescents.

We understand that organized learning opportunities like the White Stag program are not for every youth, and that many youth grow into fine, mature adults and leaders in their communities without participating in organized youth groups.

However, participants in the White Stag program strongly feel that the program helps young people realize their full potential, assists them in developing positive concepts of self esteem, self evaluation, and the ability to get along with others in the widest variety of situations. The White Stag program plants a seed in some who then grow it themselves; others return to partake again and again of the distinctive spirit which nurtures growth, that is marrow to the bone of White Stag.

Growth in leadership capacity does not happen in isolation as a member or learner in the program. The support and understanding of peers and adults in the youths' home environment is critically important.

The opportunity to apply what he has learned, to experiment, is essential if the leadership competencies are to be transferred out of the White Stag program. It is at home, in the school, in their church or temple, in the community, and at work while helping others grow, that the youth applies the leadership competencies and captures the White Stag Spirit.

### The Focus is on the Learner

We have shifted our attention from instruction to learning. This does not mean that we minimize the importance of instruction or the role of the instructor. The significance of instruction is not questioned here at all. The point that is made here is that the learning task is the nucleus around which to design instruction. The role and function of instruction should be viewed in its proper relationship to learning. It should be planned for and provided for accordingly. Instruction is a means to an end and not an end in itself. Its function is to facilitate learning. The effectiveness of the program is not measured by the effort made by the instructor but by the amount of learning achieved by the learner.

### Leadership is a Property of the Group

Leadership is a combination of three dynamic factors: the group, the environment, and the task. More than one member of the group will perform leadership functions. Several members may contribute to goal achievements, depending on the requirements of the situation and the resources it offers, including the people, time, and material available. The task in which the group is engaged also affects the type of leadership needed. Leadership, therefore, may be looked upon as the property of the group.

### What is a Group?

The group is "an assemblage of persons or objects gathered or located together; an aggregation."We believe that when two or more people gather for the purpose of accomplishing a task, leadership emerges. This is the concept of leadership with which we concern ourselves in White Stag. It is vital in all cultures that groups are able to work together to achieve the maximum benefit for society.

### How do Groups Come About?

The most basic and obvious group is our family.

Leaders are needed in all circumstances, even for the most routine tasks, in the most common affairs of every day...In the family the leadership function of a parent is most basic. There is scarcely any leadership role in society which would be of greater significance than parenthood.

With the many challenges facing society today, it is abundantly clear that many families lack leadership.

Beyond the family, people band themselves together for numerous reasons. Some involve simple interpersonal relations such as neighbors organized to form a neighbourhood association. Others may involve quite complex interrelationships, such as a large integrated manufacturing enterprise. In each case the group has been organized to meet a need that is recognized by or is common to all the members of the group.

## About Leaders

What constitutes leadership? How can a leader be recognized? Leadership in most dictionaries is simply the "capacity or ability to lead." In White Stag, we argue that it is not quite so simple or that obvious.

### *The Leader's Function*

Some groups persist and prosper and some blow up or wither away. Those that prosper are characterized by having a leader, someone who functions in two ways.

- The leader helps the group meet the needs of the individuals.
- No two members join for exactly the same reason. The leader helps knit the individuals into a cooperating group. The leader helps them all to see a common reason, a common goal that is mutually desired, and he delegates responsibilities among the individuals so they can see how their efforts will lead toward reaching the goal.
- The leader helps the group realize the purpose for which it was created. The leader helps the group:
    - o Define the purposes for which it exists.
    - o Keep its activity within the defined purposes and goals.
    - o Find alternative ways of attaining their goal.
    - o Grow to a more progressive organization in its own eyes.
    - o Clarify the responsibilities of its officers and members to carry out the program.

o Evaluate itself—why it exists, where it is headed, how much progress it is making.

Simply put, leadership is...

...influencing the group to accomplish a mutually agreed-upon task while advancing the group's integrity and morale.

In the language of an eleven-year old, it's "getting the job done and keeping the group together." The group remains in existence only as long as these two needs are being fulfilled. The leader is not the same as the boss. The following poem says it well.

### The Leader

The boss drives group members; the leader coaches them.

The boss depends upon authority; the leader on good will.

The boss inspires fear; the leader inspires enthusiasm.

The boss says "I"; the leader says "we."

The boss assigns the task, the leader sets the pace.

The boss says, "Get there on time"; the leader gets there ahead of time.

The boss fixes the blame for the breakdown; the leader fixes the breakdown.

The boss knows how it is done; the leader shows how.

The boss makes work a drudgery; the leader makes it a game.

The boss says, "Go"; the leader says, "Let's go."

—Author unknown

### A Leader's Key Functions

The leader accepts three key functions in his role:

- Authority: the right to make decisions.
- Responsibility: assignment for achieving a goal.
- Accountability: acceptance of success or failure.

You may at times be asked to accept a leadership position but are granted only two of these three responsibilities. If this happens, watch out.

When you do not possess any one of the three functions, just imagine you are sitting on a three-legged stool—and you've just had one of the legs broken off from under you. You know what's going to happen next.

### What the Leader Must Know

What must you, as the leader, know to be able to help the group? You must know:

- The members and be interested in their welfare.
- Their hopes, ambitions, abilities, limitations and prejudices.
- The things the members want to learn, or at least where and how to get the knowledge, such as woodcraft skills.
- How to motivate members to want to learn new skills and gain new attitudes. Without motivation no learning takes place and without learning the member stagnates and consequently finds no satisfaction from being a part of the group.
- How to establish communication between the members of the group.
- How to conduct or supervise meetings, discussions, and informal activities. Within White Stag, these include campfires, singing, Sunday services, troop leader councils, work parties and so forth. Common experiences that the group enjoys or that they are proud of help weld the group together.
- How to assess his own effectiveness, how to get the group to evaluate itself, its goals and its progress toward them. This in turn becomes a powerful motivating force for further learning.

### Can a Group Have Several Leaders?

This leadership capability is usually assumed by the world at large to rest in a designated individual. He or she, in modern democratic social structures, typically governs with the consent of the governed for a specified period of weeks, months or years.

In White Stag we implicitly include as a leader any member of the group who possesses the knowledge, skill, and ability needed by group members to help the group achieve cooperative results. While there is usually a designated leader—someone appointed or elected to that role—for our purposes a leader is someone who is exerting more influence on the group than anyone else at that moment.

At any specific moment, one person is exercising more influence than anyone else on the group and therefore by definition is the leader. This functional take on leadership assumes that different leaders exercise different roles in keeping the group moving towards its purpose. The leader of the moment does not automatically usurp the responsibility and authority of any designated leader, although in certain crisis situations this may in fact take place. The leader of the moment is usually fulfilling only one of the many functions necessary to the group's continued success. The leadership control of the group continues to rest with the person selected to function in most of the required roles. Some leaders excel in several leadership functions and neglect others. Those women and men who are recognized and acclaimed as outstanding leaders have cultivated excellent skill in many areas, are in effect multi-disciplinary leaders.

To give you a practical example, take a group of Scouts on a hike. The Patrol Leader is the designated individual in charge. But perhaps one of the members had just been hiking in the same area last week. That person then might assume temporary leadership in guiding the group towards its campsite over the next ridge.

If, during the hike, a Scout falls and sprains his ankle, yet another Scout with superior skills in first aid may assume leadership in treating and managing the care of the injured Scout. Everyone, including the designated leader, willingly takes direction from another member of the group who demonstrates the leadership skills necessary in the moment.

Some might say that map reading and first aid are practical skills and not a demonstration of leadership. True for only a moment. For the Scout familiar with the terrain, or the knowledgeable first aider, what must each be able to do to persuade the others that he really knows what he's talking about? If either is non-communicative, uncertain, cannot articulate a plan, does not demonstrate resourcefulness, fails to be sensitive to group members' needs—then they fail as leaders. To implement the practical skill in a group setting requires something more, which we conceive of as a specific set of leadership skills.

The real measure of leadership excellence is evident when members of the group talk in terms of "we" instead of "I". They are identifying their personal goals as the group's goals and feel they belong to the very best group.

### *Lao-Tzu*

Of the best rulers,
The people only know that they exist;
The next best they love and praise
The next they fear;
And the next they revile.

When they do not command the people's faith,
Some will lose faith in them,
And then they resort to oaths!
But of the best when their task is accomplished,
their work done,
The people all remark, "We have done it ourselves."
—Lao-Tzu (6th century B.C.), Chinese philosopher.

A group is successful when group members believe preserving the integrity of the group has an overriding importance to each of them and they desire to stay and work together. They may not hold strong affection for every member in the group, in fact they might dislike a member or two, but the group is more important than any individual differences.

Johnson & Johnson taking cue from the failure of IBM in the early nineties formed a team of senior executives and called it *"FrameworkS"* to identify the critical factors that would drive its market leadership position built over a century.

## Frameworks as Management Process

*"FrameworkS"* has since been institutionalized in the company as a management process to help leaders understand the marketplace and how it can be served best. In 1995, the *"FrameworkS"* tasks force reported that the company lacks *"strong"* potential leaders to fill up the senior positions and that competencies different from *"command and control"* were required for future growth. The task force also defined leadership as it means to J&J and drafted the "Standards of.

### *Standards of Leadership*

Behaviours with respect to credo values, business results and leadership competencies were clearly brought out in the "Standards of Leadership" to enable leaders to demonstrate and emphasize them in their day-to-day work. The leadership competencies identified by Johnson & Johnson are:

- Customer and marketplace focus
- Innovation
- Interdependent partnering (collaboration)
- Mastering complexity (managing complexity & change)
- Organizational & people development.

## *Seven Principles of Leadership*

Also the *"FrameworkS"* team has defined *"seven principles of leadership development"* to further guide the company in building future leaders:

- Leadership development is a key business strategy
- Leadership excellence is a definable set of standards
- People are responsible for their own development
- J&J executives are accountable for developing leaders
- Leaders are developed primarily on the job
- People are an asset of the corporation; Leadership development is a collaborative, corporation-wide process
- Human resources support is vital to the success of leadership development.

The *"seven principles of leadership development"*, leadership competencies and related behavioural aspects were communicated throughout the organization. Next logical step was to help leaders assess their effectiveness as *"J&J leaders"* and from this need came the necessity of multi-source feedback mechanism. To assess the leadership behaviours with respect to the identified competencies a specially customized 360 degree feedback was introduced in the company. 360 degree feedback is used at J&J as a developmental tool and not as performance measurement tool. The need for 360 degree feedback instrument at Johnson and Johnson can be articulated as:

- To help individuals receive real feedback on leadership behaviour
- To help individuals identify the areas of development as leaders
- To help individuals create a personal development plan
- To help individuals seek continuous feedback on progress on the development plan and behaviour change.

## 13 Leadership Competency Model Competencies

These 13 competencies are going to lead you to the top of all. The 13 Competencies includes Drive for Results, Service Orientation, Quality Orientation, Planning & Organizing, Analysis & Problem Solving, Entrepreneurial Orientation, Risk Management, Relationship Management, Adaptability & Change Management, Team Leadership, People Development, Visionary & Strategic Thinking and Values & Ethics.

The 13 Leadership Competencies are:

- Drive for Results
- Service Orientation
- Quality Orientation
- Planning & Organizing
- Analysis & Problem Solving
- Entrepreneurial Orientation
- Risk Management
- Relationship Management
- Adaptability & Change Management
- Team Leadership
- People Development
- Visionary & Strategic Thinking
- Values & Ethics.

### *Leadership Competency 1 : Visioning and Strategic Thinking*

The ability to Provide direction and communicate the vision to encourage alignment within the organization. Has the skill and mindset to address issues for sustaining competitive edge and provide the relevant organizational response. The issues addressed could cover a wide spectrum of areas including people, technology, products, market opportunities, competitive threats and customers. Understands rapidly changing environmental trends at national and global levels.

### *Leadership Competency 2 : Adaptability and Change Management*

Is open and responsive to personal change. Changes the overall plan, goal or project to fit the situation. Personal willingness and ability to effectively work in, and adapt to change and adapts personal style/approaches to meet change requirements and is able to adjust to the changing needs.

### *Leadership Competency 3 : Drive for Results*

Motivated by success and passionate about working and achieving higher results. Persists to complete tasks/responsibilities, even in the face of difficulties, is optimistic and tenacious all through. Operates with personal ownership and looks for ways and means to improve performance all the time.

### Leadership Competency 4 : Team Leadership Competency

Set and champion a clear future direction and demonstrate the actions expected in others, including a high standard of performance. Takes responsibility not just for the deliverables of the department and its constituents, but also for enabling success of the business. Sets high standards of performance for self and others and provides a clear direction for the team to achieve objectives

### Leadership Competency 5 : People Development

A desire to work to develop the long term capability of others. Fostering the growth of people allows them to better meet organizational needs, to be more efficient, and gives them greater satisfaction in their job.

### Leadership Competency 6 : Entrepreneurial Skills

The ability to sight business opportunities and take them to a logical end. This is done by generating creative ideas, applying sound commercial acumen. Takes an innovative approach to problem solving.

It includes the ability to "think out of the box", to go beyond the conventional, and a willingness to try out different solutions. At the Sr. VP and above, it is the ability to champion innovation and encourage new ideas from employees.

### Leadership Competency 7 : Values and Ethics

Abide by a strict code of ethics and behaviour (i.e. chooses an ethical course of action and does the right thing, even in the face of opposition; encourages others to behave accordingly), Acting fairly (i.e. Treats others with honesty, fairness and respect; makes decisions that are objective and reflect the just treatment of others) and Taking responsibility (i.e. Takes responsibility for accomplishing work goals within accepted timeframes; accepts responsibility for one's decisions and actions and for those of one's group, team, or department; attempts to learn from mistakes).

Understanding, Identifying, assessing and managing risk while striving to attain objectives. Conducting risk assessment when identifying or recommending strategic and tactical options. Also providing organizational guidance on risk

### Leadership Competency 8 : Service Orientation

Understands and anticipates the needs of internal and external customers. Discovers and meets customer's underlying needs. Partners with the customer to create value for them.

Tracks and anticipates market trends and patterns, conceptualizes/ customizes products and services to address and shape customer needs. Provides support and resources to his team members to serve their customers. Creates and manages a positive perception of own product/organization in the mind of the customer. Becomes a trusted advisor/educator to customers.

### Leadership Competency 9 : Relationship Management & Collaboration

Leverages relationships with a diverse group of people across levels and functions for work and/or non work related goals. Gives equal attention to internal (within kotak) as well as external customer requirements. Handles disagreements and conflicts and seeks to resolve them. Understands others' underlying concerns, emotions and feelings. Focuses on building diversity as well as depth of relationship with associates and customers (internal & external). Sensitizes, educates and creates awareness in others towards the emerging needs to leverage relationships. Shows and encourages mutual respect

### Leadership Competency 10 : Planning And Organizing

Effectively organizing and planning work according to organizational needs by defining objectives and anticipating needs and priorities. Efficiently manage their time and the time of others and effectively handle multiple demands and competing deadlines. Identify goals, develop plans, estimate time frames and monitor progress.

### Leadership Competency 11 : Quality Orientation

Promotes and maintains high standards of quality at work. Applies discipline and a detail orientation to work activities and constantly looks for ways to improve the quality of products or services. Encourages others to have high quality standards in their work.

### Leadership Competency 12 : Analysis and Problem Solving

Solves difficult problems through careful and systematic evaluation of information, possible alternatives and consequences. Considers many sources of information and evaluates the information against possible courses of action, and carefully deliberates before a final decision is made.

### Global Leadership Competencies: The New Global Frontier

Significant changes have occurred since the emergence of the knowledge economy, demanding a recast of many of the roles of leaders. Today's leaders live and work in countries other than their home country, manage multinational teams, and have customers from all over the globe. Anyone who is working outside their country of origin or with others from outside their country of origin needs to demonstrate an effective blend of global competencies. This is even more critical for leaders and requires blending cultural definitions of leadership with multiple geographic influences.

More and more, the Internet and other means of rapid communication are allowing diverse groups of employees to come together to work and learn from each other. Ian Davis and Elizabeth Stephenson of McKinsey and Company believe, "More transformational than technology itself is the shift in behaviour that it enables.

We work not just globally but also instantaneously. We are forming communities and relationships in new ways. More than two billion people now use cell phones. We send nine trillion e-mails a year. We do a billion Google searches a day, more than half in languages other than English.

For perhaps the first time in history, geography is not the primary constraint on the limits of social and economic organization."

According to Tom Rath, best selling author of Strength Finder 2.0 and author of the Leadership without Borders foreword, while technology is making the dream of a truly global marketplace a reality today, we as human beings are now slowing things down. We are armed with the means for reaching out and interacting across borders, yet we do not.

Instead, many of us remain in our comfort zones, and spend most of our time working with those who are nearby. The borders that exist today are not created by a lack of transportation or technology...they are created by a lack of human connections.

Today, a leader might be from India working for an Indian-owned company and assigned to work in the United States. Another may be from France, working for an Australian-owned company and living in China. In my case, I am an American working for an Indian-owned company who relocated to India. Yet another person might work for a company headquartered in one part of the world and be assigned to a region in another part of the world. Wherever they are, all these people can connect simultaneously (with some creative and respectful time zone planning) to make key decisions that instantly influence organizations on a global scale. Welcome to the new global frontier.

# 4

# Business Acumen and Leadership

Business acumen is keenness and quickness in understanding and dealing with a business situation in a manner that is likely to lead to a good outcome. The term "business acumen" can be broken down literally as a composite of its two component words: Business literacy is defined in SHRM's Business Literacy Glossary as "the knowledge and understanding of the financial, accounting, marketing and operational functions of an organization." The Oxford English Dictionary defines acumen as "the ability to make good judgments and quick decisions". Given these textbook definitions, a strictly literal definition would be "keenness and quickness in understanding and dealing with a business situation."

Additionally, business acumen has emerged as a vehicle for improving financial performance and leadership development. Consequently, several different types of strategies have developed around improving business acumen.

## Business Acumen Characteristics

### *Business Savvy and Business Sense*

"Business savvy" and "business sense" are often used as synonyms, but they don't describe what people with business acumen do differently than those who are lacking the skill. Dr. Raymond R. Reilly of the Ross School of Business at the University of Michigan and Dr. Gregory P. Reilly of the University of Connecticut document traits that individuals with business acumen possess:

- Have an acute perception of the dimensions of business issues
- Can make sense out of complexity and an uncertain future

- Are mindful of the implications of a choice for all the affected parties
- Are decisive
- Are flexible if further change is warranted in the future.

Thus, developing stronger business acumen means a more thoughtful analysis, clearer logic underlying business decisions, closer attention to key dimensions of implementation and operation, and more disciplined performance management.

"Using Business Acumen to Understand How Your Company Really Works" is the subtitle to Ram Charan's book, What the CEO Wants You to Know. Mr. Charan builds the case that understanding business in its entirety, or "seeing the big picture" is an essential characteristic of someone with business acumen. He cites Steve Jobs as having strong business acumen because "he saw the potential of a machine that promised independence and freedom." He also suggests that Jack Welch's willingness to, "...learn from anyone, anywhere, anytime," contributes to his ability to exercise his business acumen to define the right business priorities.

### *Financial Literacy*

Financial literacy is an important tenet of business acumen, but is not a synonym. Ram Charan suggests that financial knowledge is the foundation of business acumen, and has described business acumen as, "...the art of linking an insightful assessment of the external business landscape with the keen awareness of how money can be made —and then executing the strategy to deliver the desired results.".

In a SHRM article entitled, "Business Acumen Involves More Than Numbers" Chris Berger, a principal and member of the human resources practice at CTPartners, explains that business acumen starts with the ability to understand how a company makes and loses money and that leaders must be financially literate and be able to understand numbers on company financial statements. But he says those demonstrating business acumen have the ability to take their knowledge of business fundamentals and use it to think strategically and then take appropriate action. "It's really the ability to think and act," he adds.

An October 2007 research paper based on the book The Three Financial Styles of Very Successful Leaders (McGraw-Hill, 2005) the book's author E. Ted Prince reports that, "Financial literacy is almost never the need for senior managers and high potentials. Most already possess degrees in business, including MBAs, and many have also had significant experience in the business sides of their professional roles. The real need for these managers is to understand how their actions and their behaviour impact their financial decision-making and how this in turn affects financial outcomes at the unit and the corporate level." It's evident that an individual with business acumen has some level of financial understanding and knowledge-but someone who is financially literate doesn't necessarily possess strong business acumen.

### Business Management & Leadership

Bob Selden, faculty member of Mobilizing People, a leadership development program based in Switzerland, observes a complementary relationship between business acumen and leadership. Selden states the importance of nurturing both the development of strategic skills and that of good leadership and management skills in order for business leaders to achieve effectiveness.

A study published in Human Resource Management International Digest titled, Business acumen: a critical concern of modern leadership development: Global trends accelerate the move away from traditional approaches, reveals why traditional leadership development approaches, which rely on personality and competency assessments as the scientific core of their approach, are failing.

The paper demonstrates the importance of business acumen in leadership-development approaches and contends that business acumen will have an increasing impact on leadership development and HR agendas. Research into this relationship resulted in the creation of the Perth Leadership Outcome Model, which links financial outcomes to individual leadership traits.

In a study that interviewed 55 global business leaders, business acumen was cited as the most critical competency area for global leaders.

In their book, The Leadership Pipeline, Ram Charan, Stephen Drotter, and James Noel study the process and criteria for selecting a group manager, and suggest that the process and criteria are similar for selecting a CEO. They write that an obvious criteria for selecting a leader is well-developed business acumen.

An organization full of high business acumen individuals can expect to see leaders with a heightened perspective that translates into an ability to inspire and excite the organization to achieve its potential.

## Business Acumen Development

Programs designed to improve an individual or group's business acumen have been a primary factor in fueling the growth of business acumen as a significant topic in the corporate world. Executive Development Associates' 2009/2010 survey of Chief Learning Officers, Senior Vice Presidents of Human Resources, and Heads of Executive and Leadership Development listed business acumen as the second most significant trend in executive development. A 2011 report published by Merrill C. Anderson Ph.D. explored in detail the impact of business acumen training on an organization in terms of intangibles and more tangible expressions of value.

Dr. Anderson's findings support the opinions of Dr. Raymond R. Reilly and Dr. Gregory P. Reilly that business acumen is a learned skill-developed on the job by learning the required skills from knowledge mentors while working in different employment positions. They also suggest that the learning process ranges widely, from highly-structured internal company training programs, to an individual's self-chosen moves from one position to another. The combination of these reports and surveys indicate that business acumen is a learned skill of increasing importance within the corporate world. In general, there are three different types of business acumen development programs available:

### *Business Acumen Courses*

Prominent schools, such as those at the University of Michigan Ross School of Business and the University of Pennsylvania Wharton School of Business, have programs which have been classified and presented as business acumen development courses. Ram Charan, cited as one of the top thinkers in business has promoted the idea that business acumen is a characteristic developed on the job and that proper training can help develop business acumen. In 1999 Mr.

Charan developed a business acumen course for Ford Motor Company and in 2002 partnered with Kevin Cope and Stephen M.R. Covey to develop a business acumen curriculum based on his 2001 book What the CEO Wants You to Know. In these programs, participants are generally involved in seminars, workshops, and highly condensed classes which cover a variety of topics on both the theory and practice of business. Subjects range from introductory financial training to industry-and-position-specific learning. Overall, these courses tend to stress the importance of business knowledge imparted from experienced leaders and managers in a classroom setting.

### Business Simulations

A business simulation is another corporate development tool used to increase business acumen. Several companies offer business simulations as a way to educate mid-level managers and non-financial leaders within their organization on cash flow and financial-decision-making processes. Their forms can vary from computer simulations to boardgame-style simulations.

Although these simulations provide participants with a more interactive learning experience, it is debatable as to whether these simulations reproduce the real-world sensation of actual business scenarios. These games never involve obtaining a behavioural base line for the participants so one can never know if they had any measurable behavioural impact. Often the simulation is too artificial to be of real-world relevance.

### Psychological Assessments

The advent of personal assessments for business acumen is based in the emerging theories of behavioural finance and attempts to correlate innate personality traits with positive financial outcomes. This method approaches business acumen not as entirely based in either knowledge or experience, but on the combination of these and other factors which comprise an individual's financial personality or "signature". The results from this research have been limited, but noteworthy.

## Perth Leadership Outcome Model

The Perth Leadership Outcome Model is a leadership model that aims to characterize leaders by the financial outcome of their leadership, as distinct from the two traditional leadership models of focusing on either the leader's personality or behavioural skills and business competencies. It was developed by Dr. E. Ted Prince over the period 2002-6.

### Traditional Approaches

The traditional leadership models are based on either a personality or a behavioural/competency approach (Bass, 1990). The personality approach is rooted in the "Great Man" theories popular in the early 20th century. Research in this tradition sought to identify the personal qualities that distinguished leaders from followers or effective leaders from ineffective leaders. This tradition is operationalized in the modern era by the plethora of personality tools used in leadership research and practice. Popular examples include the Myers Briggs Type Indicator (MBTI),the Fundamental Interpersonal Relations Orientations-Behaviour(FIRO-B), and assessment tools based on the Five-Factor Model of personality like the NEO PI-R or Hogan Personality Inventory (HPI). These personality measures are based on a standard psychological paradigm and were designed to show the level of interpersonal and social functioning of an individual.

These instruments were designed by psychologists and were not primarily designed to be business leadership assessments—the business application only gained traction in later years. (An exception is the Hogan Leadership Forecast tools, which were designed to predict psychological functioning in the workplace).

The behavioural/competency approaches, by contrast, were designed specifically for use in business. They are focused on individual managerial competencies such as vision, execution, and perseverance. They usually measure from 60 to over 100 individual competencies. Their intellectual heritage is the intersection of vocational guidance—which aims to show how individuals will perform in a particular job function—and a political backlash to intelligence/ability testing—following former Harvard president and entrepreneur, David McClelland's classic article, "Testing for competence rather than intelligence." Neither of these arenas—guidance counseling, downplaying IQ—were intended for application with senior leaders, although the use of competency models has been extended to this area. Examples include the competency models offered by Lominger. Hay-McBehr, Personnel Decisions International. and so on.

## Concepts

### Financial Outcome

The Perth Leadership Outcome Model differs from these in that it focuses on what types of business outcome are associated with particular types of individuals and leaders. The model defines "outcome" in strictly financial terms. It links an individual's inclinations with the type of financial objectives they are likely to pursue and in particular, the type of financial value and valuation outcome most will to occur as a result of their leadership.

This model therefore differs significantly from the traditional models in that it focuses specifically on the financial outcomes of individuals and organizations. The traditional personality and competency models do not have a specific goal of explaining a leader or organization's financial performance, as does the Perth Leadership Outcome Model.

### *Financial Signature*

The Perth Leadership Outcome Model (PLOM) identifies the concept of the financial traits of an individual, which it calls their "financial signature". The financial signature describes an innate calculus, possessed by all individuals, that drives their behaviour when they make judgments about situations involving risk and reward, cost and benefit. Each individual has a characteristic way of handling such situations.

This particular way imposes a systematic but unconscious bias on all decisions which have financial impacts and ramifications. Knowing this the model predicts the types of financial decisions they make and therefore the financial impacts of their decision-making. From this it can predict their impact on financial performance, profitability and ultimately the financial value and market valuation of organizations they run. This analysis can be extended to the team and the organizational levels.

### *Financial Mission*

The PLOM states that individuals cannot change their financial signature because it is innate, or at the very least fixed for long periods of time. However they can change their financial mission, that is how they express their financial traits in their actual behaviour. The extent to which an individual can change their financial mission compared with their financial signature varies significantly between individuals. Most will be able to change somewhat, while only a few will be able to make dramatic change. However if a critical mass of leaders in an organization change their financial mission even by a small amount, the organization may also change its financial performance and its market value.

### *Outcome Assessments*

The financial signature of an individual can be identified and measured using assessment instruments designed by the Perth Leadership Institute including the Financial Outcome Assessment. Other instruments show how a person can improve their financial mission and their leadership outcome (the Executive Outcome Assessment) and the financial signature and mission of an organization (the Corporate Financial Outcome Assessment).

### Behavioural Finance

PLOM represents a new approach in the areas of behavioural finance and behavioural economics. These two fields and their foundational assumption of economic irrationality are focused mainly on consumers, although the more recent approaches have extended this assumption to a limited class of executives involved in making investment decisions for their corporations. However the PLOM approach is focused mainly on the extension of this assumption of irrationality to all corporate executives and managers, even those who do not have corporate responsibility for financial decision-making.

### Historical Development

The PLOM model is unique in many ways. However, it is related to two intellectual precursors. The work by the great German sociologist, Max Weber, linked social and economic variables. This is reflected particularly in his seminal work "The Protestant Ethic and the Spirit of Capitalism". However Weber did not go further to link behaviour with economic outcomes at the corporate, as distinct from the social, level.

The other precursor is, again, the Harvard psychologist David McClelland. His work in the 1950s linked entrepreneurial behaviour with the emergence of capitalist society. His great work."The Achieving Society," identifies these links in societies from the Greek era to the present. However, although prescient, his work still did not model the structure of entrepreneurial and financial behaviour at the level of the individual and does not show its relevance to corporate financial outcomes, again analysing at the social, not the corporate, level. Although influential in its day, McClelland's approach has not been extended and it has only been with the emergence of behavioural finance and economics that interest in this area has been revived. The PLOM research reflects this interest.

### Validation

The work by the Perth Leadership Institute is intriguing and innovative. It demonstrates statistically the link between financial signature and company financial outcome. However definitive validation has yet to be achieved and replicated by other researchers.

### Developing Business Acumen for Better Business Leadership

We have always heard about business acumen but many of us do not have quite a clear idea of what this really means. One way to describe it is through relating it with understanding the different drivers that promote sales and profit. Simply put, business acumen is understanding how a certain business work, and what makes it profitable. It is about having knowledge about what terms like amortization, assets, balance sheet, book value, liquidity, fixed assets, cash flow, margin, and return on assets really mean and how they reflect business performance.

Many people believe that the best business leaders are those who have a strong understanding of their business or those who have business acumen. This is quite true because understanding how a business works plays a significant role in ensuring a consistent influx of money.

It can also help much in determining which kinds of opportunities to grab, and which ones to ignore. The best business leaders also understand that they should not only have a good idea of what their business is in general, but they must also have specific knowledge of the kind of business that they have, and the type of industry they are in.

Not everyone is born with business acumen but there are different ways to develop an understanding of how different businesses work. One way is through reading business publications and journals. You can also tune in to business channels that can help give you an idea of the current business trends, factors that influence various markets, economic factors, and many others that affect different kinds of businesses and industries. Being part of professional business networking organizations or associations can also give you a good idea of how different kinds of business work during conferences, networking events, and seminars.

A good way of developing business insight to help you become a better leader is through attending weekend or evening courses that focus on business topics. This can help much in building your knowledge on understanding profit and loss, financial statements, cash generation, revenue growth, and many other business and finance concepts.

If you are really determined in improving your business insight and aptitude, you can also try looking for a mentor who has a deep understanding of the world of business and finance. You can also try your hand in committees involved in developing business in your area. This can give you a first-hand experience with exciting and challenging business initiatives like improving quality, reducing costs, process re-engineering, and generating improved revenues.

## Business Acumen Training

Business acumen: a keenness and depth of perception in practical matters of financial and behavioural tendencies to enable good, quick business decisions. The target audience for business acumen skill development training are those close to the action. Where their decisions aggregated significantly impact the financial success of the organization: managers and team leaders with technical backgrounds that were promoted from within, customer service team members, program and project managers, engineers, estimators, team leaders, and any one else who does not have a financial background yet their decisions directly affect the financial health of the organization. Our effort here is to take business acumen skills, that many see as a complex issue, and break in down into a logical flow of measurements that can be applied to successfully lead a team to met the financial goals of the organization. And then use the resources of the team to analyse, dissect, and review the processes and procedures used by the team to add value to the organization.

This business acumen course is designed to apply business acumen to the day-to-day operation of the team by developing:

1. An understanding of financial metrics and tools that gauge the cost effectiveness of the team
2. Decision making skills that balance risk and consequences, keep customers happy, and maximize the contribution
3. Skills in thought leadership: to engage team members in non-defensive dialogues that creates an environment where they take the action needed to implement the change initiatives
4. Empower team members who participate in the analysis, craft alternatives and fully support implementation of the selected alternative solution
5. Balance between the emotions of great customer service and the reality of the cost structure
6. Skills to overcome resistance of team members to change

Methods:

- Instructor led on-line training
- One-on-one coaching
- National/annual Associate meeting topics with break out sessions
- Classroom instruction emphasizing technique practice with role-plays and case studies.

# 5

# Nature of Organisational Leadership

Leadership has been a major topic of research in psychology for almost a century and has spawned thousands of empirical and conceptual studies. Despite this level of effort, however, the various parts of this literature still appear disconnected and directionless. In our opinion, a major cause of this state of the field is that many studies of leadership are context free; that is, low consideration is given to organizational variables that influence the nature and impact of leadership. Such research, especially prominent in the social and organizational psychology literatures, tends to focus on interpersonal processes between individuals, nominally leaders and followers. Studies that explicitly examine leadership within organizational contexts, particularly from the strategic management literature, seem incomplete for other reasons.

They typically ignore the cognitive, interpersonal, and social richness of this phenomenon, in that they fail to come to grips with processes that would explain or account for outcomes. While model building in the strategic management literature is typically focused on the examination of leadership occurring at upper organization levels, any insights offered regarding the selection, development, and training of potential leaders are not often grounded in strong conceptual frameworks having significant empirical support. These observations sometimes leave the student of leadership with the feeling that many wheels are spinning in a deepening rut.

One reason for the lack of progress in developing an integrated understanding of organizational leadership is that theorists of all stripes have sought to offer generic leadership theories and models that use many of the same constructs to explain leadership across different organizational levels. Such an approach assumes that leadership at the top of the organization reflects the same psychological and sociological dynamics as leadership at lower organizational levels. This lack of consideration to organizational level and other structural factors has contributed to a dearth of good empirical research on organizational leadership, particularly at the executive level. Some writers have argued for qualitative shifts in the nature of leadership across organizational levels. This view recognizes that dimensions of organizational structure, specifically hierarchical level, degree of differentiation in function, and place in organizational space, moderate the nature of organizational leadership as well as its antecedents and consequences. Thus, performance demands on leaders change across organizational levels. This also means changes in the critical competencies and work requirements that form the basis for selection policies and that leader training and development programs must target. If leadership were to be studied in situ, researchers could then fully appreciate how the antecedents, dynamics, consequences, and criteria of leadership change as a function of such variables as organizational level, organizational structure, environmental complexity, and cultural and societal parameters.

## Some Defining Elements of Organizational Leadership

Stogdill (1974, p. 259) noted that "there are almost as many definitions of leadership as there are persons who have attempted to define the concept." We do not wish to add still another; indeed, we suspect that what we might offer would not satisfy all of the chapter authors, much less the entire community of leadership scholars. However, there are central defining elements of organizational leadership that have some consensus in the literature and provide a unifying perspective for the ideas offered here. For the purposes of our discussion, we make the following arguments:

- Organizational leadership involves processes and proximal outcomes (such as worker commitment) that contribute to the development and achievement of organizational purpose.
- Organizational leadership is identified by the application of nonroutine influence on organizational life.
- Leader influence is grounded in cognitive, social, and political processes.
- Organizational leadership is inherently bounded by system characteristics and dynamics, that is, leadership is contextually defined and caused.

### Leadership and Organizational Purpose

Positions of leadership are established in work settings to help organizational subunits to achieve the purposes for which they exist within the larger system. Organizational purpose is operationalized as a direction for collective action. Leadership processes are directed at defining, establishing, identifying, or translating this direction for their followers and facilitating or enabling the organizational processes that should result in the achievement of this purpose. Organizational purpose and direction becomes defined in many ways, including through mission, vision, strategy, goals, plans, and tasks. The operation of leadership is inextricably tied to the continual development and attainment of these organizational goal states.

This perspective of leadership is a functional one, meaning that leadership is at the service of collective effectiveness. Describing a similar approach to team leadership, Hackman and Walton argued that the leader's "'main job is to do, or get done, whatever is not being adequately handled for group needs'. If a leader manages, by whatever means, to ensure that all functions critical to both task accomplishment and group maintenance are adequately taken care of, then the leader has done his or her job well." These assertions can be made whether leaders are leading groups, multiple groups combined into a department or a division, the organization as a whole, or conglomerates of multiple organizations. This defining element of organizational leadership also means that the success of the collective as a whole is a (if not the) major criterion for leader effectiveness.

It should also be noted that functional leadership is not usually defined by a specific set of behaviours but rather by generic responses that are prescribed for and will vary by different problem situations. That is, the emphasis switches from "what leaders should do" to "what needs to be done for effective performance". Thus, leadership is defined in terms of those activities that promote team and organizational goal attainment by being responsive to contextual demands (Mumford, 1986).

Senior organizational leaders generally carry the construction of organizational purpose and direction. The leadership performance imperatives that derive from the organizational context become entwined in this obligation as well as in the content of organizational directions. For example, the complexity of the senior leader's operating environment requires considerable cognitive resources to build the frame of reference that provides the rationale for organizational strategy. Similarly, organizational goals and strategies need to be responsive to the requirements of multiple stakeholders and constituencies, indicating the social imperatives confronting senior leaders. Finally, a little-noted observation about organizational goal setting is that when such directions are created, they reflect in part the senior leader's personal and self-defined (career) imperatives. Thus, when leaders develop and implement organizational strategies, they do so from and within the context of these and the other imperatives discussed here.

### *Leadership as Nonroutine Influence*

Leadership does not reside in the routine activities of organizational work. Instead, it occurs in response to, or in anticipation of, nonroutine organizational events. This defining element was suggested by Katz and Kahn (1978), who considered "the essence of organizational leadership to be the influential increment over and above mechanical compliance with the routine directives of the organization".

Nonroutine events can be defined as any situation that constitutes a potential or actual hindrance to organizational goal progress. Thus, organizational leadership can be construed as large-(and small-)scale social problem solving, where leaders are constructing the nature of organizational problems, developing and evaluating potential solutions, and planning, implementing, and monitoring selected solutions within complex social domains. This is not to suggest that leadership (as social problem solving) is necessarily reactive. The boundary management obligations widely assigned to organizational leaders require that leaders be attuned to environmental events, interpreting and defining them for their followers, anticipating the emergence of potential goal blockages, and planning accordingly. Thus, successful organizational leadership is quite proactive in its problem solving.

This defining element of leadership as involving nonroutine influence reflects two other points. First, critical organizational leadership is more likely to be reflected in responses to ill-defined problems. defined as those for which the starting parameters, the permissible solution paths, and the solution goals are unspecified (Holyoak, 1984). In such situations, leaders need to construct the nature of the problem, as well as the parameters of potential solution strategies, before they can begin to devise resolutions to the problem. In well-defined problems, solutions are grounded mostly in the experience of the leaders in prior similar situations. Such solutions are also not likely to require significant large-scale change in organizational routine.

The second point is that leadership typically involves discretion and choice in what solutions are appropriate in particular problem domains. Thus, as Jacobs and Jaques argue, "Leadership must be viewed as a process which occurs only in situations in which there is decision discretion. To the extent discretion exists, there is an opportunity for leadership to be exercised. If there is no discretion, there is no such opportunity." Team or organizational actions that are completely specified by procedure or practice or are fully elicited by the situation do not usually require the intervention of leaders. Such actions are likely to be encoded as part of the organizational rule or normative structures (although, leadership is involved in the evolution of these structures). Instead, leadership is necessitated by organizationally relevant events that present alternative interpretations and by problems in which multiple solution paths are viable or requisite solutions need to be implemented. Individuals in leadership roles are then responsible for making the choices that define subsequent collective responses.

In this sense, the performance imperatives we highlight can be construed as representing a cluster of ill-defined discretionary problems or obligations requiring collective action for organizational success. For example, the nature and rate of technological change can pose a number of challenges to organizational leaders: how information is to be gathered and distributed, how to interpret the resulting flood of data, and how to gain competitive advantages from technological advances in both production and human resource systems are just a few of these. In the same way, financial imperatives challenge executives to make and integrate a variety of long-and short-term strategic decisions. Senior staffing imperatives follow these challenges as executives strive to create the right human resource combinations for their strategic choices. Thus, a functional or social problemsolving perspective of leadership is necessarily grounded in a contextual framework that presents fundamental performance imperatives demanding organizational choices.

## Leadership as Managing Social and Cognitive Phenomena

Most definitions of leadership stress social or interpersonal influence processes as key elements. Thus, persuasion, the management of social and political processes, and the use of social power are ubiquitous constructs in the leadership literature. In addition, as suggested by the problem-solving perspective, the execution of effective cognitive processes is equally critical to leader effectiveness. To illustrate, cognitive requirements include interpreting and modelling environmental events for organizational members, determining the nature of problems to be solved, and engaging in long-term strategic thinking. In general, models of leadership, particularly those in the psychological literature, have focused on social processes directed toward the implementation of solutions to organizational problems. A full exposition of leadership must also include the cognitive processes leaders use to plan collective action.

Some researchers in the organizational and management literatures have indeed emphasized the role of leaders in organizational sense making, where collective actions are given meaning through the leader's interpretation and cognitive modelling of environmental events. Along these lines, Jacobs and Jaques noted: Executive leaders "add value" to their organizations in large part by giving a sense of understanding and purpose to the overall activities of the organization. In excellent organizations, there almost always is a feeling that the "boss" knows what he is doing, that he has shared this information downward, that it makes sense, and that it is going to work.

Such understandings, defined as frames of reference by Jacobs and Jaques, become crucial mediators of leadership influence in organizations. An organizational frame of reference is a cognitive representation of the elements and events that comprise the leader's operating environment. Such models contain the pattern of relationships among these events and elements. Accordingly, the logic and rationale for an articulated organization strategy become grounded in the causal relationships interpreted by top executives as existing among the critical events in organizational space.

These frames of reference are not the sole province and responsibility of senior leaders. All leaders need to interpret their operating environment and convey that understanding to their constituencies. However, Jacobs and Jaques. relying on the notion of requisite variety (Ashby, 1952), argued that the complexity of the organizational causal map must correspond to the complexity of the operating environment being patterned. Therefore, the frames of reference or causal maps that senior leaders develop must be more complex than those of leaders at lower organizational levels. That is because executive leaders must accommodate many more causal elements, and the connections among these elements are decidedly more complex at higher levels. The required development of increasingly complex frames of reference at upper organizational levels compels the need, then, for higher-order cognitive processes.

We do not mean to argue that the use of cognitive and social leadership processes is entirely independent. In many instances of effective leadership, these processes become inextricably entwined. For example, functionally diverse teams (where members have varied specializations within the organization) can help leaders interpret environmental ambiguity and reduce uncertainty. This is particularly true in top management teams, where environmental complexity is typically stronger than for lower-level leaders (Zaccaro, 1996). If the top executive team is constructed with individuals of varying functional expertise, the team as a whole has considerably more resources to develop more complex representations of the organization's operating environment. However, team members will often stay silent and defer to the CEO unless social processes permit them to contribute to environmental interpretation.

### Leadership and the Organizational Context

Most theories of organizational leadership in the psychological literature are largely context free. For example, leadership is typically considered without adequate regard for the structural considerations that affect and moderate its conduct. We maintain, however, that organizational leadership cannot be modeled effectively without attending to such considerations.

One particularly strong influence is the organizational level at which leadership occurs. Not only do the fundamental demands and work requirements of leaders change at different levels; the hierarchical context of leadership has profound effects on the personal, interpersonal, and organizational choices that can be made, as well as the import that a given choice might have. Clearly a CEO's stating a preference for a site for a new factory is different from the case of a department manager's stating his or her preferences. Organizational level matters profoundly yet, surprisingly, has been ignored in all but a few leadership models in the literature.

What has been argued about leadership at different organizational levels? Katz and Kahn (1978) specified three distinct patterns of organizational leadership. The first pattern concerns the administrative use of existing organizational structures to maintain effective organizational operations. If problems arise to disrupt these operations, existing organizational mechanisms and procedures are used to resolve them. Indeed, Katz and Kahn note that "such acts are often seen as so institutionalized as to require little if any leadership" (p. 537). This leadership pattern occurs at lower organizational levels. The second leadership pattern, occurring at middle organizational levels, involves the embellishment and operationalization of formal structural elements. Such actions require a two-way orientation by the leader (that is, toward both superiors and subordinates), as well as significant human relations skills.

The third pattern of organizational leadership, which occurs at the top of organizations, concerns structural origination or change in the organization as a reflection of new policy formulations. Taken together, the distribution of separate leadership patterns across organizational levels that Katz and Kahn proposed suggests significant qualitative differences between the nature of junior and senior leadership. Similar models specifying differences across levels of organizational leadership have been proposed in separate theoretical formulations by Jacobs and Jaques (1987), Mumford, Zaccaro, Harding, Fleishman, and Reiter-Palmon (1993), and Bentz (1987).

In our view, a contextual model of leadership would be different from approaches that emphasize context as implying situational moderators. In the latter, the situation is viewed as determining which leadership response is likely to be the most effective. Generally, these models produce classifications of leader-situation matches that produce effectiveness. Such conceptualizations are important and do contribute to understanding organizational leadership. However, they tend to understate the role of the organizational context in influencing and mediating the fundamental nature of leadership work, including those forces that animate or retard leader initiatives or behaviours, themselves. This context shapes the performance imperatives that both stimulate and define the parameters of appropriate leadership action.

It implies qualitative shifts in the ways that leaders acquire information in their roles and go on to make sense of this information. It changes if and when (and then how and what) leaders plan appropriate collective responses. It changes the nature and role of key processes such as how leaders influence and manage their followers. It clearly affects the range and scope of their influence. The organizational context even changes the mechanisms by which leaders acquire their role and develop their legitimacy. These effects extend beyond those typically modeled in situational contingency approaches in the current leadership literature. Thus, unlike the situation as moderator, we view situation or context as boundary conditions for theory building and model specification.

### Major Conceptual Approaches to Leadership

These defining elements and the contextual perspective of organizational leadership were our guiding principles when we planned this book with the chapter authors. As such, we are promoting an alternative view in this book, or perhaps more accurately, we are angling for a more holistic perspective in modelling organizational leadership, albeit at one level of the organization. By way of contrast, we have abstracted from a survey of leadership research four established traditions: social and interpersonal exchange, strategic management, organizational systems theory, and performance effectiveness models of leadership. We examine each of these briefly and highlight their major limitations. We do this not to discredit established traditions in research on leadership but to argue for the value of the approach we have chosen to follow in this book.

### Social and Interpersonal Exchange

The social exchange approach to leadership is perhaps the most popular and pervasive perspective in the literature. The major unit of analysis in this approach is the relationship between the leader and his or her followers: leaders provide direction, guidance, and activity structuring to a collective; members of the collective in turn grant the leader permission to influence them (therefore conferring legitimacy), as well as reverence and respect. Leader effectiveness is defined as a function of the dynamic that occurs between leader and followers.

As might be expected, models from this approach focus on one or more of three elements: characteristics of the leader, characteristics of the followers, and characteristics of their relationship. In defining key leader characteristics that contribute to a successful exchange, researchers have focused mainly on the leader's predominant interaction style. Specifically, leaders vary in terms of their primary tendency to adopt a structuring taskoriented style toward their subordinates or a considerate, socioemotional style. For example, Fleishman and his colleagues defined initiating structure and consideration as key leadership behaviours. Likert (1961) argued for task-oriented and relationship-oriented behaviours as differentiating effective from ineffective managers. In his contingency model, Fiedler (1964, 1971) used his leastpreferred coworker (LPC) scale to define a similar task (low LPC) versus group-oriented (high LPC) dimension. Similar stylistic differences have been proposed by Blake and Mouton

(1964), House and Dessler (1974), Katz, Maccoby, and Morse (1950), and Hersey and Blanchard (1969).

Other leadership theorists within the social exchange tradition have focused heavily on characteristics of the subordinate. Hollander examined the role of followers in granting "legitimacy" to the leader to be innovative. Lord and his colleagues have taken these notions further to describe the leadership schemas that followers develop and use to bestow leadership status on individuals. Hersey and Blanchard (1969, 1982) argue that the maturity level of subordinates determines what behavioural style the leader should adopt when seeking to influence a group. Leadership substitutes theory cites the experience, ability, and commitment of subordinates as moderating the efficacy of leadership influence.

The characteristics of leader-subordinate relationships that have been investigated include their overall quality. the degree to which they are mutually influential. Their variability across individual subordinates and the sense of empowerment they engender. Fiedler conditioned the situational favorability for leadership influence on whether the leaders and followers experienced good versus poor relations. Vroom and his colleagues examined the factors that determined whether the exchange between leader and follower was a participative one, where influence flows in both directions, or a directive/autocratic one, where influence flows solely from leader. While most of these models emphasize an average leadership behavioural style displayed across subordinates, Dansereau, Graen, and their colleagues argued that the quality of leader-follower relationships varied across members within the same collective unit. Some relationships were participative, close, and characterized by a high level of trust, while others were more formal, directive, and less trustful. Finally, research on inspirational leadership by Bass and his colleagues has focused on a dynamic established between leader and follower that reflects an intense reverence and loyalty to the leader and a strong sense of empowerment in the follower. Taken together, these models and theories constitute a huge proportion of research in the leadership literature. They have contributed to a broad and deep understanding of the following topics:

- What constitutes an effective exchange between leaders and subordinates
- How leader qualities and behaviours facilitate subordinate and small group effectiveness

- How the contributions of various leadership styles to subordinate effectiveness are moderated by a variety of situational factors
- How the characteristics and information processing of subordinates contribute to effective leadership.

The social exchange approach has greatly enhanced our fundamental knowledge about leadership. Nonetheless, this approach has several limitations that constrain an understanding of organizational leadership. Social exchange models and theories emphasize individual, small group, and direct leadership. The focus is on the direct interaction of leader and followers. Such leadership does reside at all levels of the organization, but other forms of indirect or mediated leadership also exist. For example, middle-level managers are typically tasked with providing meaning and direction to subordinates several levels down whom they rarely see face-to-face. At the top of the organization, executives are engaged in sense making and direction setting for followers they may never meet. Most of the theories noted do not attempt to model or explain this form of influence. Indeed, these theories do not fundamentally explain executive leadership very well.

Day and Lord (1988) observed of the existing leadership literature that "the topic of executive leadership... has not been a major concern of leadership researchers or theorists. Their focus has been primarily lower-level leadership". Although several of the social exchange theories do provide what can be called a contingent or contextual perspective. they do not significantly account for organizational contextual variables. For example, none of these theories explicates how the processes and relationships they model would (must) change at different organizational levels. Along this line, Zaccaro (1995, 1998) argued that the postulates of Fiedler's contingency model and his cognitive resources model do not apply easily to the executive leader effectiveness.

As a final illustration, the functional leadership behaviours and processes that are necessary for effectiveness at different organizational levels and in different kinds of organizations are broader than the stylistic approaches typical of this tradition (Day & Lord, 1988). Thus, the social exchange models either do not consider, or obscure in their theorizing, the importance of such leadership processes as information acquisition, sense making, sense giving, systematic social networking, boundary spanning, and long-term and long-range strategic decision making.

### Strategic Management

Models of strategic decision making and management argue that organizational effectiveness emerges from a coalignment between the organization and its environment; the role of senior organizational leaders is to create and manage this fit. The major unit analysis in this leadership research tradition is the strategic decision-making activities of top executives. Thus, strategic management models describe how executives make the strategic decisions that are intended to facilitate organization-environment coalignment. Researchers in this approach focus on key leadership processes: environment scanning, sense making and sense giving, the specification of strategic choices, and the selection and implementation of appropriate strategies.

Some models within the strategic management tradition actually deemphasize the contributions of top executives to organizational effectiveness. Arguing that organizational and environmental parameters (such as resource availability, the fit of the organization with its environmental niche, and the strategic predisposition of the organization) primarily account for organizational outcomes. Other theorists have adapted a contingency model in which effectiveness is a product of the fit between the organization's strategic orientation and the characteristics of its top managers. Thus, this approach defines strategy as a determinant rather than a consequence of executive selection and action. For example, Gupta noted:

By definition, the notion that matching executives to organizational strategies enhances organizational performance assumes that strategies get specified prior to executive selection; in other words, for most CEOs, strategies are assumed to be a given and the CEO's primary task is assumed to consist of the implementation rather than formulation of strategies.

Other leadership models have placed a more central role on the thought processes and characteristics of top leaders. Rational and normative models argue that the responsibility of executives is to make strategic decisions based on a careful analysis of environmental contingencies and organizational strengths and weaknesses and an application of objective criteria to strategic choices to determine the most appropriate organizational strategy. Thus, strategic leaders are viewed as mostly rational and optimizing informational processors. An alternate or augmenting view suggests that the personal qualities and characteristics of top leaders play an inordinate role in strategic decision making. For example, Hambrick (1989, p. 5) noted:

In the face of the complex, multitudinous, and ambiguous information that typifies the top management task, no two strategists will identify the same array of options for the firm; they will rarely prefer the same options; if, by remote chance, they were to pick the same options, they almost certainly would not implement them identically. Biases, blinders, egos, aptitudes, experiences, fatigue, and other human factors in the executive ranks greatly affect what happens to companies.

Recent work has also focused on the top management team processes and characteristics that influence strategic decision making. Such research adds team processes and demographics to executive values and belief systems as primary determinants of executive decision-making processes.

The strategic management approach has greatly increased our understanding of organizational and executive leadership. Unlike the social exchange perspective, the emphasis here is primarily on the cognitive and planning processes of executives. In particular, researchers in this tradition consider environmental scanning and analysis as key leadership processes, a point not readily apparent in most leadership literatures. Further, this body of research deals with large-scale leadership, that is, leadership of large collectives and organizations. Thus, it showcases indirect or mediated leadership processes that are prominent in any but smallsized organizations. In addition, several of the models in this tradition feature a contextual perspective that specifies the environmental and organizational forces shaping strategic decisions. As such, this perspective is represented within several chapters in this book.

Despite these strengths, several limitations are clear. Strategic management models do not describe the direct interpersonal processes, so prominent in the social exchange tradition, but still vitally important in strategic implementation. This is readily apparent in the research on top management teams, where much of the focus is team demographics and their meaning for strategic outcomes. Few studies have examined team processes in these settings, and even fewer explore the role of top executives in shaping these processes.

### *Organizational Systems*

In common with the strategic management approach, the models in this leadership research tradition emphasize the boundary spanning and internal coordination responsibilities of leaders within open social systems. However, unlike the strategic management approach, these models postulate guiding principles that apply to leaders at different organizational levels, but also describe the differences in performance requirements at successive levels.

This perspective is grounded heavily in the work of Katz and Kahn (1978), who described organizations as open systems in close transactional relationship with their resource-providing environments. Organizations convert environmental inputs into usable outcomes through a set of interlocking throughput processes. These processes become the basis of connected subsystems within the organization-in particular, the production subsystem that is most directly responsible for resource conversion. The production subsystem is buttressed by two other subsystems, supportive and maintenance, that are responsible for procuring material and personnel resources, respectively. Adaptive subsystems are established to look outward, providing environmental outreach and input for the organization. Managerial subsystems overlay all of these patterned activities.

Katz and Kahn (1978) noted two critical aspects of social behaviour patterns that are particularly defining for managerial subsystem roles. First, the system character of organizations means that "movement in one part leads in predictable fashion to movement in other parts"5. Further, discrete patterns of functional responses are collectively interconnected to define the responses of larger units and subsystems. An essential function of management is to coordinate the activities of integrated units. Although this requirement exists in fundamental form at all organizational levels, the complexity of such coordination increases at successive levels as the number and variability of interacting social units also increases.

The second aspect of social behaviour patterns is their susceptibility to shifting environmental dynamics. The embedding environments of organization are rarely in stasis, and their fluctuations can have profound implications for resource procurement and output receptivity. Accordingly, a major responsibility of organizational leaders is to monitor the external environments of their units and promote system adaptation to critical changes. Again, this responsibility extends to leaders at all organizational levels. However, the "external environment" for the first-line supervisor is the larger organization, whereas the top executive needs to span the boundary between the entire organization and more complex and unstructured environment. Nevertheless, both are responsible for facilitating system responsiveness.

For top executives, the responsibility for facilitating system coordination extends to other organizations that are linked in a partnering arrangement with their constituent companies. Such "interorganizational relationships" also reflect a systemic response to environmental demands that operate on all members of a particular niche. A response by one organization in such an arrangement clearly has implications for the activities of other linked organizations. Their actions also often require careful coordination to gain industry-wide advantages (such as political lobbying efforts).

The organizational systems approach, then, emphasizes the role of the leader in coordinating and maintaining system interconnectiveness and promoting system adaptiveness to external change. This perspective places a premium on both the unity and distinctiveness of leadership functions across organizational levels. Earlier, we provided a brief summary of models that describe qualitative differences in upper-and lower-level organizational leaders. After reviewing the executive leadership literature, primarily from the organizational systems perspective (but including models from social exchange and strategic management traditions), Zaccaro offered the following conclusions:

- Leader performance requirements can be described in terms of three distinct levels in organizational space.
- All organizational leaders engage in direction setting (such as goal setting, planning, strategy making, and envisioning) for their constituent units. Such direction setting incorporates an increasingly longer time frame at higher organizational levels.
- All organizational leaders engage in boundary-spanning activities, linking their constituent units with their environments. At lower organizational levels, this environment is the broader organization. At upper levels, boundary spanning and environmental analysis occur increasingly within the organization's external environment.
- All organizational leaders are responsible for operational maintenance and coordination within the organization. At upper levels, operational influence becomes increasingly indirect.
- The effective accomplishment of executive performance functions facilitates organizational performance and success.
- Characteristics of the operating environment influence the nature and quality of executive performance requirements.

These conclusions reflect the leader's responsibility at all levels to maintain system effectiveness and viability. They also highlight the dual external and internal systemic perspective of the leader's requisite functions. This approach is a significant addition to the other traditions.

It provides an organizationwide perspective, while denoting how leadership changes at successfully higher organizational levels. Thus, it can speak to both small group and large-scale leadership. Organizational systems models describe contextual influences on leadership by virtue of specifying key environmental dynamics that alter system requirements. As such, this perspective is reflected in several chapters in this book.

Nonetheless, like the others, this approach too has some limitations. Although it does provide a contextual perspective, models in this approach rarely distinguish the range of performance imperatives in the leader's operating environment that influence leadership activity. Further, these imperatives are often systematically linked, just as are the organizations they influence. That is, the intensity and quality of one imperative (say, technological) can have reverberations that alter the intensity and quality of other imperatives (say, cognitive, social, and staffing).

The nature of this interconnectiveness also changes across organizational levels. The strategic management tradition attends more closely than the systems approach to these dynamics (although not in a thorough, finely grained sense), but does not specify how they change across levels. The systems approach provides some fundamental constructs for cross-level model building but needs to attend specifically to the nature of contextual imperatives that impinge on organizations' systems.

Finally, the organizational systems approach emphasizes the importance of leadership processes for organizational effectiveness. This assumption is also apparent in several of the models within the strategic management perspective. Nonetheless, despite some wellarticulated exceptions.

There has not been sufficient attention given to the links among leader attributes, the leadership functions articulated by systems models, and organizational effectiveness. Further, the models do not consider systematically leader training, development, and selection systems that have as their ultimate end the improvement of organizational functioning. That is the focus of the last leadership research tradition described here.

### Leader Effectiveness

A central assumption in organizational leadership research is that leaders and leadership processes make a difference in organizational effectiveness. Although a number of theorists and researchers have offered countering notions or evidence. The predominant view, supported by empirical findings, is that "top executives matter". Accordingly, some perspectives of organizational leaders emphasize the connections between leader attributes and organizational effectiveness. A result of this tradition is a focus on leader assessment, selection, training, and development systems that enhance these attributes.

Zaccaro (1996) defined executive attributes as personal qualities that facilitate the successful accomplishment of executive performance requirements, which in turn drive organizational success. These attributes also provide a framework for the construction of measures and tools that can be used for executive selection and assessment and training and development programs that target one or more of them. Thus, a key focus in this research tradition is identifying and validating personal qualities linked to indexes of leadership and organizational effectiveness.

Perhaps the oldest tradition in leadership research is the search for critical leader traits. Early forms of this research, although prodigious, did not yield consistent evidence for particular attributes, and hence researchers moved in other directions. More recent efforts have renewed the argument for leader attributes by correcting for earlier methodological and statistical limitations. Updating reviews of this literature and highlighting consistent patterns and by offering conceptual models linking key attributes to leadership performance processes required for organizational effectiveness. Unfortunately, research that validates the connections between particular attributes and key leadership processes and organizational effectiveness, respectively, has lagged behind this theoretical interest.

The performance effectiveness approach emphasizes leader assessment and development. Two examples of this focus are the longitudinal assessment Centre research conducted at American Telephone & Telegraph (ATT) and the investigations of leader development by the Centre for Creative Leadership (CCL). The ATT research developed assessment Centre procedures in which a number of exercises and tasks are used to identify managerial characteristics that purportedly predict career advancement. In a longitudinal research program, these researchers associated scores from assessment Centres with managers' rate and level of promotion over a twenty-year span. They found that such characteristics as need for power, interpersonal and cognitive skills, and motivational orientations were significant predictors of attained level. Although this research has been important for identifying characteristics relevant for one index of leader effectiveness, it also provided a viable means of leader assessment, albeit one that has been fraught with debate.

Research by CCL has focused on identifying the characteristics of top executives who succeed versus those who derail in their career. They found that managers who were emotionally unstable and not able to handle high pressure were defensive, and those who put personal advancement ahead of personal integrity, had weak interpersonal skills, and were narrowly focused in terms of technical and cognitive skills were more likely to fail after reaching higher levels of management. Note that these were managers who were as successful at lower organizational levels as those executives who tended to succeed in their careers. Their shortcomings emerged, presumably as critical predictors of effectiveness, only when they attained top executive positions. This research therefore argues for different effectiveness models at successive levels of the organization.

The development of executives is a difficult task. Research by McCauley and others at CCL has focused on the role of work experiences and developmental relationships as key antecedents and mediators of executive growth. A consistent premise in this work and in related research is that the complex cognitive and social competencies required for effective executive work emerge from training and work experiences that push the leader to the limits of his or her retained schemas and ways of behaving. When these comfortable patterns of thinking and behaving no longer suffice in completing required work assignments, individuals who are likely to succeed at higher levels of organizational leadership can develop new functional schemas and behaviour patterns.

In sum, the performance effectiveness approach has promoted research on the attributes linked to leader and organizational success, as well as the means of assessing and developing these attributes. Nonetheless, it has not yet contributed a level of understanding commensurate with the conceptual advances in the other traditions described. One limitation has been a lack of consideration given to the diversity of organizational imperatives that will influence the leader's performance efforts. Such imperatives create a rich operating environment for the leader that renders as insufficient narrowly defined leader assessment and development systems. Validation research, so vital to affirming leader performance effectiveness models, has consistently lagged behind the conceptual models that have emerged in this tradition (Zaccaro, 1996).

### Summary

These four research traditions in leadership have made tremendous contributions to our understanding of leadership; nevertheless, each has limitations, particularly in terms of modelling, assessing, and developing executive leadership. We believe that a more thorough specification of the performance imperatives that operate for organizational leaders, particularly at the top, will begin to address some of these limitations and perhaps promote a greater integration of these research approaches.

Performance Imperatives for Organizational Leadership An operational imperative is analogous to a functional requirement, derived from factors or forces that coexist in the context or operating environment of a senior leader. Our list of imperatives has been gleaned from the descriptive, theoretical, and inferential literatures in the area (Zaccaro, 1996). Although there may be alternative ways of characterizing them, we believe the following are a reasonably complete set.

### Cognitive Imperative

This imperative refers to the complex information processing and problem-solving demands that organizational leaders, particularly executives, need to confront to be successful. These demands derive from the multiplicity and interconnectiveness of causal factors operating to affect corporate success. In addition, the recent rapidly burgeoning advances in information technology have resulted in exponential increases in the data flowing to executive decision makers.

Attending to, processing, and interpreting these factors are central to resolving such problems as organizational sense making and charting long-term strategic directions. Moreover, the environment for executive leaders is typically unstructured and ill defined; thus, successful performance in such environments requires qualitatively different cognitive skills and capacities than leadership at lower levels.

### Social Imperative

This imperative reflects the behavioural complexity that is required of organizational leaders. Such complexity results from the social complexity (that is, the number, nature, and variability of relationships) in the leader's operating environment. For example, executives need to coordinate and supervise the activities of multiple (or even all) units within the organization. This leads to greater social complexity because leaders need to integrate these units, even when their members have conflicting goals and demands. Executives are also required to adopt multiple organizational roles simultaneously when relating to constituencies, with many of these roles specifying competing behavioural requirements.

Further, executive leaders have the responsibility for maintaining relationships, even while implementing organization-wide change, a responsibility that involves the development and nurturance of large social networks and the acquisition of social capital. These social imperatives suggest that the social skills and competencies required for executive leadership also differ qualitatively from those required for lowerlevel leadership. At lower levels, social demands are less complex because leaders are typically in charge of fewer subordinates and organizational units, and they supervise more functionally homogeneous units.

### Personal Imperative

This imperative refers to demands on leaders for the timely and skillful execution of such activities as career and reputation management and the acquisition of power. This is especially true as executives seek to place their own stamp on the organization. These imperatives become critical forces during periods of executive succession and CEO transitions. They are also reflected in the personal values that executives bring to organizational visioning and strategic decision making. Some crucial questions reflect personal imperatives: How does a new CEO develop or staff a new top management team without disrupting important and functional dynamics that carry over from previous CEO tenures? How does the nature of departure by the previous CEO influence the selection, entry, and tenure of the new CEO? What are the critical reputation and impression management techniques that contribute to successful CEO succession and transition?

### Political Imperative

Closely related to the personal imperative is pressure coming from the political environment within which most organizational leaders need to operate. Such pressures stem from the role that power plays in organizations. The acquisition of power, the timely and judicious use of power, and even the appropriate application of power sharing are part of the story. A special aspect of the political imperative has to do with the routine need for building and maintaining coalitions.

Thus, paradoxically, the operation of executive leadership is often described as more collegial and less authoritative than at lower levels. Such leadership requires more persuasion as an influence tactic and coalition building among top decision makers. The use of power inevitably gives rise to a significant amount of conflict at top organizational levels.

How CEOs confront and resolve these dynamics plays an important role in organizational performance and adaptation. Finally, most, if not all, of the strategic and tactical decisions made by organizational leaders, particularly those in top executive teams, will be influenced in part by the political network within which the organization is embedded. That is, organizational strategic decisions are determined not only by internal political dynamics but external ones as well.

This last point means that political imperatives are also driven by the interorganizational relationships executives need to establish and maintain on behalf of their organizations. Well-constructed interorganizational relationships are highly instrumental for organizational success. The acquisition of resources and political advocacy are two critical reasons for the development of interorganizational relationships (Galaskiewicz, 1985), and power plays a crucial role here as well. Top executives need to apply the judicious use of power and persuasion to position their organization close to the Centre of interorganizational networks, where links are strongest to resource bases. Effective political advocacy also requires the welding together of diverse and common interests into a powerful coalition. This imperative will drive much of the strategic implementation efforts of top executives.

### Technological Imperative

Today's organizations operate in the context of an information age in which technology has revolutionized the operating environment of organizational leaders. This technology, with its corresponding impact on organizational information flow, presents leaders with challenges and opportunities that can fundamentally restructure how they accomplish the tasks of organizational leadership and change. Key questions regarding technological imperatives need to be considered in a theory of organizational leadership. How does information technology change the strategic decision processes of leaders, particularly top executives? What kinds of support systems (such as decision support systems and control systems) are available to assist in leadership and decision making? How do executives use technology in the service of organizational transformation and change? How does technology operate to change or deny traditional leadership roles or functions.

### *Financial Imperative*

This imperative is perhaps the most fundamental source of pressures on senior organizational leaders. Financial and industry factors in an executive's operating environment may prompt an orientation toward short-term thinking, in which decisions regarding acquisitions and mergers are made in the context of fairly immediate gain rather than long-term organizational investment and adaptation. Competitive dynamics in the organizational environment also provide financial imperatives that may force a shortterm perspective on top organizational executives.

Most theories of executive leadership promote the idea that effective leaders adopt a long-term perspective-one that is strategic and visionary. However, such theories need to consider the financial and competitive imperatives that shorten this perspective. Thus, executive compensation as well as investor pressures interact here. Furthermore, the links among such imperatives, executive actions, and organizational decline need to be noted.

### *Senior Staffing Imperative*

The previous imperatives imply a set of forces that would require that the staffing of senior organizational positions be done with individuals who possess a particular set of skills, dispositions, and capabilities. This, in turn, demands that renewed attention be given to the traditional staffing concerns of recruitment, assessment for selection, training and development, and performance assessment as they are applied to senior organizational leaders.

More specifically, given that the nature of work at the top is problematic in the ways so described, just how should we go about measuring and preparing organizational leaders of the future? Thus, whereas the previous imperatives can be used to describe the context of the modern senior leader, this last imperative represents, in the abstract, pressure on the organization to respond appropriately in its senior staffing demands.

Staffing imperatives also embrace the CEO's management of the executive team. Much of the popular literature and current models and theories in organizational studies tend to treat senior organizational leadership as a solitary phenomenon. However, much of the CEO's work is collective work emphasizing the coordinated contributions of multiple executives.

Although some of the forces that operate here reflect social imperatives, the CEO's management of this process represents another aspect of staffing imperatives. Thus, key questions associated with this imperative include how staffing decisions contribute to and shape top-level human resource management concerns and how the senior leader is responsible for, interacts with, and indeed is affected by the top management team.

# 6

# Value Leadership

A new global economic paradigm is taking shape, triggering a broad and fundamental shift in the underlying competitive dynamics of local and global businesses. This catalytic transformation is changing the rules of the competitive game for businesses – regardless of their size, the industry in which they operate, and the country in which they are located. Companies can no longer seek protection in the traditional positions they have built in their domestic markets. In the new global economic paradigm everything is up for grabs.

The rapid expansion of offshoring and the corresponding rise of India to a world class global services and value cluster within the course of just one decade, show that the very nature of globalization is changing too. The slow and bureaucratic way of globalizing belongs to a bygone era. Today, a formidable mix of powerful macro-and micro-level forces including – deregulation, new technologies and the internet, the free flow of capital and ideas, and a new cadre of globally minded entrepreneurs with the intent to disrupt traditional markets – are together creating a fast paced and rapidly changing global competitive environment that is challenging the status quo.

## *Companies Face Complex Strategic and Operational Challenges*

In many industries traditional firms in Europe and the USA now face powerful new challengers from India and other emerging markets. These challengers are leveraging large highly qualified talent pools, low operating costs and operating model innovations to bring into play a new system of assets that is difficult for many incumbent firms to emulate. Many firms have been caught off-guard by the rapid pace at which these challengers have expanded and encroached their business.

Tactical cost cutting and conventional efficiency improvement initiatives will not solve the competitive dilemma many companies face. As the rules of the game change, companies must develop a broad and complex mix of new strategic and operational initiatives that cut across corporate functions, build new capabilities and perspectives, and most importantly, deliver more client value. In short, many companies have to recalibrate their executive mindsets and rethink their business strategy, alliances, market positioning, value proposition as well as their operating and business models.

Moreover, strategies for winning in this new environment come with significant implications for the soft factors of a successful business requiring new forms of global leadership, governance, organizational culture, and team management. Managing large culturally diverse organizations across distance and time in an integrated way calls for a more sophisticated, entrepreneurially oriented, and nimble set of managers. That is, a new kind of global mindset and mix of capabilities are required to win in the new global competitive paradigm.

### *Leadership Values and Ethics*

Leaders know what they value. They also recognize the importance of ethical behaviour. The best leaders exhibit both their values and their ethics in their leadership style and actions. Your leadership ethics and values should be visible because you live them in your actions every single day. A lack of trust is a problem in many workplaces. If leaders never identified their values in these workplaces, the mistrust is understandable. People don't know what they can expect. If leaders have identified and shared their values, living the values daily, visibly will create trust. To say one sentiment and to do another will damage trust-possibly forever. In *Trust Rules: The Most Important Secret*, three constructs of trust are explored. Dr. Duane C. Tway calls trust a construct because it is "constructed" of these three components: "the capacity for trusting, the perception of competence, and the perception of intentions." Workplace ethics take the same route. If the organization's leadership has a code of conduct and ethical expectations, they become an organization joke if the leaders fail to live up to their published code. Leaders that exhibit ethical behaviour powerfully influence the actions of others.

### *Choose Your Leadership Values*

The following are examples of values. You might use these as the starting point for discussing values within your organization: ambition, competency, individuality, equality, integrity, service, responsibility, accuracy, respect, dedication, diversity, improvement, enjoyment/fun, loyalty, credibility, honesty, innovativeness, teamwork, excellence, accountability, empowerment, quality, efficiency, dignity, collaboration, stewardship, empathy, accomplishment, courage, wisdom, independence, security, challenge, influence, learning, compassion, friendliness, discipline/order, generosity, persistency,optimism, dependability, flexibility.

As a leader, choose the values and the ethics that are most important to you, the values and ethics you believe in and that define your character. Then live them visibly every day at work. Living your values is one of the most powerful tools available to you to help you lead and influence others. Don't waste your best opportunity.

### *Characteristics of a Successful Leadership Style*

Much is written about what makes successful leaders. I will focus on the characteristics, traits and actions that, I believe, are key.

- Choose to lead.
- Be the person others choose to follow.
- Provide vision for the future.
- Provide inspiration.
- Make other people feel important and appreciated.
- Live your values. Behave ethically. (Current article-you are here.)
- Set the pace through your expectations and example.
- Establish an environment of continuous improvement.
- Provide opportunities for people to grow, both personally and professionally.
- Care and act with compassion.

Most people recognise true leadership when they see it but ask them to articulate exactly what it is that they admire and we immediately come up against issues of perspective and definition. Even if we were able to define leadership, in commonly understood and agreed terms, would it help us to identify and develop leadership capabilities? Paul Kearns builds a case for a model of leadership definition and development that comprises three key components-value, strategy and measurement.

### *What's the Difference between a Good Leader and a Bad One?*

Anyone given the task of dissecting leadership is at a serious disadvantage before they even start. The word itself defies any attempt at accurate or precise definition. It also comes with other complications-it is not a constant; can only really be judged within a unique, historical context; and this usually means we have to judge leadership with the benefit of hindsight. Churchill's leadership being one of the most obvious examples.

His potential only really found its outlet during the Second World War and even then he had plenty of critics and detractors. Nevertheless, we all still tend to believe we can recognise true leadership when we see it even if we realise that, as with beauty, any assessment of leadership remains firmly in the eye of the beholder. Yet the fact that there is no universal measure of leadership does not stop us trying to search out, nurture and develop leadership. The potential rewards for getting it right and the risk of getting it wrong are both just too huge to ignore.

So if we do manage to put leadership under the 'microscope' would even the most powerful magnification be able to identify the defining and distinguishing features and characteristics behind the leadership abilities of a John F. Kennedy or a Nelson Mandela? More worryingly, would a detailed look at their DNA only conclude that there is not much difference between the famous and the infamous? Perhaps there is only an infinitesimal, biological quirk that distinguishes them from a Hitler or a Stalin. Leaders come in all shapes, sizes and hues so do we just hope that we get the ones who share our own views? Do we ever know what value they might bring to society or can we actually do something to make that happen? Maybe this whole subject needs a really different perspective if we are to gain any fresh insights.

## The Value of Leadership

The Leadership Trust has a view that "... business performance is driven by effective leaders-those who can truly inspire their people to release their personal and collective potential" amend it slightly to offer a variation on their theme-

### *The Leadership Measurement Proposition*

So why are we interested in leadership? Because if we can reproduce or replicate it society will benefit. The microscope analogy has particular relevance here. Whatever apparatus we choose must be able to bring leadership into sharp focus with clear definition. We have to be able to observe leadership and analyse it. This microscope not only has to show us how leadership works at an elemental level but also, more importantly, what makes this organism grow. How does reproduction actually take place? Only then can we hope to spot leadership potential and have any chance of cultivating and nurturing it. Is such a piece of equipment beyond our comprehension? Do we have the technology? If so, what might the main components be?

As someone who has spent the whole of his professional life working in the human resource management (HRM) arena I have always seen the role of HRM as attempting to get the right organisational configuration; with the right people; in the right role and performing at the height of their capabilities. Such an obvious and eminently sensible goal and yet one that is fraught with a multitude of issues, diversions, distractions and downright political subterfuge at every turn.

This is particularly true as you move up through organisations to try and ensure the right 'leaders' are in place. The Peter principle of promoting people above their level of competence appears as prevalent today as it has ever been-we only need to consider the average tenure of a CEO, or even a Government minister, to see plenty of evidence of this principle in action. Is this fallout just an inevitable consequence of the Machiavellian attitudes of those clawing their way to the top of the greasy pole or is the answer much more prosaic? Maybe those 'leaders' who profess to having to 'play politics' have really just been using it as a good cover story to hide the fact they were never up to the job in the first place? If so, then we can only blame the methods we use to select and develop effective leadership.

After all, we seem to have arrived at a situation where the most powerful jobs in the country, including the Prime Minister, all MP's and Chief Executives, require no formal qualifications at all. No wonder we still have a serious leadership problem and the only way out of this problem is to have a stab at measuring leadership ability both before and after the fact.

Perhaps even a subjective measure of leadership, but based on a commonly agreed scale, is better than no measure at all. Ask any measurement question of any people variable such as height, weight, intelligence and this theory says there will only be a very small number at the top end of the range. If this holds true for leadership ability then the challenge to society can be expressed simply as 3 options (*):-

1. How can we, in some way, raise this level of leadership ability (shown by the dotted line shift)?

2. How do we ensure that only the best (those with 8 and above) find their way into positions of leadership so that they can make their greatest contribution?
3. What can we do to ensure that the worst candidates (anyone with less than 3) do not get into such positions?

As you are considering these questions it might be worth just reminding ourselves of a particularly irksome but, unfortunately, unalterable fact of life. We can only manage what we measure. So, while such a construct is of great interest, conceptually, there is no way of producing or managing this curve unless we can develop meaningful measures of leadership ability. We have already identified a host of issues that bedevil the subject of leadership definition, and they are all thorny, but a failure to grasp the nettle of measurement will inevitably be the biggest obstacle to progress.

It might be problematic but when the only other option is for leadership to happen by chance or default what do we have to lose? Could we not raise the probability of getting better business and political leaders simply by trying? Our recent track record is certainly nothing to be particularly proud of, especially if judged against our prime criterion of societal value.

## Leadership, Strategy and Value

If we pull together several of the strands of this article we can see that if leadership is about creating societal value we need to have a consensus view in society on what is valuable. Not everyone will perceive value in the same way but that is precisely what an effective leader would do. Let us look at the NHS from this perspective as an example.

What is the value of the NHS? Is that a philosophical question or one of hard numbers of patients treated per million £'s spent? Maybe the very fact we have trouble answering it is proof that the NHS has had little clear leadership since its original vision from people like Nye Bevan at its launch in 1948? Is its purpose to provide health? Or do IVF treatment and cosmetic surgery have an equal right to its resources, even though they may not fit the original definition of 'health' problems? The answer in reality is it depends and, in some cases, is dependent on nothing more than either where you live or how loudly you shout.

Now before this inflames any readers I am not putting a case for or against IVF on the NHS. All I am highlighting is the fact that we have no clear leadership on these issues. You can only lead if you know exactly where you are going. Without clear leadership we cannot have coherent policies and without clear policies those who work in the NHS will always be open to criticism for the way they allocate resources. Hence we will have no way of gauging the value of the extra billions of £'s being poured into the NHS and no employees in the NHS will be able to look at how they might add more value.

Leadership is about making choices. The consensus for supporting cancer treatment on the NHS is probably taken, quite rightly, as a given. IVF is a much more difficult choice because it is not a 'matter of life or death'. Every penny spent on it means a penny less spent somewhere else, where society's consensus may put a higher value. Political decisions aim to win votes. Real leadership decisions aim to maximise societal value from limited resources. These two aims do not have to be mutually exclusive. Two-a-penny politicians will always choose the votes option. True political *leaders* will aim to make both causes mutually inclusive and reinforcing.

The one step that we have missed out here though is 'strategy'. A strategy, for the sake of brevity, is a grand plan that pulls together competing demands towards a common goal. Strategy always involves very difficult choices (IVF or more cancer screening equipment?) and it is those difficult choices that only effective leaders can reconcile in the eyes of the majority of the interested parties. The opposite of strategy is knee-jerk reaction. Short-term solutions that aim to placate the most vociferous at the expense of dealing with underlying issues. NHS waiting lists are a symptom of a whole range of organisational issues. Setting targets to reduce waiting times and allocating resources to achieve that target might score 1 out of 10 in strategic terms but 10 out of 10 for the person actually waiting for the operation.

These are different perspectives but only one is a gauge of leadership and that is the value added per £ spent. Let us apply the same thinking to a very mature sector-the car industry. Market values tell us that Toyota ($127 billion) has left its erstwhile rivals standing (Ford and GM $22 and $19 billion respectively, as at March 2005) and the trends are up for Toyota and down for the Americans (at the time of writing GM's credit rating is at 'junk bond' status and is in danger of filing for bankruptcy). Yet we have already questioned the validity of the macro financial picture in gauging leadership effectiveness so we need to increase the magnification and look in more detail at what is happening behind the crude numbers. In GM's case the huge burden of pension and healthcare costs are cited as one of the reasons why the company is now in such a parlous state. In other words, senior GM management must have bowed to employee pressure in the past to offer a level of benefits that their ineffective management could not deliver. In effect, they did not enable their employees to create enough value to pay themselves what they felt they deserved. Put this way it makes GM's leadership look like it deserves a score at the bottom end of the leadership ability scale.

Toyota, on the other hand, would never offer its employees anything it felt it could not deliver. It would also point out to its employees that only they, ultimately, can create the value required to pay themselves. Clear leadership that is willing to tell both sides of the story: the good news as well as the bad. But this leadership approach and the solid 'psychological contract' on which it is founded did not happen overnight. Here is a quote from one of the founders of Toyota, Eiji Toyoda, when he wrote his biography of the company on its $50^{th}$ anniversary, on the subject of employee relations:-

"Mutual trust is the basis of labour relations. Labour relations at Toyota were initially marked by doubts and disbelief, but with time differences were ironed out. The labour-management declaration we signed was simply a written statement of this rapprochement. The purpose of this document was to uphold and sustain the trust that had been built up... and to prevent backsliding by either side from this position. It also was intended as a reminder to those who came after to guard the fruits won through the sacrifices made by both sides. ...it took about 10 years for that relationship of mutual trust to take hold. The spirit of this declaration still lives on at Toyota."

Eiji Toyoda, "Toyota-50 Years in motion" Harper & Row 1987.

Now, if we compare this with their other erstwhile competitor Ford, does Ford have a leadership with a coherent view of employee relations? How strong a leader would Ford now need to start a change in attitudes that might take 10 years, when the markets are demanding immediate action to stem losses? Even if Ford found such leaders would they actually know what to do? Charismatic leadership can often appeal to the masses, and even shareholders, in the short term but leadership that comes without a depth of knowledge and understanding of how to get the best value out of people cannot hope to provide society with what it needs in the long term.

### Leadership Development

Against this background we have finally arrived at the issue of actually developing leaders and this has to be an area that demands urgent attention. Very little, serious effort is made to provide the organisational leaders of the future with the real skills and knowledge they will need to do the job effectively. Henry Mintzberg in his book "Managers not MBA's" berates business schools for providing theory and not practice. Leadership can and should be studied but it can only be truly developed in a real time situation and context. Managers in a car company can learn all about Six Sigma and how to apply it but only leaders will ensure that everyone works together towards a common goal. Employees who see their own redundancy as an inevitable consequence of efficiency improvements will need some strong leadership to turn their natural, personal perspective from negative to positive.

Conversely, business leaders or politicians who only introduce popular policies or have to use spin to get unpopular policies accepted have already broken two of the golden rules of leadership. Popularity does not guarantee that the policies are valuable (e.g. curbing immigration could reduce value for everyone) and hiding the truth (i.e. fiddling the figures) will only 'lead' people in a false direction. So where does this leave us? I am conscious that I don't want to finish this article with more questions than answers so let me at least provide an answer to the 3 specific options I posed earlier (*). The answer to the first question is the simplest. Leaders need much more knowledge and understanding than they currently possess and this can be prescribed and delivered to a wider audience and in more depth and detail than currently happens. We need to spend much more time on it and also help future leaders gain a deeper understanding of, for example, the *philosophy* of kaizen (continuous improvement) and its human implications, than the mechanistic techniques associated with such thinking (e.g. Six Sigma). But this is most certainly not an argument for more MBA's. Once the basic knowledge content of the job is evident there needs to be an honest and clear-headed assessment of actual leadership ability (e.g. coherent strategy, clear articulation of how value will be created, gaining commitment to a common cause).

The second answer is that such attributes can and should be tested and assessed in real time, and continuously over time, so that our picture of the 'best' is as accurate and as meaningful as it can be. The measures we use may not be perfect but the very attempt to measure leadership will, in itself, apply a discipline that should result in a higher probability that leadership will result. What gets measured gets done. But time and attention has to be built into busy operational schedules to allow this to happen. A couple of days out of the office every year on a leadership course is not the solution we should be seeking.

If my proposed answers to the first two questions provide no easy options then the answer to the third question is probably the most unpalatable of all. Leadership is only really a key issue when a long-term, value creation context is present. The NHS, law and order, foreign policy and international competitiveness are all examples of the areas that can significantly raise levels of societal value. That value will only come when everyone working in these organisations is agreed on what constitutes value and then how they can all work together to improve it.

This is a lesson that the commercial world still has to learn and re-learn. Organisational 'leaders' who ask middle managers to cut costs with no counter-balancing measure of a potential loss in service or quality will not drive behaviours that produce more value. Managers themselves have a leadership role in such circumstances. They can stand up and be prepared to be counted in telling their organisations that value is being destroyed (e.g. the local authority shutting down a library saves money but removes its service and value to the community).

Either way, it is high time that leadership and value were more closely connected in everyone's eyes. We need to make sure we can recognise the potential value that is on offer and distinguish it from meaningless targets and PR spin. If we can do that then the leaders we appoint and choose to follow will know that we can judge them accordingly and hold them to account.

## Value Based Leadership

If we treat people as they are we make them worse. If we treat them as they ought to be, *we help them become what they are capable of becoming* (Goethe).

Leadership must be the most used and multifaceted word in business at the moment. There are hundreds of different labels for leaders and leadership styles, where do values fit in and what does Value based leadership mean? Who is a leader? It's not someone who tells you what to do. Someone who simply tells you what to do is a boss. You do it because they say so. A leader is someone you want to follow, not who you have to follow. Authority is necessary as part of living in society and working in business but on its own, it's not enough to make a leader. The original meaning of the word 'leadership', is to go on a journey in the company of others. So a leader is going somewhere, they have a goal and a vision. They attract others, so they appeal to others, and influence others. Those who join them on the journey trust them to know the road.

So being a leader comes from the natural human striving to reinvent yourself. It means developing yourself. It involves the ability to see the big picture and the wider system as well as paying attention to where you are putting your feet on the road. And it means inspiring others to join you on the road. Authority is given, but leadership needs to be earned.

Picture this company. In one department they have a boss, who tells them what to do and expects them to obey. He is not interested in his people, only as a means to an end – getting things done. He takes little interest in his people, does not help them connect what they do to the company vision, and is not interested in what is important to them. 'My way or the highway' is his motto. He has the authority, but strangely enough people often seem to find excuses not to do things. The people in his department are unhappy, and behind on their work. When things get behind, he responds by doing more of what he is doing already. This is the archetypal boss. Luckily they are going extinct very fast, because their methods simply do not work. However some elements of this dinosaur can still be found in many companies.

Contrast this with a leader. He takes an interest in his people, he knows them as individuals and he knows and respects what is important to them. He knows that the same incentive does not work for everyone and so he does not try to impose it on everyone. He coaches his people, not only those who are not performing well, but also those who are. People feel they are contributing to the organization and they respect this manager. He gets the job done, but does not rely on his authority alone, but on the fact that his people want to do the work well. He inspires them to their best. This is the manager who is a leader. Would that every manager was like this, but every manager can pay attention to leading based on values – their values of respect and fairness and motivating and inspiring others by what is important to them, not what is important to him or her. A boss has power, a leader has influence. A boss depends on their position of authority; a leader gains authority by being respected by his people.

A boss gets people to do things and a leader gets people to want to do things. Why do they want to do things? Because they are motivated and inspired by what is important to them and this is value based leadership.

There are two paradoxes about value-based leadership. First is that it can only be given and not taken. A person may have power and authority, but this is not the same as leadership. People follow a leader because they want to, not because they have to. A leader without followers or fellow travellers is like the sound of one hand clapping. The second paradox is that the first person a leader has to inspire is themselves. How can they inspire others to join you on a journey if you cannot inspire themselves? So how do leaders make people want to follow them on the journey? They appeal to what is important. All leaders have a vision, a vision of how the world could be, we all have our individual visions, but leaders tap into something more than just their vision, they tap into a common vision. They are on a journey and that journey is important to them. And when we talk about important we are talking about values, values are quite simply what is important to you. Values provide the energy to get out of bed in the morning; they provide the fuel for the journey towards the goal. Without value, the journey cannot start.

Take a moment to think of some leaders that you admire. People that you resonate with. They can be in any area, business, religious, military or any area of life. They may be famous people, or friends or family you know well, but others do not. What do these people have in common? One thing they must have in common is they appeal to something that is important to you. If they did not, you would not admire them. You recognize them as leaders because what they do and what they stand for is important to you.

Their values resonate with yours. Good managers will deal with problem behaviour from the point of view of values. Rather than simply challenging the behaviour, they make it clear that the behaviour is unacceptable while pacing and acknowledging the values behind it. Behaviour is purposeful. We always act to achieve something that is important to us, something we value. Unfortunately, the actions or behaviour may not be a very good way of getting it and may cause a lot of trouble for others.

For example a manager we know had a lot of trouble with one member of his team. This person would constantly challenge the thoughts and proposals of other members. He played the Devil's advocate, finding faults with details. This got very wearing. The other members of the team started to resent him, one of them said, 'I would not feel so bad, if he contributed something positive every now and then, but it is always so negative.' This person's behaviour was destroying team rapport, yet his area of expertise was essential and could not be replaced in the current project.

We suggested the manager take this man aside, ask him what he wanted to achieve through his questioning, and why this was important to him. It turned out that hevalued safety very highly. A project in his previous job had ended in disaster, because plans were not properly checked, and crucial details were left out. The company lost a lot of money.

He vowed this would never happen again in any work he was engaged on. 'I want the plan to be absolutely fool proof in every detail.' was how he expressed it. Safety and accuracy of detail were very important to him and our friend shared these values and said so. Now came the $64,000 question. 'Is your constant challenging getting you what you want?' The answer was no. The other team members were not paying attention to his contribution, they were not listening, paying him lip service only in their attempt to move on. This made him more nervous still and he challenged all the more. The manager suggested that he had a very useful role as Devil's Advocate of the group, but should wait until plans were at a reasonable stage of formation before asking for details. He agreed. After that the group's effectiveness was greatly increased. The others knew that they had the space they needed to develop plans and they had better be good ones. Challenges came later and were more constructive, and very valuable. Several small improvements were made that made the project more cost efficient. Our friend paced the man's values and utilised them for the benefit of the group.

An extensive study of leadership in medium sized European companies showed that about two thirds of major decisions were taken in line with declared company strategy. However only about one third of decisions of middle importance were in line with company declared strategy.

This seems reasonable from the outside, but remember that the big decisions were taken behind closed doors by a small group of top people and the full implications were often kept secret for good commercial reasons. The smaller day-to-day decisions that affected the employees were out in the open and the majority of these were not consistent with the company strategy. People saw every day that the companies were not walking their talk, this can lead to disillusionment and cynicism. At the extreme there is the example of a large United States organization that had published its values one of which was putting employees first. This same organization cut employees health benefits payments and increased spending on country club membership for the top executives. This is not value based leadership and this organization can hardly complain if the people see this and get cynical. There is an important lesson – stick to your values. People do notice. And it is important.

Value based leadership can come from anywhere in the organization. What is sure is that if the people at the top do not demonstrate it, and then they will lose respect. People will become cynical about the values and even scoff at them. Ten they will start working just for money and every survey has shown that while it is important to pay people a fair wage, once this is reached, then other values are more important than money, particularly, challenge, career advancement and respect. Unless a manager leads their people by making their work challenging and fulfilling and giving them respect, they might well change jobs, taking all that highly prized and painstakingly earned knowledge and expertise to their old employer's competitor. In this way it is easy to see that value-based leadership is not an abstract ideal, but enlightened self interest and good management.

## Value Human Relationships

Before long, we notice that the value of nearly all products and services is wholly derived from the value of human interaction with the object. So where exactly is the true value of our economy, in the object or in the human interaction? Wall Street would say "object", but Main Street would say "human interaction".

An interpersonal relationship is an association between two or more people that may range from fleeting to enduring. This association may be based on limerence, love, solidarity, regular business interactions, or some other type of social commitment. Interpersonal relationships are formed in the context of social, cultural and other influences. The context can vary from family or kinship relations, friendship, marriage, relations with associates, work, clubs, neighborhoods, and places of worship. They may be regulated by law, custom, or mutual agreement, and are the basis of social groups and society as a whole.

A relationship is normally viewed as a connection between two individuals, such as a romantic or intimate relationship, or a parent–

child relationship. Individuals can also have relationships with groups of people, such as the relation between a pastor and his congregation, an uncle and a family, or a mayor and a town. Finally, groups or even nations may have relations with each other, though this is a much broader domain than that covered under the topic of interpersonal relationships.

See such articles as international relations for more information on associations between groups. Most scholarly work on relationships focuses on romantic partners in pairs or dyads. These intimate relationships are, however, only a small subset of interpersonal relationships. Interpersonal relationships can also include friendships, such as relationships involving individuals providing relational care to marginalized persons.

These relationships usually involve some level of interdependence. People in a relationship tend to influence each other, share their thoughts and feelings, and engage in activities together. Because of this interdependence, most things that change or impact one member of the relationship will have some level of impact on the other member. The study of interpersonal relationships involves several branches of the social sciences, including such disciplines as sociology, psychology, anthropology, and social work. The scientific study of relationships is referred to as relationship science and distinguishes itself from anecdotal evidence or pseudo-experts by basing conclusions on data and objective analysis. Interpersonal ties are also a subject in mathematical sociology.

### *Flourishing Relationships*

Positive psychologists use the term "flourishing relationships" to describe interpersonal relationships that are not merely happy, but instead characterized by intimacy, growth, and resilience. Flourishing relationships also allow a dynamic balance between focus on the intimate relationships and focus on other social relationships.

### *Background*

While traditional psychologists specializing in close relationships have focused on relationship dysfunction, positive psychology argues that relationship health is not merely the absence of relationship dysfunction. Healthy relationships are built on a foundation of secure attachment and are maintained with love and purposeful positive relationship behaviours. Additionally, healthy relationships can be made to "flourish." Positive psychologists are exploring what makes existing relationships flourish and what skills can be taught to partners to enhance their existing and future personal relationships.

### *Adult Attachment*

Healthy relationships are built on a foundation of secure attachments. Adult attachment models represent an internal set of expectations and preferences regarding relationship intimacy that guide behaviour.

Secure adult attachment, characterized by low attachment-related avoidance and anxiety, has numerous benefits. Within the context of safe, secure attachments, people can pursue optimal human functioning and flourishing.

### *Love*

The capacity for love gives depth to human relationships, brings people closer to each other physically and emotionally, and makes people think expansively about themselves and the world. In his triangular theory of love, psychologist Robert Sternberg theorizes that love is a mix of three components: (1) passion, or physical attraction; (2) intimacy, or feelings of closeness; and (3) commitment, involving the decision to initiate and sustain a relationship.

The presence of all three components characterizes consummate love, the most durable type of love. In addition, the presence of intimacy and passion in marital relationships predicts marital satisfaction. Also, commitment is the best predictor of relationship satisfaction, especially in long-term relationships. Positive consequences of being in love include increased self-esteem and self-efficacy.

## Theories and Empirical Research

Confucianism is in fact a study or a theory of relationship.

### *Minding Relationships*

The mindfulness theory of relationships shows how closeness in relationships may be enhanced. Minding is the "reciprocal knowing process involving the nonstop, interrelated thoughts, feelings, and behaviours of persons in a relationship." Five components of "minding" include:

1. Knowing and being known: seeking to understand the partner
2. Making relationship-enhancing attributions for behaviours: giving the benefit of the doubt

3. Accepting and respecting: empathy and social skills
4. Maintaining reciprocity: active participation in relationship enhancement
5. Continuity in minding: persisting in mindfulness.

### Culture of Appreciation

After studying married couples for many years, psychologist John Gottman has proposed the theory of the "magic ratio" for successful marriages. The theory says that for a marriage to be successful, couples must average a ratio of five positive interactions to one negative interaction. As the ratio moves to 1:1, divorce becomes more likely. Interpersonal interactions associated with negative relationships include criticism, contempt, defensiveness, and stonewalling. Over time, therapy aims to turn these interpersonal strategies into more positive ones, which include complaint, appreciation, acceptance of responsibility, and self-soothing. Similarly, partners in interpersonal relationships can incorporate positive components into difficult subjects in order to avoid emotional disconnection.

### Capitalizing on Positive Events

People can capitalize on positive events in an interpersonal context to work toward flourishing relationships. People often turn to others to share their good news (termed "capitalization"). Studies show that both the act of telling others about good events and the response of the person with whom the event was shared have personal and interpersonal consequences, including increased positive emotions, subjective well-being, and self-esteem, and relationship benefits including intimacy, commitment, trust, liking, closeness, and stability. Studies show that the act of communicating positive events was associated with increased positive affect and well-being (beyond the impact of the positive event itself a). Other studies have found that relationships in which partners responded to "good news" communication enthusiastically were associated with higher relationship well-being.

### Other Perspectives

### Neurobiology of Interpersonal Connections

There is an emerging body of research across multiple disciplines investigating the neurological basis of attachment and the prosocial emotions and behaviours that are the prerequisites for healthy adult relationships. The social environment, mediated by attachment, influences the maturation of structures in a child's brain. This might explain how infant attachment affects adult emotional health. Researchers are currently investigating the link between positive caregiver–child relationships and the development of hormone systems, such as the HPA axis.

### Applications

Researchers are developing an approach to couples therapy that moves partners from patterns of repeated conflict to patterns of more positive, comfortable exchanges. Goals of therapy include development of social and interpersonal skills. Expressing gratitude and sharing appreciation for a partner is the primary means for creating a positive relationship. Positive marital counseling also emphasizes mindfulness. The further study of "flourishing relationships could shape the future of premarital and marital counseling as well."

### Organizations Benefit from Nurturing Human Relationships

From engineering teams of just a few members, to global companies with tens of thousands of employees, organizations must constantly search for new ways to reinvigorate stressed-out workforces. You may be familiar with corporate initiatives that pop up every few years announcing new (often expensive) employee programs or software purchases intended to make working life easier. However, a lack of tools may not be the root of the problem. Maybe it's a lack of trust in human relationships.

If trust seems too touch-feely a concept, you may be surprised to learn that it has caught the attention of the US Army. After a decade of continuous engagement around the world, military commanders are faced with "employees" who have been asked to maintain a near-constant state of fighting readiness. In this state, soldiers are often called upon to exert hard power over other human beings. According to author Ori Brafman, this means a workforce overwhelmed by exposure to the stress hormone cortisol. If you can't avoid exposing workers to stress, how do you create an organization better prepared to deal with this exposure?

Brafman's suggestion to the Army was to develop the capacity to create more soft power and trust-based networks. In the video below, Brafman describes his experiences working with military personnel to help them relate their feelings and experiences in a more humane way. Between the participants, these interactions actually developed a greater level of intimacy, says Brafman, a concept that doesn't often come to mind in business or the military. If you're dealing with stressed-out workers, perhaps you should hold off on purchasing that new collaboration tool with all the bells and whistles, and instead, invest your energy into improving the relationships between the human beings that make up your company's human capital.

## Foster Teamwork

Teamwork is work performed by a team towards a common goal.

In a business setting accounting techniques may be used to provide financial measures of the benefits of teamwork which are useful for justifying the concept.

In health care teamwork has been defined as:

A dynamic process involving two or more healthcare professionals with complementary backgrounds and skills, sharing common health goals and exercising concerted physical and mental effort in assessing, planning, or evaluating patient care.

Teamwork is increasingly advocated by health care policy makers as a means of assuring quality and safety in the delivery of services.

### *Teamwork Activities*

A challenge for leaders of groups of people, such as in a work department, is to get everyone to pull together and function as a team instead of going in separate directions. One way to foster teamwork is to engage the members in activities that require them to work together. Activities can be physical in nature or require the use of team brain power to solve a problem. Fun activities such as sports or games can allow the team members to relax and enjoy working with one another.

- Social Activities: Part of the challenge of developing teamwork is to get team members to become comfortable with each other. Informal social activities allow the team members to relax and have fun while developing the rapport necessary to function as a unit. Examples of social activities include team sports such as volleyball or bowling or a group picnic, where everyone is responsible for a task such as bringing food or planning a game.
- Charitable Endeavours: Working together for a charitable cause builds teamwork and gives the participants a good feeling from working together. An example of a team charitable activity is

planning and organizing an event like a walk or run to raise money or a bake sale that promotes a cause.

- Workplace Activities: Because teamwork is important to a productive and healthy work environment, teamwork activities should be a part of the workplace. Possible activities include job swapping, where workers swap jobs with each other to develop empathy. It also requires workers to help each other to learn the jobs. Another idea is to start a team newsletter that provides the latest information on activities and accomplishments of the team members.
- Projects: Projects require that team members work together to achieve a common goal. Projects can involve activities like putting puzzles together or cleaning up or rebuilding a property. Projects typically involve assigning each team member a specific task that he is responsible for completing, which helps to develop trust within the team.
- Outdoor Activities: If members of the team are relatively fit, outdoor activities are a way for the team to get away from the "normal" environment. Activities such as camping, hiking, mountain biking or whitewater rafting allow the team members to relax while enjoying the fresh air, and the sense of being "away from it all" can lead to bonding within the team.

Today, most business owners use a team approach to solve problems, generate ideas and complete tasks. But before building a team, the entrepreneur needs to resolve these key questions: Can I complete the task myself? Do I have the time and resources to complete this task? Can some other person or group be even more effective than I can?

If the answers favour getting others involved, it's time to consider the advantages and disadvantages of teams. On the upside, teams combine various employee skills, ideas, knowledge bases and perspectives. Teams usually increase individual productivity and workplace satisfaction. Simply being on a team can be a key source of employee motivation, status and pride for having been selected to participate. Team output is generally higher in quality and quantity than individual performance.

However, all is not necessarily rosy—there are some disadvantages to using teams as well. For example, teams may take longer to achieve a goal than an individual would, and teams grow through predictable stages that are time-consuming, such as member selection, organization, socialization and creation of final products or ideas. Key resources (time, money, people and equipment) are restricted to the team and not available to others. Some of the team members may lack interest, necessary skills or abilities, or motivation. They may have been appointed or self-appointed to the team for political reasons or merely to enjoy themselves while others do the work. This "social loafing" can be a source of tension among productive team members. Finally, people dynamics can complicate the team process, replete with conflicts, group pressure to reach a fast or unanimous conclusion, and taking risky stances.

The good news is, with effective direction and facilitation from the right team leader, team-building can be a very productive and cost-effective process. To help ensure success, the team needs to consider six crucial success factors: clear identification and ownership of the team goal; clear definition and acceptance of each person's role and responsibilities; clear delineation of team processes, such as decision-making, conflict resolution, communication and participation; clear opportunities to build trust between participants; and finally, clear acceptance of each other's strengths and limitations in a manner that encourages positive working relationships.

The key word here is clear. When goals, roles, processes, trust and relationships are clear, then success almost always follows.

## Growth Matters

Corporate growth can be defined in numerous ways and be achieved in several strategic forms. In general, the matter of whether—and at what rate—a company is growing can be highly ambiguous. A company can experience strong sales growth, but simultaneously be losing market share and experiencing financial losses. In such a case, the company's volume is rising, but that of its competitors is rising even faster. And, on the bottom line, sales growth means little when the company cannot turn a profit.

The same company may be gaining market share, but losing sales volume and money. This suggests that volume is falling throughout the industry, but only less so for this company. In any case, it still loses money on its operations. Consider a third case, where a company's earnings are rising, but it's losing sales volume and market share. This is quite possibly the only favourable scenario, because it suggests that the company is cutting marginal operations to concentrate on what it does best—in effect, becoming smaller but more profitable.

While these criteria can provide some insight into the true nature of the firm—whether it really is growing or not—they also can provide some indication of what type of firm the company is: a dog, a question mark, a cash cow, or a star. A dog is a company with low or declining market share and low or declining market growth, typically a description of a dying firm. A company with low or declining market share but a high rate of sales growth is a question mark, because its success depends on whether it can outperform competitors in terms of sales growth and eventually gain market share.

Alternatively, a company with low or declining sales growth but high or increasing market share is a cash cow because its position in the market is secure even though the industry in which it operates has matured. Such a company is typically overrun by successful question marks and becomes a dog. In the meantime, however, it generates a healthy income.

A company with high or growing market share and high or growing sales volume is called a star because it is outperforming its competitors. Dogs typically lose—or will lose—money, while stars typically make—or will make—money.

Whether in terms of market share or sales volume, growth may be pursued in one of three ways. In a high-growth company, either or both market share and sales volume growth are pursued vigorously, even at the expense of short-term profitability. This is a risky strategy because the company risks going bankrupt before it can achieve commanding positions in terms of market share and/or sales volume.

A slow-growth company concentrates on maintaining profitability while pursuing incremental gains in market share and/or sales volume. The slow-growth strategy emphasizes financial longevity.

The third growth strategy is based on negative growth, or retrenchment. A company in retrenchment is purposely sacrificing market share and sales growth with the singular goal of emphasizing short-term profitability. In other words, the company is abandoning operations in markets where it has the fewest advantages, vis-a-vis competitors.

When the retrenchment has run its course, the company is left with a core business in which it enjoys solid advantages over competitors, and may take advantage of its superior profitability to pursue either a high-or slow-growth strategy. In effect, retrenchment strategies establish bases for the other growth strategies.

## Other Aspects of Corporate Growth

Whether a company is in a growth industry or a mature market, corporate growth is necessary for a company to remain healthy. Companies that compete in a growing market must grow in order to maintain market share. Without such growth, they fail to realize benefits of growth such as economies of scale and the ability to attract talented managers and employees. Especially in global markets, economies of scale allow growing companies to make significant investments in research and development and worldwide marketing.

Similarly, companies competing in mature markets must find ways to grow. Otherwise, they are forced to compete on the basis of price and face declining margins. In order to achieve growth such companies typically exit slow-growth products or market segments that aren't very profitable and enter those markets or related markets that are growing more quickly. They may develop and nurture new businesses that will replace or complement their maturing core business. Other growth strategies for companies competing in mature markets include acquiring smaller competitors or consolidating fragmented industries into a single-source operation. Growth companies in mature industries may include electric utilities, large retailers, and railroad companies.

As desirable as corporate growth may be, a study, conducted by the Corporate Strategy Board, of 3,700 U.S. and international companies for the period from 1990 to 1997 found that only 3.3 percent of those companies had consistent profitable growth in revenues, net income, and shareholder returns for the period.

Of the companies studied, only 21, or less than I percent, achieved consistent growth over the past 20 years.

### An Overview of Corporate Growth Strategies

Every business wants to grow, and there's a good reason why. Continued, sustainable growth is important for the survival of your company and for your well being. However, it can be hard to figure out what to do to get your business beyond the level of basic subsistence. Here are a few corporate growth strategies that others have successfully used to get their businesses where they need to go.

1. Take a look at your existing markets. Getting new customers is something than many businesses focus on when they want to grow. However, your existing customers can be a much better place to look for more sales. After all, they're already

buying from you. It's a lot easier to get them to buy again than it is to convince new customers to buy.

2. Referrals are valuable. Your existing customers can also help you find new ones. By referring you to their friends and relatives, they can help your business grow and your reputation improve. However, you shouldn't assume that just because you do a good job, your existing customers are passing on the word. Seek referrals actively to get the best results.
3. Find new uses for your services or products. One way to find new markets and get more purchases from existing customers is to discover new, innovative uses for your service or product. After all, many things have multiple uses – you just have to find them. Diversifying what you offer is another version of this that can be very effective.
4. Find new customer pools. Extending your reach to new customers can be a big help. This can include opening new physical or virtual locations so that you can reach more people, or by increasing your advertising. Choosing to advertise in media that targets a new market can be very profitable.
5. Look for niche markets. If you're capable of dominating a small, unique sector, it's a lot more effective than being a small fish in a big pond. Specialization can be a very good idea if you can find needs that aren't being met.
6. Trade shows are valuable. Trade shows can be an extremely effective way of helping your business grow, by drawing in people who already have an interest in what you do. Your bottom line can improve significantly. Just make sure that you choose your shows with care and find the ones that go best with your company.
7. Keep costs down. Remember that growing your business is actually about improving the bottom line. If you can reduce costs and make things more efficient, things will improve.

Of course, these are just a few ways to help your business grow. There are plenty of others that'll help you increase your bottom line and become a real success. Use these tips with a smart strategy to keep on expanding.

## Trust is Vital

In a social context, trust has several connotations. The typical definition of trust follows the general intuition about trust and contains such elements as:

- the willingness of one party (trustor) to rely on the actions of another party (trustee);
- reasonable expectation (confidence) of the trustor that the trustee will behave in a way beneficial to the trustor;
- risk of harm to the trustor if the trustee will not behave accordingly; and
- the absence of trustor's enforcement or control over actions performed by the trustee.

Trust can be attributed to relationships between people. It can be demonstrated that humans have a natural disposition to trust and to judge trustworthiness that can be traced to the neurobiological structure and activity of a human brain, and can be altered e.g. by the application of oxytocin.

Conceptually, trust is also attributable to relationships within and between social groups (families, friends, communities, organisations, companies, nations etc.). It is a popular approach to frame the dynamics of inter-group and intra-group interactions in terms of trust.

When it comes to the relationship between people and technology, the attribution of trust is a matter of dispute. The intentional stance demonstrates that trust can be validly attributed to human relationships with complex technologies. However, rational reflection leads to the rejection of an ability to trust technological artefacts.

One of the key current challenges in the social sciences is to re-think how the rapid progress of technology has impacted constructs such as trust. This is specifically true for information technology that dramatically alters causation in social systems.

In the social sciences, the subtleties of trust are a subject of ongoing research. In sociology and psychology the degree to which one party trusts another is a measure of belief in the honesty, fairness, or benevolence of another party.

The term "confidence" is more appropriate for a belief in the competence of the other party. Based on the most recent research, a failure in trust may be forgiven more easily if it is interpreted as a failure of competence rather than a lack of benevolence or honesty. In economics trust is often conceptualized as reliability in transactions. In all cases trust is a heuristic decision rule, allowing the human to deal with complexities that would require unrealistic effort in rational reasoning.

When it comes to trust, sociology is concerned with the position and role of trust in social systems. Interest in trust has grown significantly since the early eighties, from the early works of Luhmann, Barber and Giddens. This growth of interest in trust has been stimulated by on-going changes in society, characterised as late modernity and post-modernity.

Trust is one of several social constructs, an element of the social reality. Other constructs, frequently discussed together with trust, are: control, confidence, risk, meaning and power. Trust is naturally attributable to relationships between social actors, both individuals and groups (social systems). Because trust is a social construct, it is valid to discuss whether trust can be trusted (e.g.), i.e. whether social trust operates as expected.

Society needs trust because it increasingly finds itself operating at the edge between confidence in what is known from everyday experience, and contingency of new possibilities. Without trust, all contingent possibilities should be always considered, leading to a paralysis of inaction. Trust can be seen as a bet on one of contingent futures, the one that may deliver benefits. Once the bet is decided (i.e. trust is granted), the trustor suspends his or her disbelief, and the possibility of a negative course of action is not considered at all. Because of it, trust acts as a reductor of social complexity, allowing for actions that are otherwise too complex to be considered (or even impossible to consider at all); specifically for cooperation.

Sociology tends to focus on two distinct views: the macro view of social systems, and a micro view of individual social actors (where it borders with social psychology). Similarly, views on trust follow this dichotomy. Therefore, on one side the systemic role of trust can be discussed, with a certain disregard to the psychological complexity underpinning individual trust. The behavioural approach to trust is usually assumed while actions of social actors are measurable, leading to statistical modelling of trust. This systemic approach can be contrasted with studies on social actors and their decision-making process, in anticipation that understanding of such a process will explain (and allow to model) the emergence of trust.

Sociology acknowledges that the contingency of the future creates dependency between social actors, and specifically that the trustor becomes dependent on the trustee. Trust is seen as one of the possible methods to resolve such a dependency, being an attractive alternative to control. Trust is specifically valuable if the trustee is much more powerful than the trustor, yet the trustor is under social obligation to support the trustee.

Modern information technologies not only facilitated the transition towards post-modern society, but they also challenged traditional views on trust. Empirical studies confirms the new approach to the traditional question regarding whether technology artefacts can be attributed with trust. Trust is not attributable to artefacts, but it is a representation of trust in social actors such as designers, creators and operators of technology. Properties of technological artefacts form a message to determine trustworthiness of those agents.

The discussion about the impact of information technologies is still in progress. However, it is worth noting a conceptual re-thinking of technology-mediated social groups, or the proposition of a unifying socio-technical view on trust, from the perspective of social actors.

### *Psychology*

In psychology, trust is believing that the person whom is trusted will do what is expected. It starts at the family and grows to others. According to the psychoanalyst Erik Erikson development of basic trust is the first state psychosocial development occurring, or failing, during the first two years of life. Success results in feelings of security, trust, and optimism, while failure leads towards an orientation of insecurity and mistrust. Trust is integral to the idea of social influence: it is easier to influence or persuade someone who is trusting. The notion of trust is increasingly adopted to predict acceptance of behaviours by others, institutions (e.g. government agencies) and objects such as machines. However, once again perception of honesty, competence and value similarity (slightly similar to benevolence) are essential. There are three different forms of trust. Trust is being vulnerable to someone even when they are trustworthy; Trustworthiness is the ability to trust, and trust propensity being able to rely on people. Once trust is lost, by obvious violation of one of these three determinants, it is very hard to regain. Thus there is clear asymmetry in the building versus destruction of trust. Hence being and acting trustworthy should be considered the only sure way to maintain a trust level.

Increasingly much research has been done on the notion of trust and its social implications:

- Barbara Misztal in her book attempts to combine all notions of trust together. She points out *three basic things that trust does in the lives of people*: It makes social life *predictable*, it creates a *sense of community*, and it *makes it easier for people to work together*.

- In the context of sexual trust Riki Robbins describes four stages of trust.
- In the context of Information theory Ed Gerck defines and contrasts trust with social functions such as power, surveillance, and accountability.

In addition to the social influence, in organizational settings, trust may have a positive influence on the behaviours, perceptions, and performances of a person. Trust has a circular relationship with organizational justice perceptions such that perceived justice leads to trust which, in turn, promotes future perceptions of justice. One factor that enhances trust in a human being is facial resemblance. Evidence shows through manipulation of facial resemblance in a two person sequential trust game that having similar facial features (facial resemblance) enhanced trust in their partner. Structure often creates trust in a person that encourages them to feel comfortable and excel in the workplace. Working anywhere may be stressful and takes effort.

By having a conveniently organized area to work on, concentration will increase as well as effort. Structure is not just a method of order. It increases trust and therefore makes a workplace manageable. A structured, ordered environment produces trust as one may contain increased cooperation and perform on a higher level. People may work together and achieve success through trust while working on projects that rely on each individual's contribution.

Conversely, where trust is absent, projects can fail, especially if this lack of trust has not been identified and addressed. This is one facet of VPEC-T analysis: This thinking framework is used when studying information systems. Identifying and dealing with cases where information providers, information users, and those responsible for processing information do not trust one another can result in the removal of a risk factor for a project.

One's social relationship characterized by low trust and norms that discourage academic engagement are expected to be associated with low academic achievement. Individuals that are in relationships characterized by high levels of social trust are more apt to openly exchange information and to act with caring benevolence toward one another than those in relationships lacking trust.

An important key to treating sexual victimization of a child is the rebuilding of trust between parent and child. Failure for the adults to validate the sexual abuse contributes to the child's difficulty towards trusting self and others. Trust is often affected by the erosion of a marriage. Children of divorce do not exhibit less trust in mothers, partners, spouses, friends, and associates than their peers of intact families. The impact of parental divorce is limited to trust in the father.

### Philosophy

Some philosophers argue that trust is more than a relationship of reliance. Philosophers such as Annette Baier have made a difference between trust and reliance by saying that trust can be betrayed, whilst reliance can only be disappointed (Baier 1986, 235).

Carolyn McLeod explains Baier's argument by giving the following examples: we can rely on our clock to give the time, but we do not feel betrayed when it breaks, thus, we cannot say that we trusted it; we are not trusting when we are suspicious of the other person, because this is in fact an expression of distrust (McLeod 2006). Thus, trust is different from reliance in the sense that the truster must accept the risk of being betrayed.

### Economics

Trust in economics is treated as an explanation for a difference between actual human behaviour and the one that can be explained by the individual desire to maximise one's utility. In economic terms, trust can provide an explanation of a difference between Nash equilibrium and Pareto optimum. Such an approach can be applied to individuals and well as societies.

Trust is also seen as an economic lubricant, reducing the cost of transactions, enabling new forms of cooperation and generally furthering business activities, employment and prosperity. This observation created a significant interest in considering trust as a form of social capital and has led research into closer understanding of the process of creation and distribution of such capital. It has been claimed that higher level of social trust is positively correlated with economic development.

Even though the original concept of 'high trust' and 'low trust' societies may not necessarily hold, it has been widely accepted and demonstrated that social trust benefits the economy and that a low level of trust inhibits economic growth.

Theoretical economical modelling demonstrated that the optimum level of trust that a rational economic agent should exhibit in transactions is equal to trustworthiness of the other party. Such a level of trust leads to efficient market. Trusting less lead to the loss of economic opportunities, trusting more leads to unnecessary vulnerabilities and potential exploitation.

Economics is also interested in quantifying trust, usually in monetary terms. The level of correlation between increase in profit margin or decrease in transactional cost can be used as indicators of economic value of trust.

Economic 'trust games' are popularly used to empirically quantify trust in relationships under laboratory conditions. There are several games and game-like scenarios related to trust that have been tried, with certain preferences to those that allow to estimate confidence in monetary terms. Games of trust are designed in a way that their Nash equilibrium differ from Pareto optimum so that no player alone can maximise his own utility by altering his selfish strategy without cooperation while cooperating partners can benefit.

The classical version of the game of trust has been described in as an abstracted investment game, using the scenario of an investor and a broker. Investor can invest a fraction of his money, and broker can return only part of his gains. If both players follow their economical best interest, the investor should never invest and the broker will never be able to re-pay anything.

Thus the flow of money flow, its volume and character is attributable entirely to the existence of trust. The game can be played as one-off, or as a repetitive one, between the same or different sets of players, to distinguish between a general propensity to trust and trust within particular relationships. Several other variants of this game exist. Reversing rules lead to the game of distrust, pre-declarations can be used to establish intentions of players, while alterations to the distribution of gains can be used to manipulate perception of both players. The game can be also played by several players on the closed market, with or without information about reputation.

Other interesting games are e.g. binary-choice trust games, the gift-exchange game and various other forms of social games. Specifically games based on the Prisoners Dilemma are popularly used to link trust with economic utility and demonstrate the rationality behind reciprocity.

The popularisation of e-commerce opened the discussion of trust in economy to new challenges while at the same time elevating the importance of trust, and desire to understand customer decision to trust. For example, inter-personal relationship between the buyer and the seller has been dis-intermediated by the technology, and had to be improved upon. Alternatively, web sites could be made to convince the buyer to trust the seller, regardless of seller's actual trustworthiness (e.g.). Reputation-based systems improved on trust assessment by allowing to capture the collective perception of trustworthiness, generating significant interest in various models of reputation. Leadership and trust go hand-in-hand. Whether you are a minister or a corporate CEO, you cannot expect people to trust you—you have to prove it first. We have become skeptical and callous.

## "In God we Trust, all others Bring Data"

Furthermore, maintaining trust is like walking on eggs—slow going and easily crushed. Even before Enron, my experience as a management consultant shows many executives unintentionally damage their credibility and trust. Here are some ways to maintain a high trust level within your organization.

- *Your personal life is your public life.* Your personal life reflects who you *really* are. If you are in a leadership position, your personal life is open to scrutiny. Your ability to lead others will increase if people respect you. You may not like it, but that is the way it is.
- *Do what you say you will do.* How many times has someone told you, "I'll get back to you on that," but never followed up? Don't make promises you can't or won't keep. Trust breaks down when promises are broken.
- *Tell the truth.* The worst thing you can do is to not be open and honest with people. Trying to hide information will always catch up with you. Tell people everything they need to know, even if it's bad news. It's better to say too much than too little.
- *Treat everyone with respect.* You may not *like* everyone you work with, but you must *treat* them as if you do. People want to feel they have value and worth as individuals. Give everyone a chance to improve and attempt to *understand* and place their interests first.
- *Show appreciation.* Surprise people by doing something unexpected for them. When you see one of your employees

doing something good, write a note of appreciation or walk up and just tell them. They will appreciate you and trust you more.

- *Avoid favoritism.* Don't turn to the same person for help over and over again. Train and develop all your employees so everyone has equal opportunity to prove themselves and the workload is shared equally. Insure all people of color are fairly represented at all levels of the organization and provided the same opportunity for advancement.
- *Consistently enforce the rules.* Eliminate unnecessary rules, regulations, and policies, and enforce all the rest. When you selectively enforce policies, mistrust increases. No matter how clear the rules seem to you, everyone has a different perception. What appears unnecessary to you is important to someone else. Either enforce it or eliminate it.
- *Treat people as equals.* Because of the Enron scandal, there will be more pressure on boards and executives to give all employees the same privileges normally reserved for executives. If executives can sell their stock options, why can't other employees? Privileges and perks will be under greater scrutiny by both the media and rank and file.
- *Don't tell jokes at others' expense.* Telling jokes is a good way to lower your trust quotient. The most harmless joke will offend someone. Even *Dilbert* cartoons damage the credibility and trustworthiness of management. They create a perception that all managers are stupid.

The business community faces a crisis in confidence. Many are asking: how can corporations govern them-selves more effectively? This Policy Brief describes six fundamental, inter-related tasks which boards of directors and business leaders should discharge in governing publicly held corporations in order to regain the vital trust upon which business is based.

As discussed in more detail below, the *first task* is to redefine the corporate mission away from short-term maximization of shareholder value towards three reinforcing objectives: creation of durable value for shareholders and stakeholders through:

a. sustained economic performance
b. sound risk management and
c. high integrity.

From this general restatement of mission flow the *five other tasks*:

1. revamped leadership development;
2. refocused CEO selection;
3. reformulation of operational goals to reflect the broader mission;
4. revision of compensation to reward attainment of those operational goals; and
5. re-alignment of board oversight to track the highest priority performance, risk and integrity issues.

Boards of directors in particular should focus on these six tasks in clarifying a "right-sized" role going forward. This will require energy and intensity within the normal time parameters of board service. But, this laser-like board focus will only be possible if the CEO and other senior company executives also make these tasks the core of their leadership and management efforts as they "govern" the company on a day-to-day basis. This Policy Brief is not just about the role of boards of directors but also about the importance of a powerful board/business-leader partnership in directing the destiny of publicly held corporations.

By showing how closely, indeed seamlessly, these six tasks relate to each other, this Policy Brief hopes to provide an affirmative, *actionable* framework which boards and business leaders can apply, as appropriate, in their own corporations. Such a framework is of special importance in orienting the company towards the essential in an era when any commonality among shareholders has broken down—indeed shareholders have many conflicting objectives and agendas—and when stakeholders, too, make many competing demands on the corporation.

The forward trajectory of corporations involves a balance between many competing objectives and claims—not pursuit of one simple goal—and, at the end of the day, only boards and senior executives can make the complex decisions to find the right balance. Although written in a prescriptive form, this paper, prepared in the aftermath of the greatest economic down-turn in 60 years, seeks to stimulate an important discussion on the essentials of corporate governance, not to exhaust or end it, by arguing for the primacy of the six fundamental tasks. It encourages debate on the *substance* of what a corporation should do, not just on the *processes* for how to do it. It discusses illustrative concepts to provide context but hopes to avoid mind-numbing or rote box-checking detail.

This crisis of confidence in corporate governance has many origins. Major financial institutions (banks and investment banks) and industrial companies (automobiles) have gone bankrupt with significant injury to all stakeholders. Important financial service companies contributed to the credit melt-down and severe recession (through, among other things, poor risk management, high leverage, inadequate liquidity, creation of ill-understood products). High, poorly structured corporate compensation has drawn sharp criticism as a cause in excessive risk taking and as out of proportion to good judgment and common sense. And other corporations in both the financial and industrial sectors, even those which are well-run, are not immune from general reputational harm to business caused by almost two years of headlines about corporate problems, excesses and failures.

To address these real and perceived issues about corporate leadership, about corporations' ability to govern themselves effectively and about corporate accountability, there are two broad options:

- more public-sector regulation to limit private-sector self-determination either in the financial sector or across all publicly held corporations; and
- more broad-gauged, transparent and effective private-sector leadership to articulate the core purposes of public corporations and to carry them out with rigor.

This Policy Brief focuses on the second option: enhanced corporate self-governance at all publicly held companies. It builds on prior policy statements from leading governance groups and on recent reports about the causes and cures of the financial and auto-mobile company melt-downs.

It hopes to make a singular contribution by defining the six essential governance tasks, by emphasizing their interrela-tionship, and by showing that these seamless tasks are the touchstone of corporate accountability.

A company culture that truly makes the six intercon-nected tasks a reality is necessary whether or not there is additional public-sector regulation. Some companies discharge some of these tasks; some may discharge all. But, to meet the demands of the times, all companies may find it helpful to re-assess their current approach against these six priority actions. At the end of the day, whatever the result of the public-policy debates about governance structure and process, only out-standing boards of directors and outstanding business leadership can together make corporations work.

## *Restoring Trust with Six Essential Governance Tasks*

In this period of economic upheaval and change, boards of directors and CEOs are buffeted from many sides with conflicting demands about what they should do. A common board lament is being overwhelmed with too little time and too much complexity. In arguing that boards of directors and business leadership must discharge six core tasks in order to regain public trust, this Policy Brief underscores that these are seamless, building upon and reinforcing each other. While the details of discharging these tasks will necessarily vary with company, industry, geography and competition, focusing on them together as action-able, core functions will help answer the pressing question asked by boards and business leaders: what should be our priority tasks? Attempting to draw the line between board-of-director and business-leader responsibility is not the purpose of this Policy Brief.

The long-standing proposition that the board of directors sets the corporation's direction and oversees implementation—and the CEO and senior executives lead and manage the corporation it-self—continues to apply. Too much of the governance writing, especially since Enron, has emphasized the board's role in being a check and balance on manage-ment, as if they are necessarily in perpetual opposition. But—*and this must be emphasized*—if the board correctly defines the jobs of the CEO and top business leaders and chooses the right people, the primary relationship should be a questioning but affirmative partnership. That partnership critically but constructively tests the reasonableness of *both* the fundamental systems and processes instituted by management *and* the high priority decisions and results flowing from those systems and processes.

## *Redefining the Mission of the Corporation—and the Roles of the Board of Directors and the CEO*

Far too much emphasis has been placed in recent years on the single corporate goal of maximizing short-term earnings per share, stock price and shareholder value. As discussed below, this is due, in important part, to pressures exerted by the change in institutional investors who are increasingly preoccupied with short-term results, with beating composite industry benchmarks and with their own absolute profitability, rather than company fundamentals.

A statement of the mission of publicly held companies, appropriate to these times, is creation of durable shareholder and stakeholder value by:

- *Attaining high performance* which means: strong, sustained economic growth; through the continuous provision of high quality goods and services; which in turn provide durable benefits for shareholders and other stakeholders (creditors, employees, customers, suppliers, communities, regulators) upon whom the company's health depends.
- High performance entails an essential balance between risk-taking (the creativity and innovation so essential to the growth of our economy) and economic risk-management (the financial, commercial and operational disciplines so essential to the soundness and durability of business institutions).
- *Creating a culture of high integrity* which means: robust adherence to the spirit and letter of the formal rules, legal and financial; adoption of global ethical standards which are in the company's enlightened self-interest and which bind it and its employees as if they were formal rules; and securing employee commitment to the core values of honesty, candor, fairness, reliability and trust-worthiness in all internal and external relationships.
- High integrity has positive benefits inside the company, in the marketplace and in a global society but it also addresses serious legal, regulatory, reputational, communications and public-policy risks which are also important facets of contemporary business.
- *Fusing high performance with high integrity.* This fusion of sustained economic performance with a strong commitment to law, ethics and values is the foundation of the contemporary corporation.
- *Properly addressing business-in-society issues.* In balancing risk-taking with risk management and in fusing high performance with high integrity, contemporary CEOs, and their top business associates, need to pay systematic attention to business-in-society issues: how society can and will affect the conduct of business; how business has an impact on society; and how business leaders should shape and communicate the alignment of business with societal interests through the concept of corporate citizenship.

As emphasized, each company will give detailed meaning to these concepts of performance, risk and integrity, but together they constitute the core mission of the contemporary corporation and define the fundamental role of the board of directors, the CEO and other senior executives.

## Revamping the Leadership Development Process

Corporations often provide highly specialized training in such business skills as sales, marketing, finance, IT, business development, manufacturing, engineering and product or technology development. They also may provide less specialized, more general training for P&L (profit-and-loss) managers, who are promoted from positions of narrow expertise to assume broader operational responsibilities. Such general manager training customarily focuses on achieving commercial goals in different environments.

- But, with careful board oversight, the CEO and other top business leaders must *institute management development processes* for corporate P&L and functional leaders that, at early stages in their careers, put strong emphasis not just on developing specialized expertise or on achieving commercial goals but on developing the experience and skills to do this through balanced risk-management and performance with integrity. This emphasis on risk management and an integrity culture should be a talent-management imperative as individuals rise within the corporation and face increasingly broader challenges requiring integration of all three dimensions of corporate mission.
- Such development will involve *broader and different educational courses offered by the corporation during an individual's career* on the interrelationship between performance, risk and integrity in the context of a global society. Such courses may be offered inside the company or in executive MBA or executive education programs—but a rethinking of such courses, both in the company and in academia, may be necessary, given a broader definition of the CEO and business-leader role and the robust debate about necessary changes in business education as a result of recent business failures.
- Such leadership development will also entail *giving high-potential individuals a broader range of assignments earlier in their careers*—e.g., working on a team scrubbing a new product line for its risks; being integral to a major internal investigation of potential wrongdoing; helping to ascertain the geopolitical issues, as well as the business issues, in locating a new manufacturing facility in one of three or four Southeast

Asian nations; assessing supply-chain risks and opportunities—and third-party suppliers—in emerging markets. Establishing the theory and practice of systematically implementing cross-functional assignments for up-and-coming leaders is a vital role for the CEO and senior HR leader working with the management development and compensation committee of the board of directors.

### Refocusing the Process for CEO Selection—and for Other Promotions into High Corporate Positions

The ultimate result of the initial tasks—redefining the mission of the company and the CEO and revamping leadership development—should be a CEO-succession process which expressly searches for and then selects a new leader for the company whose personality and career reflect the combination and integration of the necessary performance, risk and integrity dimensions.

- As it begins this succession process, the board of directors should restate and reiterate the mission of the company and the key characteristics of balancing risk taking with risk management and fusing high performance with high integrity in a company-specific articulation of purpose aimed at both inside and outside audiences.
- In exercising this function—which has historically (and properly) been viewed as its most important task—the board should hopefully (ideally) be able to choose from a strong talent pool inside the company.
- Similarly, promotions to senior corporate leadership jobs which the CEO recommends and the board of directors approves should be awarded to individuals who have the broad constellation of talents and skills required by the contemporary corporation with a redefined mission.

The need for core economic performance skills—financial, commercial, operational, strategic—are as important as ever in the CEO and top business leaders. Nothing said here is intended in any way to diminish the primacy of high economic performance in a business organization. But failures of business leadership in the recent past have frequently been due to serious weaknesses in risk assessment and management, or to serious lapses in adhering to legal, financial or ethical standards.

These failures have had significant, even catastrophic, impacts on shareholders, creditors, employees, custom-ers, suppliers and communities. They have, over time, eroded the trust upon which successful conduct of business depends. A contemporary CEO must have proven skills in risk management, in creating a culture of integrity and in understanding business-in-society issues which pose both threats to, and opportunities for, the corporation. Strength in commercial operations and strategy is absolutely necessary, but not sufficient, in today's business environment.

### *Reformulating Operational Objectives for Performance, Risk and Integrity*

How the company measures commitment to its fundamental mission over the short, middle and long term is, of course, a critical task in driving desired behaviour and setting the terms for corporate accountability. Boards of directors and business leadership must together define a concise, comprehensive and robust set of operational objectives across the dimensions of economic performance, risk management and high integrity which can be clearly communicated inside and outside the company. Some will be enduring, like fundamental systems and processes. Others will need modification as the competitive, regulatory and geopolitical landscape changes.

This annual process of translating the broad articulation of mission into operational objectives requires great care and sustained attention. It should measure both financial and non-financial factors. It must become a core feature of the board/business-leadership relationship—a joint "deliverable" at the end of one year to provide an accountability test in the next.

Some important, illustrative measures follow. Each company will, of course, explicitly articulate and clearly explain the ones which it chooses to use because each, by itself, can create or hide problems.

***Sustained Economic Performance:*** These measure-ments should be insulated as much as possible from bookkeeping manipulation and short-term stock price fluctuations.

- The efficient use of capital through such measurements as return on assets and return on invested capital.
- Operational excellence as reflected in cash flow or operating margins or productivity increases.
- Strong connections to customers, through such measures as: market share, increases in revenues, repeat customer percentages, assess-ments of customer satisfaction, new products as percentage of offerings, brand strength. For all the

past focus on shareholders, the core activity of the corporation is selling quality goods and services to *customers,* the stakeholders upon whom the company truly depends.

- Employee motivation, satisfaction and individual productivity.
- The more traditional performance measures of net profits, earnings per share, stock price increases, total shareholder return and return on equity. While these metrics of economic performance should not overwhelm all others, they will continue to be important. One of the challenges is how to give them their due, not make them dominant and thus put them in context with the many other measures of performance which make for a strong, growing company.
- How, and to what degree, changes in new technologies, new products, new acquisitions (or dispositions) and new geographies positively impact economic performance.
- Performance against peer companies in all the measurements mentioned above whenever possible.

***Systematic Risk Management for Economic Performance:*** Risk disciplines must be matched with decisions about setting and implementing economic performance objectives. This Policy Brief discusses, in this section, *direct economic risks* relating to capital adequacy, leverage, liquidity, interest rates, currency, credit-worthiness of counterparties, products and operations. Other critical risks which can *indirectly affect economic performance* such as legal, reputational, ethical, IT, supply chain, country and geopolitical issues are discussed in the next section (on integrity measurements and processes).

The goal, of course, is not to eliminate economic risk taking—risk is the very nature of business. Indeed, the drumbeat of risk discussions in the recent past, while understandable, should not obscure the essential role of business in creativity and innovation. Rather the purpose is to understand risks to the extent possible, mitigate to the extent practicable and to ensure that there is adequate spread of risk so if large known or unknown adverse events occur the company is protected, not from decline but from destruction.

A prefatory note on risk organization: there are many different ways to organize risk functions both inside the company and at the board level. This Policy Brief does not attempt to say what is the best organizational form. That will depend on company mission and culture. As indicated below, it does say that, inside the company, there need to be independent experts on various direct and indirect economic risks. At the board level, each of these independent company experts should be directly connected to a committee (be it Audit, a new Risk Committee or a Public Affairs or Public Responsibility Committee). Ultimately pulling all the threads of risks together for the enterprise is, however, the responsibility of the CEO (the "chief" risk officer in a very real sense) and of the board of directors as a whole.

### *Within the Company*

- Inside the company, the economic risk function must be independent of operational business leadership. It must have direct access to the CEO—and, on highest priority matters, to the board. Assessing whether such an independent risk function exists, the quality of its people, and where it reports are all part of a risk measurement process.
- The fundamental job of financial risk management directed at economic performance is to assess major, direct and discrete economic risk dimensions of the firm—e.g., capital, leverage, liquidity, credit, currency, market, operations—through process-mapping, identification of important risk areas, and development of risk-mitigation measures and controls. Activities covered range from new products, to new geographies, to new customers, to major areas of existing operational exposure. Companies must also rigorously assess off-balance-sheet risks as part of this activity. These fundamental risk systems and processes can be assessed and measured.
- As a matter of business decision-making, the risk function should have an opportunity in front of top leadership (separate from the business leaders proposing a course of action) to present important issues. The risk function doesn't make the decision: top business leaders and (on high priority matters) the board of directors must expressly balance well-articulated reward and risk. But boards and top business leaders must understand as clearly as possible not just the rewards, but also the risks through candid, systematic presentations by those expert in risk. *A healthy, candid debate is critical.* Again, it is possible to assess whether such interaction took place during the course of the year on the right set of priority issues.
- Risk management must also ascertain the systemic risk to the corporation from the combination of financial, commercial and operational risks. Without entering the voluminous and spirited

debate about mathematical risk models, it is fair to say that, while they have utility in measuring some types of systemic risk, they are not better than their assumptions and the past data from which they are constructed—which can well be inadequate in times of future stress or dislocation. Systemic risk assessment involves some scenario-planning around worst-case critical issues—such as leverage, liquidity, currency, credit and operational risks—including those occasioned by major global economic dislocations.

- The company must decide how to spread risk prudently so that even an unknown, low-probability event in a particular area or activity cannot sink the company. Articulation of this spread-of-risk philosophy and adherence to it is also an important risk objective.
- Similarly, the company should institute early warning systems on economic risks—whether in regular valuation of assets, or changes in markets, or unforeseen moves from competitors—which trigger a high-level discussion of risk-taking/risk-management issues that could lead to changes in course.

### Inside the Company

A company can measure the integrity promotion efforts of its CEO and other senior executives across at least five dimensions. Have leaders:

- *adopted key principles* such as consistency and commitment in both words and actions; embedding integrity disciplines in business operations; having systematic processes for surfacing, analysing and deciding ethical issues; giving employees voice to express concerns; protecting company security?
- *adopted key implementing practices* to make those foundational principles a reality (risk assess/risk manage fundamental business processes intersected by variety of legal requirements; insure that systems for preventing, detecting and responding to integrity issues are robust across businesses and geographies)?
- *created an affirmative culture of integrity* where employees are not just afraid of violating rules but affirmatively want to do the right thing? Culture can be assessed by a number of techniques, including anonymous internal surveys, external reputational surveys and 360 evaluations of key leaders.

- *performed well against peers* (comparisons to other divisions inside companies or to external peer companies, in, for example, environmental compliance)?
- *established and met annual goals and objectives* (how are hard problems handled, key people hired, identified weaknesses remedied)?

As with financial, commercial and operational risks, companies should establish "integrity" early-warning systems to identify important, emerging risks which can have indirect economic impact (as well as other adverse effects):

- Changes in broad public-policy architecture (e.g., tax, trade, environment, health care etc.).
- Changes in important but more fine-grained legal or financial rules that can have a significant impact on the company.
- Changing ethical expectations and demands.
- Security threats to people, facilities, information and supply chain.
- Changing geopolitical or country risk. In particular, an understanding of geopolitical context is critical because low-probability but high-impact events (military action, currency devaluations, political upheaval) can, of course, have dramatic impact on business operations.

Properly designed, such early warning systems gather information systematically and present issues on periodic basis to business leaders for decision. Is detailed analysis beyond issue identification needed?

Business leaders must decide. If so, should the business take anticipatory action to get ahead of the curve (e.g., adopt consumer protections in financial services to anticipate regulatory change and avoid enforcement actions and consumer law suits)? Both the process (does every appropriate business unit have such processes relevant to their product mix?) and the results (were challenges anticipated, if not why not?) can be assessed.

### At the Board Committee and Full Board Level

As with financial risk, a committee of the board of directors should be responsible for reviewing and agreeing upon the fundamental measures for promoting integrity and the systems, processes and measures for assessing, mitigating and monitoring integrity, country and geopolitical risk. As noted at the outset of this section, whether this is the Audit Committee, a special Risk Committee or a Public Responsibilities or Public Affairs Committee will turn on each company's culture. (Joint committee meetings may be appropriate on such topics as country or geopolitical risk which have multiple causes and impacts.)

*Finally, as with economic performance, it is ultimately the responsibility of the full board to oversee basic integrity risk-mitigation systems, processes and priority results and assess whether an integrity culture exists.*

In sum, these basic operational goals and measure-ments across performance, risk and integrity dimensions are essential for allocating responsibility and ensuring accountability *inside* the corporation. But they also should provide a public template for account-ability that is a meaningful alternative to the reductionist, at times misleading, metric of short-term share price as indicator of company value and performance.

### *Revising Compensation for CEO, Senior Executives and Other Key Employees*

A revised approach to compensation flows from a redefinition of the CEO role, revamped leadership development, a new process for CEO selection, and development of broader operational objectives to hold executives accountable. It should reinforce and be reinforced by those other tasks. The broader purpose is to change compensation based on short-term results that ignore long-term risks and to use compensation to incentivize short, medium and long-term value creation attained with sound risk management and with high integrity. The purpose of compensation is, of course, to attract and retain talent, *but* within that balanced framework. Select companies are moving explicitly in this direction.

The setting of compensation for the CEO and top business leadership is a fundamental role of the compensation committee and then the full board. But, development of the overall compensation philosophy and its application to top company talent should be a joint board and senior executive function.

This Policy Brief advances the following concepts for a revised approach to compensation. These concepts are consistent with those advanced in other recent analyses and reports as a consensus is beginning to form on new pay principles (if not yet on critical details and methodologies).

- Compensation for the CEO and top business lead-ers should turn on actions and results in the three separate operational areas comprising corporate mission: sustainable, durable economic performance; effective risk assessment and mitigation; and promotion of an integrity culture through systems and processes embedded in business operations. Each should be a discrete element in a comprehensive pay regime which then uses them in combination to determine total awards.
- Although top business leadership will receive substantial annual cash compensation, significant compensation *in a particular year* will be variable cash and variable equity which will be paid out or held back over time as performance, risk and integrity objectives are met, exceeded or missed. These objectives should generally reflect relative effort of leaders—compared to past results within the company (positive or negative trends) or against peers or both. Deferred cash has the advantage of avoiding stock price manipulation and providing necessary liquidity to individuals. Deferred equity has the advantage of tying employees to the long-term creation of shareholder value.
- Variable cash granted in a single year will be some multiple of annual cash and should be paid out in increments on a multi-year schedule. Some misses due to negligent or intentional acts—a significant misstatement of financials upon which company results were based or a serious failure to weigh risk or a major integrity lapse—can lead to complete cancellation of the variable out-year compensation. Others misses due to serious, avoidable mistakes may lead to a diminution but not cancellation of variable compensation.
- Variable equity should also be granted in one year but only vest in out-years depending on attainment of performance, risk and integrity measurements, although the mix might be tilted more to balanced economic performance (in the different categories summarized above, efficient use of capital, operational efficiencies, relationships with customers etc.). Stock price increases and total shareholder return should be a factor but not the factor. Again, these performance options or RSUs should be withheld or clawed back for serious negligent or intentional acts similar to the cancellation of variable cash grants. So, too, lesser mistakes may lead to diminution, not cancellation. To minimize manipulation of business for short-

term stock gains even in the out-years a holding period, beyond the vesting period, may be appropriate.

- Variable cash and variable equity awards may also be designed in the year they are granted with incentives for sustained performance in the out-years. For example, if future operational objectives set in year one are exceeded in subsequent years, then cash and equity awards from year one which are vesting in those subsequent years could be increased.
- In cancelling variable cash or variable equity awards for performance, risk or integrity misses due to negligent or intentional acts, boards should utilize “hold-backs” and “claw-backs.” A “hold-back” occurs during the vesting period of the award: the cash or equity never goes to the recipient. A hold-back occurs at the discretion of the company, and employees have to bring an action if they believe the corporate action was improper or unfair. A “claw-back” occurs after the vesting period and requires some type of formal company action to demonstrate that clearly articulated standards triggering a claw-back were breached.
- Similarly, compensation plans must risk assess jobs below the top business leaders and apply new compensation design for individuals, not just top officers, with the ability to commit resources with significant long-term opportunities and risks for the corporation (e.g., those who sell instruments creating long-term obligations for the company). Compensation design will turn on specific performance, risk and integrity parameters applicable to those individuals. But, the variable cash and equity compensation will outweigh annual cash compensation. Here too, the board should have the power to hold-back or claw-back variable cash or equity for negligent or intentional misses within a defined sphere of responsibility, as well as providing for diminution or augmentation of target compensation in the outyears depending on enhanced or poor results.
- But, even for those individuals important to company performance, compensation should have an important element built on company and division results, not on solo contributions alone, to help create a strong and loyal culture.
- Application of these principles would sharply reduce two problematic compensation mechanisms which, in the view of

a number of commentators, drove short-termism and excessive risk-taking:

- the "naked" stock option which rewards a simple increase in share price disconnected from attainment of priority operational goals; and
- the huge annual cash bonus awarded without regard to risk consequences in the out-years.

- Such a compensation redesign—like establishing measurements for risk, performance and integrity accountability—requires new thinking and hard work.
  - One problem is devising multi-factor measurements (performance, risk, integrity) in the right proportions that reflect the mission of the company but are not so complex as to be confusing or opaque nor so simplistic as to be a distortion of reality.
  - A second difficulty is ascertaining when company leaders or individual performers have made a difference by their efforts—the kind of differentiation which should be at the core of all compensation—or whether exogenous conditions have affected results, either on the positive or the negative side. Leaders and key employees should not be penalized for events beyond their control, but neither should they be rewarded excessively for such occurrences.
  - A third *critical* issue is pay equity (which has drawn tremendous fire in the financial sector): both the absolute amount and the amount relative to other key personnel inside the corporation. Companies need to face into the question: how much is too much?

All these issues should be addressed in a revised compensation regime.

- The revised approach to compensations should be communicated in clear, understandable terms to shareholders and others. Meaningful, nuanced discussion with appropriate groups about the approach to compensation, including but not limited to shareholders, is more important than a blunt "advisory vote" of compensation philosophy, measurements and results at shareholders' meetings.

## Obstacles

Boards of directors and business leadership must honestly confront key obstacles to this basic reorientation of corporate governance. A brief enumeration of salient problems follows, which is intended to raise issues for further discussion, action, research and analysis.

***Labour Markets:*** Can individual corporations which define short, medium and long-term performance, risk and integrity operational objectives—and base significant deferred compensation on their attainment— compete in the labour market for business talent? Other business entities willing to use large amounts of cash and options, with fewer pay-out requirements, may seek to attract top leaders and performers in a very competitive labour market.

One approach, beyond individual firm initiatives and well short of comprehensive public regulation, is for corporations in a particular industry group (or in a more general business association) to develop a code of compensation principles (in a manner that must avoid antitrust concerns). A corporation's commitment to such a code and subsequent implementation could be reported in sequential Proxy Statements. Such codes must have principles which are specific enough to guide action. They must also avoid "leakage" either through an inability to ascertain clearly whether signatories are keeping their commitments or through the refusal of peer entities to sign up in the first place.

A less difficult, more traditional approach is to rely on institutional loyalty spawned by strong leadership. Such leadership can create exciting, empowered, growing corporations serving custom-ers with great products and services and meeting fascinating challenges in the global marketplace.

Many people have important values, other than money, that need to be served in an institution— and great leadership can make those values come alive, can create loyalty and can, thus, attract, retain, promote and challenge outstanding individuals from all over the globe. For those employees motivated solely by greed, little can be done by an individual firm dedicated to the changes in measurements and compensation described above.

***Differing International Standards:*** Because of its centrality to the effective functioning of the global economy, the financial sector is the subject of procedural or substantive regulatory debates ad-dressing some or all of the governance issues raised above—as well as important questions relating to broader issues of safety and soundness. For example, the G-20 recently announced a set of broad principles covering risk and compensation practices which should be subject to national regulation. But, the prospects for genuine harmonization of national laws—or even significant convergence—are mixed, at best. Until that happens across major capital markets, there is a genuine risk that companies or talented individuals in the financial sector will take advantage of "regulatory arbitrage" to avoid governmental pressures for the types of changes outlined above, even if those changes are undertaken voluntarily by financial institutions. Similar regulatory arbitrage may occur with non-financial public companies as a result of different regulatory regimes across the globe relating to governance (and other impactful) regulatory issues. Companies concerned about the issues in this Policy Brief need to consider political action in their major markets to urge as much uniformity as possible. Such political action could be directed at regulation which they believe is a necessary floor under private action. But it could also be aimed at regulations with which they may differ but which will have greater adverse impact if lacking in uniformity (e.g., capital requirements or liquidity protections).

***Change in Board Compensation Advisors:*** Many compensation advisors to boards are expert in comparing executive compensation delivered at one company to compensation delivered at "peer" companies. They are expert in designing various mechanisms for delivering that compensation—salary, bonus, deferred salary, deferred bonus, stock options or restricted stock units. But, for boards of directors to revise compensation of senior executives and to oversee broader company compensation regimes, they need their own advisors with *additional* expertise. Many reports focus on the advisers' independence. That is important. But a revised skill set is of equal importance.

Compensation advisors to boards need to have a detailed understanding about how the company works in the context of global markets and global society so that they can help the board have its own perspective, when working with management, to define the operational performance, risk and integrity objectives which are appropriate to the company and upon which a revised compensation regime must be built. Finding such an advisor—with business as well as compensation expertise—may require boards to go beyond the traditional compensation consulting firms. Eventually, a new cadre of independent consultants can emerge, but only if boards of directors make clear that they want advisors who can help analyse the business goals which must necessarily precede compensation sound design.

***Short-Termism of Institutional Investors:*** Perhaps the most difficult of these difficult issues is how do corporations resist the short-termism of certain, important institutional investors? Such investors today own more than 60 percent of U.S. equities and drive the direction of the stock markets.

Institutional investors—whether traditional ones like pension, insurance and mutual funds or newer more ones like hedge funds or micro-second traders—*may* be primarily, even exclusively, interested in short-term profits to beat composite bench-marks or to attain highly remunerative "2-and-20" absolute returns. Individual investors place their funds with institutional investors and are likely to care more about how the institution manages their money, than about the underlying performance of the companies owned by various funds. There is now substantial debate about whether (or over what period) the stock market accurately reflects the "value" and "performance" of a company, especially as the average holding period for equities is now less than a year.

Two seasoned observers describe the problem. In a new book, economist Henry Kaufman says: "Most investment relationships today are very fickle. Portfolio performance is measured over very short-term horizons....Day trades and port-folio shifts based on the price momentum of the stock—rather than anything having to do with the underlying fundamentals—are commonplace." Ira Millstein, a pioneer in the governance movement and proponent of shareholder voice, has recently expressed similar views. So have the Federal Reserve and regulatory bodies in Europe.

One answer is to begin a much closer examination of the governance of these various types of institutions, the compensation of fund managers and the need for greater transparency.

But, given the variety of institutional investors, it may be a long process to evaluate governance, fund manager incentives, the different market impact of different types of institutional investors and, ultimately, whether any private or public, substantive or procedural, "governance" reforms are necessary or appropriate.

# 7

# Elements of Effective Leadership

Everything rises and falls on leadership. The reason why some families and Corporations seem to have it all while others struggle along is a result of good leadership and bad leadership respectively. Many Successful people acknowledge the importance of good Leadership practices and the impact they can exert on the people they lead and the organization as a whole. Leadership skills are a very vital component in any entity.

It can be defined as leading or influencing others. In other words, where there is a leader there is a follower. I would like to mention here that, we are all leaders in one way or another. We are influenced by other people and we also have people in our circle of colleagues that we influence. We might also be an older or younger sibling and we influence those under us. So it is very important that we influence the people we lead in a positive way so that they may influence others in a similar manner. At the end of the day we may live in harmony and lead productive lives. So, what are the 10 elements of effective leadership?

1. They appreciate who they are: One of the mistakes a leader can make is try to act like someone else. A leader understands that he or she is a unique and original individual and can not imitate another person. A leader has to learn from other leaders before him but never should he think he is a Malcolm X, Martin Luther King or Winston Churchill etc.
2. They posses a positive attitude. Attitude can be defined as the way you habitually think and react to life's situations or circumstances. Attitude is everything and can do wonders in

your life. Attitude is what makes one person succeed and another fails. The difference between successful people and people that are less successful is because the successful ones have a lot of attitude and the other minimal or non existent. Effective Leaders have a great deal of positive attitude. They are not shaken by circumstances or mishaps as they do not dwell on negatives. They always look on the bright side of life and they see something good in any misfortune. They are in control of their lives. "When you control your attitude you control your life."

3. They believe in themselves. They have a firm belief in themselves and they value and regard themselves highly. They believe that they can conquer anything. If you are a leader and do not believe in yourself, how do you convince another person to believe in you?
4. Change is their way of life: In order to grow and develop, effective leaders put themselves in situations that are going to make them change and mature and keep on growing. They are not scared or intimidated by change and in many circumstances, they initiate change. They act rather than react.
5. They plan ahead: Effective Leaders know where they are going. They have their goals and destiny in defined long before they motivate others to follow. They have a plan for their lives and are not free styling. They have the future in perspective and are clear where they are going before they lead others.
6. They build relationships with quality people. A leader influences people and is influenced by others. It is in this view, therefore, that a leader ought to network with people who are going to nurture and motivate him. These are people who will tell him what he has to hear not what he wants to hear. These people often put him in the hot seat and he will learn from their counsel.
7. They are optimists: Optimism is one of the qualities of an effective leader. He needs to have a positive outlook towards life. To an Optimistic Leader white is black and bad is good. He always has something to learn from every bad situation.
8. They do not take issues personally. When disciplining a subordinate, a leader does not get personal or do it in front of others but rather finds an appropriate time and place to have a friendly chat with them.

9. They build the people they lead. The greatness of a leader is not determined by the power he possesses but his ability to empower others. Many leaders want to be feared and revered but a leader who will win the peoples' heart is one who is keen on empowering them. He wants to build his people to become better employees, citizens and colleagues.
10. They love and respect the people they lead. Without love and respect, a leader can not be effective and all efforts to control or influence the followers may be in vain. Love and respect when given out are the exactly what you receive in return. You do not receive disrespect when that you give out respect. So what you give is what you get.

In a study of over 8,000 leaders, the Corporate Leadership Council measured effectiveness based on four dimensions:

- People Management: The skills and attributes associated with leading through others, such as clearly communicating expectations; inspiring others and holding people accountable
- Personal Characteristics: A diverse set of characteristics and attributes associated with individual, personal leadership such as confidence, intelligence, and perseverance
- Process Management: The skills and attributes required to successfully manage an organization on a day-to-day basis, such as creatively solving problems, measuring results and properly managing budgets and timelines
- Strategic Management: The skills and attributes necessary to successfully devise and execute strategy and vision, such as identifying and articulating a long-term vision, understanding markets, competitors and customers, and correctly assessing the risk and return of decisions.

Based on the survey results, the following characteristics were rated as most important for Leadership Effectiveness:

1. Honesty and integrity
2. Clearly communicate expectations
3. Recognize and reward achievement
4. Adapt to changing circumstances
5. Inspire others
6. Put the right people in the right roles at the right time

7. Passion to succeed
8. Identify and articulate long-term vision for future
9. Persuade and encourage others to move in desired direction
10. Accept responsibility for success and failures

When you shift the focus from individual characteristics back to the major four dimensions of effective leadership, there are some interesting implications.

- People Management Is the Most Important Category to Effective Leadership. People-management skills – including clearly communicating expectations, recognizing and rewarding achievement and inspiring others – together represent the single most important category to effective leadership.
- Strategic Management Is Important, but It Is Second in Importance. Strategic management skills, such as identifying and articulating a long-term vision, understanding markets, competitors, and customers, and understanding the strengths and weaknesses of the company – are second in importance to effective leadership. The surprising finding stands in sharp contrast to the notion that effective leadership is only about formulating strategy. Leadership is more people-centred in the eyes of leaders.
- Personal Characteristics Rank Third in Importance. Personal characteristics, such as intelligence, confidence, and perseverance, rank third in importance. Moreover, the importance of personal factors is clearly bolstered by the high value placed on honesty and integrity. Without that characteristic, the overall importance of the category falls.
- Process Management Is the Least Important Category to Effective Leadership. The least important category to effective leadership is process management: resource allocation, measuring results, and managing work plans and timetables. Given the importance of the items in this category to day-to-day business management, it is clear that leaders see a distinction between effective management and effective leadership. The two are not the same. It is also apparent that leaders think leadership is more about leading other people than managing business processes.

One final analysis – do different demographic breakdowns show any significant differences in the importance of the categories?

- Comparison of Men and Women: Men feel that having a passion to succeed and inspiring others are more important to effective leadership than women do. On the other hand, women valued the ability to adapt to changing circumstances and recognizing and rewarding achievement. Overall, on the 40 characteristics that were measured there was an overwhelming similarity between men and women.
- Older Versus Younger Leaders: The differences between generations are very minimal. Much more commonality than differences. Older leaders attached more value to honesty and integrity, while younger leaders attach slightly more value to personal characteristics, such as personal development.
- Senior Level Executives Versus Middle Level Leaders: The predominant difference was in the importance of long-term visioning and a passion to succeed – both of which were valued more highly by senior executives. Less senior level leaders indicated a higher value for personal characteristics and process management.
- High Performers Versus Non-High Performers: Two characteristics that high performers viewed as having higher value were commitment to staff development and clear communication of expectations.

The research found that elements of effective leadership are universal. It is very clear that leaders agree on the elements of successful leadership. Differences were minimal across gender, age, organizational level, and performance status. Furthermore, the elements of effective leadership are viewed similarly across different types of companies and industries.

Finally, there were no significant differences by countries surveyed. Stay tuned for future leadership articles where we will focus on the individual leadership characteristics that make a difference to the success of your employees!

## Leadership and Decision Making

Decisions are at the heart of leader success, and at times there are critical moments when they can be difficult, perplexing, and nerve-racking. However, the boldest decisions are the safest. This source provides useful and practical guidance for making efficient and effective decisions in both public and private life. Nothing succeeds a success better than another sweet success.

"Somewhere along the line of development we discover what we really are, and then we make our real decision for which we are responsible. Make that decision primarily for yourself because you can never really live anyone else's life." — *Eleanor Roosevelt*

Enlightenment is man's emergence from his self-imposed immaturity. Immaturity is the inability to use one's understanding without guidance from another. This immaturity is self-imposed when its cause lies not in the lack of understanding, but in the lack of resolve and courage to use it without guidance from another. Have courage to use your own understanding! Enlightenment means taking full responsibility for your life.

Declaration of Independence in American Revolution contains the beauty and cogency of the preamble, reaching back to remotest antiquity and forward so an indefinite future, have lifted the hearts of millions of men and will continue to do. These words are more explosive and revolutionary than anything written ever those are a continual inspiration to the entire oppressed individuals around the world.

The total effect of the culture and industry is one of anti-enlightenment that is the progressive technical domination of nature, becomes mass deception and is turned into a means for fettering consciousness. It impedes the development of autonomous, independent individuals who judge and decide consciously for themselves.

You are free to decide within certain limits: A free person is the one who know and recognizes his/her feasible region e.g., set by his/her society. The slave is not aware of such limits. A free person is wise to recognize what is under his/her control and what is not, and has the ability to accept the first and extend the second one. You may have heard that "If there is a will, then there must be a way". In fact the advice should be in the opposite order, i.e. "If there is a way, then there might be a will". It is right because the feasible region might be empty, and one might ignores one or some constraints, and then being in a big trouble, e.g., willing beyond ones' ability.

The unrealistic expectations of freedom and rights to make your own decisions will destroy a person unless it is recognized that these ideals are privileges and not necessities and therefore they are accompanied by responsibilities.

Fear is not in the habit of speaking the truth; when perfect sincerity is expected, perfect freedom must be allowed. Nor does anyone who is apt to get angry when hearing the truth should wonder why he does not hear it. For example, when I asked a business manager what had made his organization one of the best in his industry, he pointed to his CIO and said "Joe is a millionaire. He can quit any time. He says what he thinks is right!"

Mind is what your brain does consciously. Our minds perform a series of information processing in order to form strategies needed to live our daily lives. This process is known as decision making. However, aside from making decisions, because of many kinds of uncertainties we also face a problem called decidophobia, which is the fear of making the wrong decisions combined with nervous agitation. Moreover, fear of judgement by others is a sure path to unhappiness which is a state of mind. Decisions are at the heart of success, and at times there are critical moments when they can be difficult, perplexing, and nerve racking.

This site provides help and guidance for making efficient and effective decisions by putting to use a well-structured approach and well-focused process known as the modelling or paradigm process. The word paradigm comes from the Greek word paradeigma, meaning "model" or "pattern." A model represents a way of looking at the world, a shared set of assumptions that enable us to understand or predict behaviour. Models have a powerful influence on individuals and on society because our view of the world is determined by our set of assumptions about it. To put it another way, our vision is often affected by what we believe about the world; our beliefs often determine the information that we "see."

Decision-making is about facing a question, such as, "To be or not to be?", i.e., to be the one you want to be or not to be? That is a decision. Humanity has always lived in the shadow of fears. Yet almost nothing was known about fear until Freud began the study of unusual phobias. A little later, some psychologists suggested that one dread is common to all mankind: the dread of death.

Decisions, decisions and more decisions! The fear of making serious decisions is a new kind of fear, called decidophobia, proclaimed by Walter Kaufmann at Princeton University in 1973. The fear of making the wrong decisions is well known to any responsible manager. As Eleanor Roosevelt said, "You gain strength, courage, and confidence by every experience in which you really stop to look fear in the face." Wherever you see a successful business, someone once made a courageous decision. There has never yet been a person in the history of mankind who led a life of ease whose name is worth remembering. The difficulty in life is the choice.

The Latin word Decido has two meanings. It can mean to decide and also to fall off. Hence plants are called deciduous if their leaves fall off in the fall. The word fall started as "leaf fall" for autumn in the 15th century. The expression "take the plunge" suggests the relevance of both meanings. Making a wrong decision provokes the fear of falling.

An effective and proven decision process has been developed over the last 70 years and is known as Operations Research/Management Science/Decision Science/Success Science (OR/MS/DS/SS). In the serious decisions that mold the future of your business, freedom becomes tangible; serious decisions are objects of extreme dread. Serious business decisions that ultimately shape, guide, and direct our future are extremely fearful to business managers. These decisions involve norms, standards, and the comparison and choice of goals.

Learning the structured, well-focused approach to the decision-making process lessens decidophobia. The gem of Applied Management Science is that it turns the old adage that "business managers are born, not made" into myth. If one can master management science applications, then no problem is too big nor any decision too overwhelming. The goal of management science experts is to wipe out decidophobia.

The first requisite for success science is the ability to apply your physical and mental energies to one decision problem/opportunity incessantly without growing weary. Just being worried about making serious decisions is like sitting on a rocking chair—it gives you something to do but doesn't get you anywhere. Therefore worrying about making a decision is a waste of time. A decision is something you have the capability of changing. Anything else is a fact of life. The first principle in making good decision is that you must not fool yourself, and you are the easiest person to fool.

Moreover, making a decision and implementing one are two different things. Here is a question for you: Five frogs are sitting on a log. Four decide to jump off. How many are left? A protracted decision is only one part of the process of choosing because it lacks the commitment to implement the decision. There is a big difference between making a decision and implementing it. The measure of success is not whether you have a tough decision to deal with, but whether it's the same decision you had before. Decide like a man of action; implement like a man of thought. It does not take much strength to decide what to do, but it requires great strength to do things.

Unlike deterministic models (risk-free decisions), the outcome of some decisions depends on the second party, as is the case in any advertising campaign strategic decisions in a competitive market. Therefore, one of the characteristics of decision analysis problems is that "good" decision-making does not necessarily bring about good outcomes. "How could I have been so stupid?" former USA president, John F. Kennedy, asked after he approved the Bay of Pigs invasion.

A decision usually involves three steps:

1. A recognition of a need: A dissatisfaction within oneself—a void or need;
2. A decision to change—to fill the void or need;
3. A conscious dedication to implement the decision.

So aside from that, we see that making the correct decisions is not only what we want to do, but includes what we have to do. The fool who repeats again and again: "I am bound, I am bound," remains in bondage. The fear of making the wrong decision is what pushes and guides us to making a decision by utilizing a scientific approach. This is what Management Science is all about.

One must distinguish between science facts and science fictions. Science fiction is a form of fiction that was developed in the 20$^{th}$ century and deals principally with the impact of imagined science upon society or individuals. Management science is a science fact which is evolving, self-correcting and, unlike science fiction, not valid for eternity. Whenever science is distorted, sensationalized or even reduced to a pseudo scientific level, a grave disservice is done to the public's attempt to understand scientific facts.

Each and every business day the manager puts many decision questions to the test. The questions must first be identified as problems or opportunities, verified; scaled into mathematical models for which an answer will abound, and then controlled by updating the solutions because of the dynamic nature of business decisions. Mathematics has been recognized as an autonomous interior constructional activity which, although it can be applied to an exterior world, neither in its origin nor in its methods depends on an exterior world. The criterion of a good mathematical model is confined to its usefulness in making good strategic decisions. This is the absolute core of Management Science approach to decision-making, which is the science of decision-making. Not all science facts have practical usefulness. For example, Darwin's insight had no practical payoff, but he was a revered figure because he changed the way humans see their place in nature.

It is this approach to decision-making that makes the business successful. But it is important to note that such a process does not come easily. Again, this process is of a three-fold origin that encapsulates doctrines of computer integration, mathematical scaling and modelling and finally re-entering new data transformations that will occur as time ticks onward. This is the complex analysis that will deduct our thinking in this regard.

Management Science can help reduce or eliminate the fear of making wrong decisions by providing help with the decision-making process. In fact, management science's goal is to eliminate decidophobia. This is accomplished through the phased processes of management science that dissects the components of the decision into workable elements and allows one to proceed to the decision-making stage with sound knowledge on which to base one's choice. However, if you choose not to use management science, there are plenty of other ways to avoid making decisions.

### How People Avoid Making Serious Decisions?

In *The Histories*, written in 450 B.C., Herodotus makes the following statement:

"If an important decision is to be made [the Persians] discuss the question when they are drunk and the following day the master of the house...submits their decision for reconsideration when they are sober. If they still approve it, it is adopted; if not, it is abandoned. Conversely, any decision they make when they are sober is reconsidered afterwards when they are drunk."

What a strange way to make decisions, you might say. Perhaps it is, but there are even stranger methods of human choice.

### Popular Strategic Methods

Recourse to someone or even something else: Examples are astrology (not astronomy which is a science), palm readings, looking up at stars, dialing 1-900 psychic friends, telepathy, telekinesis, the aura, crystals, dreams, colours, Feng Shui, numerology, fortune-tellers, etc. Physiognomy is any judgment about a person's character based on external appearance. Examples of physiognomy are: reflexology (your feet know), iridology (your eyes know). Physiognomy dates back to Aristotle.

For example, in contrast to astrology, one must accept the fact that success is not due to a fortuitous concourse of stars at our birth, but due to a steady trail of sparks from the grindstones of hard work, determination, good planning, and perseverance. When it comes to the future, there are three kinds of people: those who let it happen, those who make it happen, and those who wonder what happened.

In all these popular avoidance strategies, you are better off taking advice from Kermit the Frog. A New York City detective said, "I've gone into hundreds of fortune-tellers, and have been told thousands of things, but nobody ever told me I was a policewoman getting ready to arrest them." Fortune befriends the bold who make good decisions.

Nobody can give you wiser advice than yourself.

False hopes: Hoping for something to happen over which we have no control over its outcome. For example, hoping your airplane lands safely while you are just a passenger and not the pilot of the plane. False hope and fear are two sides of the same coin. We can promise according to our hopes that are under our control only (and have some degree of certainty on its outcome), however, we avoid making decisions according to our fears of the outcomes.

Do not think about it: The decision-makers who are waiting for something to turn up, might start with their shirt sleeves. You can either take action, or you can hang back and hope for a miracle. Miracles are great, but they are so unpredictable. Doing nothing about a problem on hand, will certainly get out of control and devour other elements of your business too. You've got to jump off cliffs all the time and build your wings on the way down.

Do anchoring: Give disproportional weights to some information instead of waiting as long as possible, to have all the information.

Sunk-cost conscious: Repeat the same decision because "you have invested so much in this approach (or your current job) that you cannot abandon it or make another decision (or look for a better position)."

Failure to reflect on the problem: Reflection before action is often resisted by some managers. They often feel that reflection takes too much time, requires too much work, or they do not know much about decision problem/opportunity. Remember that: A man should always be already booted to take his journey.

Look for confirming-evidence: Seek out the information to support an existing preselection and discount opposing ones. To put what you like against what you dislike is the hanky-panky of the mind.

Pray for a miracle: Whatever we pray for, we pray for a miracle. Every prayer reduces itself to this: "Great God, grant that twice two be not four." A miracle is an event described by those to whom it was told by men who did not see it. As Emerson said, "As men's prayers are a disease of the will, so are their creeds a disease of the intellect."

The worse things get,

the harder people pray,

the worse things get.

***Be over-confident:*** This makes you optimistic and then make high risk decisions. As Henri Poincare said, "Doubt everything or believe everything: these are two equally convenient strategies. With either, we dispense with the need to think for ourselves." Be too prudent: Be over curious long enough to delay the decision. If you are too careful, you are so occupied in being careful that you are sure to stumble over what you are going to decide. Our doubts are traitors and make us lose the opportunities, by fearing to make our decision. Indecision is debilitating; it feeds upon itself; it is, one might almost say, habit-forming. Not only that, but it is contagious; it transmits itself to others who depend on you.

***Misrepresentation:*** Use argument that "seems" scientific. For example, compute and use the average salary as a typical representative of salary rather than the median.

***Pass the buck:*** Pass off responsibility of making the decision to someone else. Do not make decisions by yourself. Bring in someone to blame if things go wrong. For example, for life's problems some may marry to constantly blame their spouse because it is easier than taking responsibility. Remember that it takes two to tango.

***Have second thoughts:*** Second thoughts have aborted more useful decisions than all the difficult circumstances, overwhelming obstacles, and dangerous detours fate ever could throw at you. Undermining your authenticity by succumbing to someone else's second thoughts is a sinister, subtle, and seductive form of self-abuse.

***Succumb to failure:*** Believe that the choices you will make are predestined and you are bound to fail (one gets used to failure) versus the result of hard work and thought.

***Set up a committee:*** To make decisions, try to set up a committee not necessarily consisting of experts. So if everything goes well, every member is proud of such a decision. But if everything goes wrong, nobody is responsible. Every member would say, "It was not I; it was the committee's decision. You see, we couldn't agree, therefore we voted". Put a face to a faceless group, call it "the committee." A committee is an animal with four back legs. The committee's members, who are wishing that just to vote in "either/or" fashion are those who are not able to contribute to the decision-making process, therefore shouldn't be trusted with an important decision. A group decision support system could be a technologically advanced version of this strategy. Of course setting up a committee could be done correctly with the proper experts. However, my experience has shown that committees are used more to displace blame and accountability. I see no good in having group decision makers. Let one person be the decision maker; let one person be responsible and accountable. A committee is a cul-de-sac down which ideas are lured and then quietly strangled. The greatest things are often accomplished by individual people, not by committees.

What does it mean to say that committee might have a responsibility? Committee cannot have a responsibility any more than the business can. The only entities that can have responsibilities are people. False decentralization:Decentralization could take place when an authoritative manager delegates accountability to a new "director of..." for every new decision-making problem, but not delegating any authority.

***Failure to define the problem:*** This certainly lends to a wrong solution. Not knowing the problem, any solution is wrong. If you know the problem then, your solution might be good. Common Sense-based decisions: If you start making decisions on the basis of conventional wisdom or chatter in the hall, generally speaking, you will make the wrong decision. What is called common sense is almost always uncommon.

***Failure to understand the problem:*** This is caused, among others, by subjectivity, irrational analysis, lateness or procrastination, lack of sensitivity, and lack of focus. Complexity is confusing to the decision maker: Simplify and even change the problem to something which you have a strategic solution for (e.g. this is committed by many OR/MS/DS/SS analysts when they change the model to fit their strategic solution algorithm).

***Rationalization to limit the course of actions:*** This strategy is very popular. Stack the cards to make one alternative clearly right and remove all risk. Reasoning by analogy: Analogies are not made for proof.

Information gathered is not valid. Decisions are often made first and information sought to support the solution, or much of the information gathered is irrelevant to the decision-making.

***False alternative:*** It attempts to box the decision-maker into a corner from which there is no escape except to accept the alternative. "If you are against abortion, you must work for a law against it." This is an example of false alternative, because you may think that a law against it is even worse.

***Decision is only symbolic:*** One will fight hard for a policy and then be indifferent to its implementation. The Decision maker has obligations: Sometimes decision makers act against integrity to meet some critical personal obligations.

***Toe the line:*** When faced with questions such as "What should I do?", "How should I live?", etc., you may "Toe the line", that is, follow the group, don't disagree and do what others are doing in your profession as men in uniform (i.e., one form) do. Best of all, decline responsibility: Some shrugged their shoulders as if to shake off whatever chips of responsibility might have lodged there. Stagnate or do nothing is another possible one. Some people do this in belief that the right strategic solution will eventually become obvious. Decline all responsibility, or better still, do nothing; i.e., status quoism. However, "not to decide is to decide". A business manager makes decisions. Whether they are right or wrong, they get made, and they are clear. A weak manager procrastinates and gives false signals, leaving subordinates to charge off in different directions. To avoid criticism do nothing, say nothing, be nothing. The choice not to choose is the choice to remain unconscious and, therefore, to wield power irresponsibly.

***Post-decision anxieties:*** The more highly desirable the alternatives that must be rejected and the faster the decision must be made, the greater are these anxieties (also known as cognitive dissonance). Most people accentuate the positive in their decision and deny or ignore the positive aspect of the rejected alternatives.

***Misattribution of causes:*** Attribute your own success to your skills and hard work and your failures to unavoidable external forces. Do the opposite for other people's success and failure.

Your anxiety is directly proportional to your mental modelling process of reality, for you bring on yourself unlimited fears and unrealistic desires. Decision-making involves a series of steps. The mental modelling process begins with the formation of goals and proceeds to the identification of problems and alternative courses of action. It does not end until well after the decision or choice is actually made and the post decision anxieties have been experienced. Decision-making, however, is one management function that is important at all points in the process of management.

### When One Should Not Make Serious Decisions?

Do not make any serious decisions because you are angry, hurt, depressed, desperate, or frightened. Do not make decisions just to get revenge or to harm someone else. Do not make decision when you are incapable of rational thought. Make decision for the right reasons and when you are calm and thoughtful.

Even at these states of mind you must decide whether making any decision is necessary or desirable. Spend some careful thought before acting, so that you will not end up making unnecessary problems. The following sets of situations for avoiding decision-making are legitimate and appropriate. These conditions include: depression and other mental illness which impairs decision-making functions, coercion, and revelation states. There are situations when you should not make serious decisions.

For example, depression is the inability to construct a future. Suppose a person in an executive position within a company has Depression, which is a mental disease, he or she should not be in charge of making serious decisions while being under medical treatment. Otherwise, it could be costly to the company For example, the well-publicized case of the Norwegian Prime Minister depression situation, he conquered his depression to assume his usual responsibilities after staying out of office for a few weeks. You might have read A Beautiful Mind: The Life of Mathematical Genius and Nobel Laureate John Nash, or seen its movie version, A Beautiful Mind. Richard Nixon claimed that, "I was under medication when I made the decision to burn the tapes."

***Coercive decision-making:*** Coercive persuasions are Mind Control tactics which are part of a Brainwashing practice. They are designed to greatly modify a person's self-concept, perception of reality, and interpersonal relations. When successful, they influence the victim's Thinking Straight ability. Brainwashing is a very intricate process that consists of two stages:

- One is *Conditioning* and used for controlling the mind of the victim, e.g., inducing manipulative guilt, covert fear, intimidation, mental and moral confusion, eliciting confessions to uncommitted crimes, and propaganda.

- The other is *Persuasion* to cause an inability to think independently, e.g., implanting suggestible impulses into the victim's mind.

Coping with such an inhumane treatment by other people requires first of all that one should never allow the feeling that he/she is a victim but rather a survivor:

- Victims ask for pity, Survivors look for challenge.
- Victims worry about who is to blame,
- Survivors find a way to make a difference.
- Victims complain; Survivors take action.

The most effective propaganda and indoctrination system is one where its victims do not think they are being propagandized and indoctrinated. We are all familiar with "mild" persuasive techniques used in commercial advertising campaigns to influence consumers' buying behaviour. "They" tell us we'll be healthier, happier, sexier, smarter if only we purchase their products. Many people are unhappy, and neurotic today partly because advertising has caused them to have unrealistic expectations of life, themselves, their jobs due to the fantasy-land products and services that are constantly pushed on them.

Solving a problem by creating a new one: Often, because of deep frustrations in facing a difficult problem, one may unfortunately solve it by creating a bigger problem. This strategy tries to get rid of a present problem with the unfortunate byproduct of forming a new problem. For example using alcohol instead of facing the difficulties of the problem courageously will only result in the realization that if alcohol kills germs it also removes personal dignity. In reality, the "happy-hours" are followed by the misery of addiction. Every solution may have a problem.

Being in a revelation state: Whenever you are feeling an extremely pleasant or very deep sadness state, characterize a revelation state of being. You should never make decisions based on whatever you said or committed yourself that you will do while being in a revelation state.

They are merely declarations made out of extreme emotions rather than results of calm, well focused thinking. The best recommendation is to never make a negative decision in the low time. Never make your most important decisions when you are in your worst moods. Wait. Be patient. The storm will pass.

### How to Make Good Decisions

Unlike the strategies used in the previous section which tell you what to do, it is possible to learn how to make good decisions. It is possible to learn the process of making good strategic decisions by practiced deciding. This Web site is about practiced deciding, to which you must give enough thought. You will learn how to use your own abilities within a focused and structured decision process to actively and pro-actively make decisions. Active decision-making involves a responsible choice that you must make, while pro-active decision making is the practice of making decisions in advance just like "in the case of fire".

***Decision Problems or Decision Opportunities:*** At one time or another, organizations develop an over-abundance of decision problems. Sometimes they can be linked to organizational trauma, like down sizing, budget restraints or workload increases, but sometimes they evolve over time with no apparent triggering event. Increased complaining, a focus on reasons why things can't be done, and what seems to be a lack of active role characterize the "problem" organization. If the manager is walking negative and talking in a negative way, staff will follow.

In many instances we forget to find positives. When an employee makes an impractical solution, we are quick to dismiss the idea. We should be identifying the effort while gently discussing the idea. Look for small victories, and talk about them. Turning a problem into an opportunity is a result of many little actions. Provide positive recognition as soon as you find out about good performance. Do not couple positive strokes with suggestions for improvement. Separate them. Combining them devalues the recognition for many people. It is easy to get caught in the general complaining and bitching, particularly in customers' complains.

Decisions are an inevitable part of human activities. It requires the right attitude. Every problem, properly perceived, becomes an opportunity. In most situations the decision-maker must view the problems as opportunities rather than solving problems. For example, suppose you receive a serious complaint letter from a dissatisfied customer. You may turn this problem into an opportunity by finding out more about what is wrong with the product/service, learning from the customer's experience in order to improve the quality of your product/service. It all depends on the decision-maker's attitude. A pessimist sees the difficulty in every opportunity; an optimist sees the opportunity in every difficulty. Each problem has hidden in it an opportunity so powerful that it literally dwarfs the problem. The greatest success stories were created by people who recognized a problem and turned it into an opportunity.

A deliberate effort to broaden your experiences is the single most helpful effort in making good decisions. By exposing yourself to a variety of different experiences causes you to look at things from different perspectives. This provides you with extra mind-eyes to see problems and issues, and compare them to apparently unrelated situations and see new opportunities.

Search process approach by diagramming: Most of your decisions can be made using your past experiences and some strategic thinking. You may encounter problems where one wrong decision could have adverse long-term effects and lead to severe mistakes and considerable failures. In many situations, small bad decisions turn out to have important consequences, as for example, in air traffic accidents. When things go wrong, one may try to discover the causes for it. In these types of decision problems that some historical knowledge and experience, the decision-maker may apply a search process to find the main factors that cause the problem. This will enable the decision-maker to make the appropriate decisions and take the necessary steps to remedy the situation.

Subjective and Objective Decision-Making: Your decisions might be categorized in two groups with possible overlaps in some cases. One category is subjective decision-making which are private, such as how you want to live your life, or decide on something just because "It feels good". In subjective decisions you might also consider your strengths, weaknesses, opportunities and threats. The other group of decisions is objective, purely unemotional decision-makings, which are public, and require one to "Step outside one" so that you can discount your emotions. For example, a CIO deciding for the company must ask among other questions, "Can I convince the shareholders?"

This group of decision-making involves responsibility, which requires rational, defensible and accountable decisions. Therefore, the first group consists of private decisions which might involve emotion, and the second is almost entirely based on rational decision-making. However, the really hard decisions involve a combination of both. The difficulty might arise from the fact that emotions and rational strategic thinking are on two different sides of the human brain, and in difficult decisions one must be able to use both sides simultaneously. The following table contains the two extreme approaches of human's mind, namely the pure-subjectivity and the pure-objectivity:

*Table 1 : Subjectivity versus Objectivity of Human's Mind*

| | ***Subjectivism*** | ***Objectivism*** |
|---|---|---|
| Decision | Voluntarism | Determinism |
| Ontology | Nominalism | Realism |
| Epistemology | Normative | Positivism |
| Methodology | Ideology | Experimental |

The Decision-Making Process: A decision-maker must first decide on his/her values and set goals to insure a fruitful decision-making process. The environment you fashion out of your decisions is the only climate you will ever live in.

Therefore, before taking any course of action one must discover/ create a set of alternative courses of action and gather information about each.

Having gathered the information with which to make a decision, one must apply information for each course of action to predict the outcomes of each possible alternatives and make a decision for implementation. Out of every good decision, comes forth a new problem that will require another effort. Each success only buys an admission ticket to a more difficult decision problem.

In the decision-making modelling process we must investigate the effects of presenting different decision alternatives retrospectively; that is, "as if" you have implemented your strategy. The decision has already been made under a different course of actions. The key to a good decision is reflection before action, therefore, the sequence of steps in the above decision-making modelling process must be considered in reverse order. For example, the output (which is the result of our action) must be considered first. The following are the decision-making sequential steps with some possible loops:

1. Value and the Objective: Consider the full range of objectives to be fulfilled and the values implicated by your action.
2. Set of Actions: Thoroughly consider a wide range of possible alternative courses of action. The above decision-making process includes the study of identifying and choosing alternatives based on the values and preferences of the decision-maker. Therefore making a decision implies that there are alternative choices to be considered, and in such a case we want not only

to identify as many of these alternatives as possible but to choose the one that best fits with our goals, desires, lifestyle, values, and so on.

3. Evaluate the Consequences: Carefully weigh whatever you know about the costs and risks of negative as well as positive consequences that could flow from each alternative.
4. Gathering Information: Intensively search for new information relevant to further evaluation of the alternatives. Information can be classified as explicit and tacit forms. The explicit information can be explained in structured form, while tacit information is inconsistent and fuzzy to explain. Decision-making process must include the reduction of uncertainty and doubt about the uncontrollable inputs. This can be achieved by gathering reliable information. Although the uncertainty cannot be eliminated in most cases, however the more useful information reduces certain amount of risk.
5. Information Processing: Correctly assimilate and take account of any new information or expert judgment, even when the information does not support the course of action initially preferred.
6. Action Assessment: Re-examine positive and negative consequences of known alternatives, including those originally regarded as unacceptable, before making a final decision.
7. Implementation of Your Decision: Make detailed provisions for implementing and executing the chosen course of action, including contingency plans for known risks and adjustments. The art of life is a constant readjustment to our situation. The decision-maker must have a set of contingent decisions at this stage. These are decisions that have been made but put on hold until some condition is met.

Finally, I would like to list some characteristics of "Good" decision makers:

- Having a high tolerance for ambiguity.
- Having a well-ordered sense of priorities.
- Being a good listener.
- Always building the consensus around a decision.
- Avoiding stereotypes.
- Remaining resilient with feedbacks.
- Being comfortable with both soft and hard input.

- Being realistic about cost and difficulty.
- Avoiding a decision minefield.

### *Other Widely Used Decision Analysis Methods*

Selection of an appropriate decision technology depends mostly on the type of information available and the technical working knowledge of the decision analyst. The most popular techniques are Pareto Analysis, Paired Comparison Analysis, Grid Analysis, Weighing the pros and cons, Force Field Analysis, Six Thinking Hats, and the Cost/Benefit Analysis, among others including the Decision Tree and Influence Diagram. which have graphical representations as effective decision-making tools. Any decision technology might be helpful in providing some insights, however, the ultimate responsibility is yours in even deciding what technique to use and what decision to make.

Paired comparison analysis: Paired Comparison Analysis helps you to work out the importance of a number of options relative to each other. It is particularly useful where you do not have objective data to base this on. This makes it easy to choose the most important problem to solve, or select the solution that will give you the greatest advantage. Paired Comparison Analysis helps you to set priorities where there are conflicting demands on your resources. In using this technique, list your options. Then draw up a grid with each option as both a row and a column header. Use this grid to compare each option with each other option, one-by-one. For each comparison, decide which of the two options is most important, and then assign a score to show how much more important it is. You can then consolidate these comparisons so that each option is given a percentage importance.

Grid analysis: Grid Analysis is a useful technique to use for making a decision. It is most effective where you have a number of good alternatives and many factors to take into account. The first step is to list your options and then the factors that are important for making the decision. Lay these out in a table, with options as the row labels, and factors as the column headings. Next work out the relative importance of the factors in your decision. Show these as numbers. You use these numbers to weight your preferences by the importance of the factor. These values may be obvious-if they are not, then use a technique such as Paired Comparison Analysis to estimate them. The next step is to work your way across your table, scoring each option for each of the important factors in your decision. Score each option from 0 (poor) to 3 (very good). Note that you do not have to have a different score for each option-if none of them are good for a particular factor in your decision, then all options should score 0. Now multiply each of your scores by the values for your relative importance. This will give them the correct overall weight in your decision. Finally add up these scores for your options. The option that scores the highest is the best.

Pros-Cons-Interesting implications method: Prior to the science of the making decision era most managers relied on the "Pros-Cons-Interesting implications method". In using this approach, simply write down the proposed decision and then below it, draw up a table with headings 'Pros', 'Cons' and 'Interesting implications'. In the column underneath the 'Pros' heading, write down all the positive points of taking the action.

Underneath the 'Cons' heading write down all the negative effects. In the 'Interesting implications' column write down the extended implication of the action, whether positive or negative. The main weakness of this approach is that the score you assign can be entirely subjective. Therefore, this approach may not help you in defending yourself if the outcome of your decision is undesirable to those whom you are accountable. It is known that, Benjamin Franklin based all his important decisions using the Pros-and-Cons methodology.

Weighing the pros and cons: To use the weighing pros and cons, draw up a table headed up 'Plus', 'Minus', and 'Implications'. In the column underneath 'Plus', write down all the positive results of taking the action, then underneath 'Minus' write down all the negative effects. In the 'Implications' column write down the implications and possible outcomes of taking the action, whether positive or negative. At this stage it may already be obvious whether or not you should implement the decision. If it is not, consider each of the points you have written down and assign a positive or negative score to it appropriately. The scores you assign may be quite subjective. Once you have done this, add up the score. A strongly positive score shows that an action should be taken a strongly negative score that it should be avoided.

The Force field analysis is a useful technique for looking at all the forces for and against a decision. In effect, it is a specialized method of weighing pros and cons. By carrying out the analysis you can plan to strengthen the forces supporting a decision, and reduce the impact of opposition to it. List all forces for change in one column, and all forces against change in another column. Assign a score to each force, from 1 (weak) to 5 (strong). Draw a diagram showing the forces for and against change. Show the size of each force as a number next to it. Often the most elegant solution is the first: just trying to force change through may cause its own problems. People can be uncooperative if change is forced on them.

Six thinking hats: Multi-perspective analysis Six Thinking Hats is used to look at decisions from a number of important perspectives. This forces you to move outside your habitual thinking style, and helps you to get a more rounded view of a situation. Many successful people think from a very rational, positive viewpoint. This is part of the reason that they are successful. Often, though, they may fail to look at a problem from an emotional, intuitive, creative or negative viewpoint.

This can mean that they underestimate resistance to plans, fail to make creative leaps and do not make essential contingency plans. Similarly, pessimists may be excessively defensive. Emotional people may fail to look at decisions calmly and rationally. You can use Six Thinking Hats in meetings or on your own. In meetings it has the benefit of blocking the confrontations that happen when people with different thinking styles discuss the same problem. Each 'Thinking Hat' is a different style of thinking. These are explained below:

1. White Hat: With this thinking hat you focus on the data available. Look at the information you have, and see what you can learn from it. Look for gaps in your knowledge, and either try to fill them or take account of them. This is where you analyse past trends, and try to extrapolate from historical data.
2. Red Hat: 'Wearing' the red hat, you look at problems using reaction, and emotion. Also try to think how other people will react emotionally. Try to understand the responses of people who do not fully know your reasoning.
3. Black Hat: Using black hat thinking, look at all the bad points of the decision. Look at it cautiously and defensively. Try to see why it might not work. This is important because it highlights the weak points in a plan. It allows you to eliminate them, alter them, or prepare contingency plans to counter them.
4. Yellow Hat: The yellow hat helps you to think positively. It is the optimistic viewpoint that helps you to see all the benefits of the decision and the value in it. Yellow Hat thinking helps you to keep going when everything looks gloomy and difficult.

5. Green Hat: The Green Hat stands for creativity. This is where you can develop creative solutions to a problem. It is a freewheeling way of thinking, in which there is little criticism of ideas. A whole range of creativity tools can help you here.
6. Blue Hat: 'Blue Hat Thinking' stands for process control. This is the hat worn by people chairing meetings. When running into difficulties because ideas are running dry, they may direct activity into Green Hat thinking. When contingency plans are needed, they will ask for Black Hat thinking, etc.

A variant of this technique is to look at problems from the point of view of different professionals (e.g. doctors, architects, sales directors, etc.) or different customers.

## Decisions Concerning Personal Life

Total quality begins with total personal quality, organizational empowerment begins with individual empowerment, and managing information system (MIS) means managing your life. The same decision-making process one faces in business arises in all other aspects of one's life, but they are obscured in other parts of life because they are not overlaid with as many complexities that arise in business. If you expect people who do not treat themselves well to treat the world well, you will be sorely and surely disappointed.

In Lee Iacocca's words: Over the years, many executives have said to me with pride: "Boy, I worked so hard last year that I didn't take any vacation." I always feel like responding, "You dummy. You mean to tell me you take responsibility for an $80 million project and you can't plan two weeks out of the year to have some fun?"

Business decision-making is a simple arena of choices expressed in dollar terms, and that simplicity is the reason for discussing the decision-making process in the context of business, though it can apply elsewhere just as well. Values, ethics, means, and social complexity must enter into the decision-making process along with the monetary evaluation such as cost-and-benefit analysis.

We all know the difference between "right" and "wrong", and we can tell "good from "bad". But we also know that the more difficult decisions come when we have to choose between good and better. The toughest decisions of all are those we have to make between bad and worse.

Many people believe that predetermined destiny rather than their own decisions govern the affairs of their lives. Personal mastery teaches us to choose. Choosing is a courageous act that entails opting for various courses of actions that will define one's destiny. Destiny is not a matter of chance. It is a matter of choice. Striving for goals (i.e., the objective of your decisions) that do not reflect your values and consequently do not make your life joyful is how we make ourselves unhappy. But if you do not know what you want, then how will you know how to achieve it? Have a very clear picture of what you want out of life and what it will take to get it. There is a popular, classic song in which a raspy female voice exclaims to her independent female audience, "*use what you got.....to get what you want.*"

Be realistic about your abilities. When there is a way, there is a will. The opposite is not true as many people unfortunately believe and have taken as the basis for decisions concerning their personal life. Thinking about strategies to strive after that are beyond your abilities can ruin your life. If a goal is unattainable and you go after it anyway, the consequential failure may cause you pain and diminish your energy (and resources of the organization). You do best in your profession and your personal life by doing well with respect to your capacity and values rather than trying to do better than another person or organization. Judge your success by what you had to give up in order to get it. Remember that, if you are attempting the impossible, you will fail; therefore ask what is possible for you.

He knows not his own strength that has not met challenge. When you are facing a decision, then you are sounding-out the depth of your own strengths and the richness of your resources. One is responsible for one's own life. Passivity provides no protection: One must accept responsibility for a decision before one can make any decision.

All religions, arts, philosophy, morality, and sciences are branches of the same tree. All these aspirations have pondered the search for what constitutes a good life. Yet only in the last decades has the study of well-being become a scientific endeavor. The results indicate that the goals and values of personal life are very subjective and mostly cultural. Most people spend a lifetime searching for happiness. They chase idle dreams, addictions, religions, even other people, hoping to fill the emptiness that plagues them. The irony is that the only place they ever needed to search was within. Moreover, once a doctrine, however irrational, has gained power in a society, millions of people will believe in it rather than feel ostracized and isolated. One must decide for oneself: Leaders and followers face different problems. The leaders have to wonder if the followers will follow them faithfully and the followers wonder if the leader will bring them to the "promised land". In essence, the leaders and the followers are slaves to each other's needs.

There are many factors that contribute to being a good decision-maker, the cardinal ones are:

1. Self-esteem (not pride): Self-esteem is a big factor in making good decisions. Some people easily pressured into doing things by others are easily told what to do because they have very low self-esteem. Never feel sorry for yourself — it has a deadly effect on your thinking. Recognize all problems, no matter how difficult, as opportunities for enhancement and/or affirmation of your life, and make the most of these opportunities. Creativity in making good decisions requires having a clear mind.
2. Courage: Courage is doing what you are afraid to do. There can be no courage unless you are scared. Courage is to think for yourself. When one has low self-esteem one can be talked into doing almost anything because one depends on others too much for advice. This is all because one may not have strength and courage to listen to his/her own thoughts. There are many ways to escape from your own strategic thinking engagement. For example, have you asked yourself why you read newspapers? Could it be an escape device? As a reporter puts it "Fact that is fact every day is not news; it's truth. We report news, not truth." It may be a shock to most of us that, Thomas Jefferson said, "I do not take a single newspaper, nor read one a month, and I feel myself infinitely the happier for it." You ought to never try to avoid the duty of making up your mind for yourself. If you do not make decisions for yourself, others do it for you: "You're legally allowed to drink now so we figured the best thing for you was a car."

   Of all the gifts that a parent can give a child, the gift of learning to make good choices is the most valuable and long lasting. It is the nature, and the advantage, of courageous people that they can take the crucial questions and form a clear set of alternatives. The weak always have to decide between alternatives that are not their own.

   It takes education and courage to gain more self-esteem to be positive or confident in decision-making. Listen to yourself and think for yourself. This won't get you into trouble because of someone else. Courage means the act of intelligent risk taking while looking forward into the future. Nothing splendid has ever been achieved except by those who dare, as something inside them was superior to circumstance in making their decisions.

3. Honesty: Honesty is to be the one you are. Be objective about yourself and others. It is important to identify your weaknesses as well as your strengths. Being honest with yourself is the most important thing you can ever do. When it comes to yourself, you have to be brutally honest.
4. Love: Love means caring about yourself and other people. It means that you go to sleep at night knowing that your talents and abilities were used in making decisions that, served others. The wonderful thing about love is that it embraces, without binding.

To be honest, you must fully accept that at this moment, you can only be what you are. No more, no less; however, with the inevitable passing of each moment of time, you will gradually, but surely change — to become more or less, better or worse, stronger or weaker. Your choice is the direction of change: it is yours alone. The only true *competition is the rivalry within* your changing self. It is the very basis of a good decision making.

Hard Decisions: Only you can change your life. No one can make decisions for you when it comes to serious questions, such as, What ought I to do?, What should I believe?, What can I know?, How should I live? What Ralph Waldo Emerson tells us is that the only good answers to such questions are personal and examined ones, rarely those adopted by large groups; conscious, reasoning minds should neither pray to strange Gods, nor encourage the vanities of the self. That alone can set us on the path to freedom. All the interest of your education should come together to make decisions for yourself. What is the use of education if you cannot face these questions to your own satisfaction?

While you are making these decisions, you feel for the time being that your life is your own. Do not envy others, because who envies others does not obtain peace of mind. Everything starts with yourself — with you making up your mind about what you're going to do with your life. The more amiability and esprit de corps among the members of a policy-making in-group, the greater is the danger that independent critical thinking will be replaced by groupthink, which is likely to result in irrational and dehumanizing actions directed against out groups.

Major decisions require courage. We must have courage to bet on our decisions, to take the calculated risk, and to act.

Finally, in personal decision-making there is no one better to talk to than yourself if you really want to get things worked out. No other person has as much information about your problems, and no one knows your skills and capabilities better.

Self-Realization: Maslow's work specifies that individuals have a hierarchy of needs ranging from basic needs for survival and safety to higher-level needs for esteem and self-actualization:

1. Physiological Needs: These are primarily biological needs. They include such things as the need for adequate nutrition, shelter, warmth and medical care.
2. Safety Needs: After physiological needs, the second most compelling needs that individuals face are safety and security.
3. Belongingness and Love Needs: When physiological and safety needs have been addressed, the next set of needs — those related to belongingness, affection and love — can emerge.
4. Esteem Needs: If the first three needs are fulfilled, the need for esteem may become dominant. This refers both to self-esteem and to the esteem a person gets from others.
5. Self-Actualization Needs: The highest level of needs, those that individuals are able to satisfy when all other more basic needs have been met, is the need for self-actualization. Self-actualization is a person's need to be what he/she is. A musician must make music, an artist must paint, a poet must write, if he is to be ultimately at peace with himself.

What does Maslow mean by his observation with respect to self-realization? My answer is: If it falls your lot to be a street sweeper, sweep streets like Michelangelo painted pictures, like Shakespeare wrote poetry, like Beethoven composed music; sweep streets so well that everybody will have to pause and say, Here lived a great sweeper, who swept his job well.

***Popular Strategies in Avoiding Personal Decisions:*** Decisions shape our personal lives, however decision-making can be a stressful, bewildering personal responsibility. Decidophobia is the fear of making your own decisions. The comparison and choice of goals and standards arouses the most intense decidophobia but the only way to ensure stability in the strategic thinking is to engender fear. In the past few decades, the field of decision-making has concentrated on showing the limitations of decision makers-that is, that they are not very rational or competent and their thoughts are clouded with a plethora of possibilities, variables and outcomes. In short, there is the lack of a well-focused structured decision-making process.

The following strategies or combination of them enable decidophobes to avoid making their own decisions.

- Religion: Religion and the proclamation of what is good and evil is the most popular one. It is through this unity that the decidophobe avoids confrontation. Instead of inviting us to evaluate alternative standards, it gives us norms as well as detailed standards. However, *moralizing and morals* are two entirely different things and are always found in entirely different people.

Every religion too, is a model for questions such as: How should I live, What should I believe? How should I behave? What should I do and so on. In Islam, for example, a man may have more than one wife (officially up to four, at any given time), but he should not drink wine. In Christianity the opposite is allowed. Here you have a choice.

Models are always changing to adapt to reality. For example, Martin Luther, and John Calvin among others, found a need for *reformations* and modified the Catholic model. The same happened with the Eastern models, such as Buddhism which is the reformed Hinduism. Models, in general, should be able to provide "insights" useful to cope with the decision problem. In the case of religious models, the question "how should I live?" is not a decision problem. The imperative and authoritative answers to almost all similar decisions are already given. However, there is only one big decision one must make first — "the leap of faith." While the organized religions are life-enhancing for those who need their services, they are not life-affirming (e.g., concepts of sin and redemption as its cure).

The source of all religion and metaphysics is the recognition of a higher power, such as a god(s), or "the-thing-in-itself", respectively. Much of what passes for religious faiths, and metaphysics idols (i.e., ideas) amounts to a side bet, covering a vague belief that "there must be something" or that man needs to believe. Philosophy and religion are accustomed in constructing models such as, metaphysics of a higher world, and another-world, in order to despise this world.

The beauty of religious mania is that it has the power to explain everything. Once God (or Satan) is accepted as the first cause of everything which happens in the mortal world, nothing is left to chance. Logic can be happily tossed out the window. Metaphysics are the concepts that empirical investigation is unable to tackle such as the nature of time and gravity, space and the purpose of our beings.

Believing in God, while is sometimes advantageous health-wise, can have the reverse effect: it can predict mortality. A study of 600 older hospital patients, 95% of whom were believers, found that people who felt alienated from God, or who blamed the devil for their illness, had a 19% to 28% increased risk of dying over the following two years.

- Drifting: Instead of choosing how to live and what to believe, The drifting person simply follows the "status quo". On the opposite end of the spectrum is the person who has no ties, no code of conduct, or purpose. These types of individuals are afraid of making any decision, no matter how small.
- Allegiance to a Movement: This strategy identifies the people who are dissatisfied both with traditional life styles and with being adrift, so they join a movement. This is an indication of a person's fear of "standing alone".
- Allegiance to a School of Thought: This strategy helps to give one an identity. People of this nature share a way of thinking and deal with problems in the same way.
- Exegetical Thinking: In this strategy one reads in the text, assumes that the text that one reads is right and therefore, treats it as an authority. This enables the exegete to read his own ideas into the text and get them back endowed with authority. The exegetical thinker fears independence and independent thinking.
- Manachaeism: For the Manachaeist, the decision is most important and generally makes itself; the choice is loaded. It is when all the odds are stacked, all the good is on one side, all the evil on the other. It ignores all other alternatives.
- Moral Rationalization: The idea is that the moral rationalist, through rational thought, can make decisions. However, that moral rationalism may involve an inadequate conception of reason and responsibility. Man — a reasoning rather than a reasonable animal.
- Pedantry: This strategy emphasizes on a "microscopic distinction". Decidophobia engulfs the pedantic person, as they never get around to considering major decisions and do not look at, or see, the big picture. Action always generates inspiration. Inspiration seldom generates action.

- The Wave of the Future: Although this strategy overlaps with religion, allegiance to a movement or to a school, and to ignore other alternatives and, like other strategies, there is a fear of standing alone and unsupported. Ideals are acceptable because they are "the wave of the future". Idealism increases in direct proportion to one's distance from the decision problem.
- Marriage: One of the most popular strategies is that of marriage. This strategy is based on the premise that in marriage, the decisions are left, in most cultures to the husband. However, either spouse can succumb. Decisions are either a consensus of the two or there is a disagreement and one ends up "going along" with the other.

### Problem of Determination of Values and Rank Among Values

Not to arrive at a clear understanding of one's own values is a tragic waste. You have missed the whole point of what life is for. Which one of the following fits your value system? The major value in life is what you get, OR the major value in life is what you become.

***Setting a Clear Goal:*** What is it you want to accomplish? Strangely enough, many decision-makers collect a set of alternatives (say cars to buy or person to marry) and then ask, "Which should I choose?" without thinking first of what their goals are, what overall objective they want to achieve. Next time you find yourself asking, "What should I do? What should I choose?" ask yourself first, "What are my goals?"

***Know Your Values and Preferences:*** Value refers to how desirable a particular outcome is, the value of the alternative, whether in dollars, satisfaction, or other benefit. However, preference reflects the philosophy and moral hierarchy of the decision-maker. Personal values determine the preferences. Some people prefer excitement to calmness, taking too much risk to a calculable risk, efficiency to esthetics, quality to quantity, and so on.

It is not hard to make good decisions when you know what your values are. However, a question that has inspired many theories conveys the impression that the numerous theories of values and valuation are deeply heterogeneous, some being rational and some irrational, some seeing values as the mere effect of social inculcation, others the effect of emotional factors, as resentment.

Moreover some theories attempt to derive values from self-interest, others from the constraints imposed by society on individuals.

***Rational Choice Model:*** Rational theory deals with one of the major "rational" theories used today to explain norms and values: the so-called "Rational Choice Model".

In the expression "Rational Choice Model" the word rational is used in an indigenous fashion, as an equivalent of "instrumentally rational." An action is "rational" in this sense if it can be held as representing objectively a good way of reaching the goal the subject is following. While its supporters see it as a potentially universally valid theory, in other words as the only one actually able to explain indistinctly all human activities, this claim seems ungrounded.

***Relativistic vs. Naturalistic Theories:*** The interest and limits of these theory deal with the question of which values should be considered as the emanation of singular cultures and, for this reason, vary from one culture to another. These models are dominant today because they defend a relativistic view of values and treat the perception people have of the reasons as to why they endorse such and such values as illusory. Some opponents of the relativistic theories have instead a naturalistic theory of values. It takes its inspiration from sociobiology.

***Axiological Rationality:*** Axiological rationality was studies by Weber in distinction between axiological rationality and instrumental rationality. The instrumental rationality deals with the relations between means and ends, the notion of axiological rationality introduces the idea of a non-consequential type of rationality. This idea can be presented as a sequential type of rationality rather axiological rationality. The explanation of axiological feelings is concerned with the cases where social actors act in conformity with their values.

***Cognitivist Model:*** Cognitivist model is a generalization of the Rational Choice Model which starts from the idea that the notion of rationality has two very different meanings: The sense of the concept in economics, and the philosophy of science. It implies that some irrational people can be interpreted rationally, provided the notion of rationality is adequately defined. It is also concerned with the development of the "judicatory" or "cognitivist" theory of rationality. The cognitivist model is also applied to the analysis of the feelings of justice in an attempt to apply the judicatory theory of values to a well-circumscribed field: the feelings of justice. Philosophers, such as Rawls, propose implicitly a theory as to what people mean when they perceive a distribution of goods as fair or unfair. They are in some circumstances Kantian (that is, they tend to follow principles of universal value), while they are rather in other circumstances utilitarian (That is, they tend to follow their interest and hold principles as valid provided they can consider them as serving their interest).

Concepts such as "local justice" or "bounded justice" are concerned with building a bridge between reality and theory on the feelings of justice. With respect to decision-making, instead of saying that man is the creature of circumstance, it would be more accurate to say that man is the architect of circumstance. It is character, which builds an existence out of circumstance. From the same materials one man builds palaces, another hotels; one warehouses, another villas; bricks and mortar are mortar and bricks until the architect can make them something else.

As my reader noticed by now, the major problems for the scientists are the problem of determination of values and the assignment of ranks among the values.

The ultimate goal of human decisions is always the satisfaction of the acting man's desire, which is almost always "growth". There is no standard of greater or lesser satisfaction other than individual judgments of "values" and determination of "ranks" among those values. The values and their ranks are different for various people and for the same people at various times.

A potential problem is deciding the importance of the things you think about most of the time. The solution to this problem is to come-up with some criteria in evaluating the degree of the values you hold dear for achieving living well. We have to give meanings to our individual life, otherwise our lives are blank and senseless.

The first task in making private and personal decisions is to find out what the "values" are, for what? The answer is for the enhancement and affirmation of your life. Moreover, one must decide about the "ranks" among these values and their relation to the other values. The following is an ordered three-category model:

1. Group A: This most important group includes all the things that you can do for yourself and no one else can do for you. Examples include "a good night's sleep", learning to think for yourself, and your health. As a Spanish proverb says, "A man too busy to take care of his health is like a mechanic too busy to take care of his tools." You know it well that "Your health is your wealth." Remember that you will be as much value to others as you have been to yourself.

2. Group B: The things which are yours and could not have been anybody else's. For example, your child belongs in this group.
3. Group C: All other things. Such as your house, your job, etc.

Clearly, the question concerning what belongs to which group is highly subjective. For example, your job could become a member of group B if you like what you do and you believe no one else can do it as well as you do. Music the supreme form of all arts, for the composers belong to this group to amuse themselves in the first place. While the other forms of arts kept in the museums to amuse others too.

### Thinkable Decisions and the Economy of Strategic Thinking

What do artists do? They make models of reality that are more beautiful than reality itself in order to make our existence bearable. However, as Michelangelo once said, "A man paints with his brains and not with his hands." Moreover, a modeler of reality is an artist with constraints.

A Japanese proverb says, "Thinking without action is a daydream. Action without thinking is a nightmare." Therefore, there are two kinds of failures: those who thought and never did and those who did and never thought. The trouble with most people is that they think with their hopes or fears or wishes rather than with their minds.

Speechless thought moves over the fibers of our brain like water over the face of the deep. That we think, we know because we think. That we are, we know because we think; but what is it to think? And what is it to know that we think? What happens when you let your mind wander? When human mind has nothing specific to think about, it becomes chaotic, flitting from one thought to another in a random way. That's why thinkers are more often in a good mood while thinking than they are in their free time.

When one faces a problem, one must always ask whether the problem is thinkable. Not every idea or concept is thinkable. Moreover, every thinkable idea deserves its own duration of time in your mind. Our senses furnish the mind only with materials of information; it is our thinking that converts information we receive to our useful knowledge for decision making. Decision-making is described as the economy of thinking. There are six steps that must be considered in making a good decision. The steps are as follows:

1. Is it thinkable? Is your problem thinkable?

2. Is it my business? Is it really necessary for you to think about it? It seems like one of the hardest lessons to be learned in life is where your business ends and somebody else's begins. The moment a question comes to your mind, see yourself mentally taking hold of it and disposing of it. In that moment is your choice made. You learn to become the decider and not the vacillator.
3. Do you have enough explicit information to start your strategic thinking? Information can be classified as *explicit and tacit* forms. The explicit information can be explained in structured form, while tacit information is inconsistent and fuzzy to explain. A good thinking resides in the capacity for evaluation of uncertain, hazardous, and conflicting information.
4. How long should I think about it? The key is in not "spending" time, but in "investing" it. Thinking does not stay in some minds very long because unfortunately they do not like solitary confinement that is needed.

   Decision does not just happen; it takes reflection and thought. Reflection time must be built into the decision process allowing ample time to ponder and rethink. For many people, unfortunately, the expectation that responding immediately is far more important than responding thoughtfully for many.
5. Implementation-taking action. Thinking without action is daydreaming. To think too long about doing a thing often becomes its undoing.
6. Monitoring my action. Since everything changes, to be in control of my problem I have to adapt and update my thinking. The art of life is a constant readjustment to our situation.

Following the above thinking process with its many loops, then it is very likely that good ideas spring into being in response to your analytical probing. This analytical thinking is the most powerful tool for the mind. Without this, recurrence relation will keep coming back to your mind to haunt you.

Mind maintains, and holds whatever has been put on it during the last few minutes. It holds and works on it, unless we replace by something new. Therefore, in order not to think about what is not worthy one must start thinking about something else immediately. That is the hygiene for the mind.

The crux is noticed in *Alices' Adventures in Wonderland*: " ' How am I to get in?' asked Alice again, in a louder tone. 'Are you to get in at all?' said the Footman, 'That's the first question, you know.' " Remember that most people waste most of their time every day majoring in minors. Time is of no account with great thoughts. Obviously, the basic problem is this: Law firms, which bill by the hour, are more profitable when less efficient. As Goethe said, "Things, which matter most, must never be at the mercy of things which matter least." Time is the scarcest resource and unless it is managed nothing else can be managed.

If you work on a nonexistent problem there are much fewer obstacles to overcome. To accomplish something noteworthy, we should look to do something worth the effort unless we are trying to relax. In times of leisure, nonexistent problems usually need to be sought out! Here is an example of an unthinkable question/problem. Is there an after life? This question is not thinkable. You must think about it as much as you think about "life before life." We can ask primal questions, but we can never stand near the beginning or the end.

In other cases, the questions are thinkable, however, one "wishes" not even raise any doubt about them that invoke strategic thinking. These cases include, e.g., our deepest beliefs. And in many cases, one even deliberately changes the perception of the problem in order that it suits ones preconceived desirable decision. This is unfortunate, but people lie much more to themselves than to others.

I studied the lives of relatively great men and famous women, and I found that the men and women who got to the top were those who did the jobs they had in hand, with everything they had of energy and enthusiasm and hard work.

On the duration of the strategic thinking, Albert Einstein said, "I think and think for months and years, ninety-nine times, the conclusion is false. The hundredth time I am right. It's not that I'm so smart, it's just that I stay with problems longer." As a general rule for strategic thinking, if you cannot describe in writing to be understood by someone else about your decision problem and what you are doing as a process about it, then you do not know what you are doing. The best place to make a decision is on paper.

Being able to control the thought process is the hardest of all, and it takes discipline and training. One must develop the ability to engage in a consecutive, and a well-focused strategic thinking for a predetermined limited time in order produce a solution to a given well defined problem. It is not that things will necessarily go wrong (Murphy's Law), but rather that they will take so much more time and effort than you think, if they are not to. The cardinal aim is to uncover the underlying logical structure of the decision problem by means of a mathematical model. All branches of human knowledge are moving towards scientific representation. These include all the —logy subjects, such as sociology, and psychology, etc., usually being taught at our liberal art and humanity colleges. Nowadays, one expects a deeper understanding from studying sociometric, psychometric, and econometric, etc.

Students often ask me if, as a thinker, I was rational or creative. Left-brained or right-brained. I consider it, and ask in reply, do I have to choose? Is it possible to be both? I did not think I could afford to discriminate. You want to be good at designing a good solution strategy, and you need all the brainpower I had available.

Well-focused strategic decision-making is the act of simultaneous thinking. However, there is no expedient to which a man will not resort to avoid the real labour of thinking.

Remember that:

Birds fly; when they get tired, they land.

Man thinks; when he gets tired, he says "I understand."

Philosophy of Creation: The fundamental project in life is engaging with the central idea that being strives for creativity. There are various ways in which being affirms the unlimited creative power. Moreover it dissolves whatever might restrict or mediate its expression, including the organisms, objects, representations, identities, and relations that this power generates along the way.

Thinking could be dangerous: The following metaphor illustrates how in some cases people prefer to not think for fear of being disappointed, adhering to the saying that "ignorance is bliss". There was a boy who lived his whole life on an iceberg. One day, he wondered what could be under the ice. He decided to dig in to find out for himself. To his greatest disappointment he discovered that he was actually living on water. From that day on, he never felt comfortable living on the iceberg and he wished he had not asked himself that question.

Mastering your fears: The major obstacle that stops people from making their own decisions is fear of making wrong decision.

When one has fear there are two primary reactions: facing the problem courageously or avoiding any commitments. However, since one has a powerful ability to analyse and understand, one can overcome the fear by self-psychoanalysis techniques to cope with the flight instinct.

Top business performers have developed a multiple-step approach to conquering their fears. First, ask yourself a few important questions. Try to identify what you actually fear. Ask yourself what's the worst that can happen if you fail. Most of the time in business, it's either a fear of loss or a fear of embarrassment. Next, identify what you could gain if the task or strategy works out well. This positive vision helps overshadow the negative fear. Last, ask yourself what the price is to you and to others if you do not overcome this fear

There are two types of people: those who try, stumble and get up and try again, and those who fear stumbling and never even try. Guess which type is more successful.

Our stomach is wiser than our brain: When one eats too much, the stomach rejects it by throwing up. However, the brain has no such mechanism. While mind controls the body, unfortunately, it is unable to control or give order to itself. The main cause for this is our habits, which are the Centres of the gravity of the mind. Habits are weighing our mind down and therefore they are shortcuts that become comfortable means to avoid thinking.

Process of thinking for yourself : Thinking for yourself has been valued ever since ancient time:

"If I am walking with two other men, each of them will serve as my teacher. I will pick out the good points of the one and imitate them, and the bad points of the other and correct them in myself." — *Confucius*

The critical thinking techniques enable us to evaluate arguments and question the quality of the reasoning that leads to a certain conclusion. Too often we accept what we see and hear, becoming passive absorbers of information rather than critical listeners or readers. We must guard our mind against adapting a belief as our own before examining the validity of arguments for or against. We should ask questions in order to reach our own personal opinion or decision including:

- What are the issue and conclusion?
- What are the reasons?
- Which words or phrases are ambiguous?
- What are the value conflicts and assumptions?
- What are the descriptive assumptions?

- Are there any fallacies in the reasoning?
- How good is the evidence?
- Are there rival causes?
- Are the statistics deceptive?
- What significant information is omitted?
- What reasonable conclusions are possible?

Unfortunately, pure uncritical thinking enables us to absorb a great deal of information and provides a foundation for more complex thinking at some future time. However, it is a passive exercise and, therefore, does not require an exhaustive mental effort, just concentration and memory skills. Clearly, this approach does not provide us with a method for discerning the facts, which could have serious consequences. Moreover, I am always fascinated by the way memory diffuses facts.

On the other extreme is the interactive approach to thinking that requires a "question-asking attitude" to determine the value of what is read and heard. If we are capable of thinking for ourselves, then the rewards are considerable and allows us to critically evaluate and then form personal opinions based on that evaluation of what makes sense and what is non-sense. We must also be aware that we bring our own personal experiences and values into the process and must not allow emotional involvement to taint our ability to think in an open-minded manner.

### *What is Man?*

The many debates over mind and matter cover much of the history of human thoughts. The main engaging question, prior to the age of Enlightenment was how a nonphysical (i.e., mind) causes a physical (e.g., movements)?

Both Spinoza and Freud among others, worked on the unity of mind and body together with their interaction with nature and society. The following chart depicts the psych-analysis of Freud and Spinoza hybrid model: Spinoza was the first to question the concept of mind-and-body, i.e., physical and nonphysical duality dominated humanity for over twenty centuries. He recognized that there is no such separation, but a manifestation of two different moods of the same thing. For example, when you have sufficient physical energy, then your mind registers it as feeling joyful. Anybody old enough has physical scars from all sorts of things. It is the same with the mind. In the above chart, the interaction of humankind with nature, society, and self are depicted inside the triangle. Humankind and Nature: Genetic engineering has shown how it is possible to splice genes from one animal to another and not just animals. So, are humans really that unique? And even if they are not, are they that special?

When one talks about humankind it is often with a tendency to separate man from the rest of animals. However, in reality there no such separation, the man is wholly nature not a kingdom within a kingdom. Humankind is not the crown and the hidden purpose of evolution.

According to the primatology, which has mounted ever more convincing bodies of evidence that there is really nothing special or unique about the human at all, that almost everything that you care to name is, to some degree or another, performed by other primates; it is all a matter of degree. And so, rather than distinct categories primatologists would rather have shifting shades of gray in the primate world and extend the term homo to a much broader population.

***Nature of the Man:*** Man has no nature, but he has history. In man the creature and the creator are one. While man is still undetermined animal, he is the strongest of all animals.

What Nietzsche realized was that man must understand that life is not governed by rational principles. Life is full of cruelty, injustice, uncertainty and absurdity. There are no absolute standards of good and evil which can be demonstrated by human Reason. There is only naked man living alone in a godless and absurd world. Modern industrial, bourgeois society made man decadent and feeble because it made man a victim of the excessive development of the rational faculties at the expense of human will and instinct.

The task is to rediscover beneath all flattering colours and make-up the frightful fixed-text homo natura, which means: To translate man back into nature; to become master over the many vain and overly enthusiastic interpretations and connotations that have so far been scrawled and painted over that eternal basic text of homo natura. To bring it about that man shall henceforth stand before man as he now, hardened by the discipline of science, stands before the other forms of nature. He is, in truth, anything but the crown of creation: beside him stand many other animals, all at similar stages of development.

***Humankind and Society:*** When man found himself bounded within the wall of society, all his instinct had to be broken to be replaced by the social norms. However, not all the instinct gave up their demand easily. The two most pervasive of all are: Anger, and Reproduction. Man derives the highest pleasure from sexual fulfilment, says Freud, but unconstrained sexuality drains the individual of psychic energy needed for a creative and intellectual life. Hence, it was society, working through the family, the priest, the teacher and the police, who imposes rules and restricts our animal nature which, because it is animal, demands release. Such an existence is painful and so causes anxiety and frustration.

But the violation of the rules of civilization also gives us guilt. Either way, we suffer torment and pain. Civilized life simply entails too much pain for people. It seemed, for Freud, that the price we pay for civilization is neuroses. Man has to find some sublimated means of satisfying the instinct. For example, our sexual fulfilment is allowed by means of engaging in e.g., "Passionate-dancing", which is accompanied by the feeling and imagination of making love in bed but vertically. There are many other "acceptable means" for sexual fulfilment, such as sexual virtual-reality as a substitute for the real-reality.

***Humankind and the Self:*** We are particularly interested in the relation between anthropology and psychology. The difficulty of the Anthropology is how to articulate an analysis of what Homo Natura is on the basis of a definition of man as subject of liberty. More specifically, in its pragmatic character, the Anthropology aims to study what man makes of himself. So the realm of its investigation will neither be morality, metaphysics, nor the society, but what makes man, — or what he can and should do of himself. Foucault observed that even though the anthropology posits man neither as homo natura nor as subject of freedom, but rather as he is given within the already operating syntheses of his relation with the world, i.e. as a citizen of the world, he/she then goes on to understand the dynamic of the inner sense.

Nature proceeds throughout the whole infinite series of its possible determinations without outward incentive; and the succession of these changes is not arbitrary, but follows strict and unalterable laws. Whatever exists in Nature necessarily exists as it is. Nature's relation to human beings is neutral while human's relation to nature is very complex process and yet undetermined. Consider for example in the animal kingdom, all creatures are striving to eat, survive, and reproduce. However, when it comes to man, he wonders and hopelessly looking for hidden purpose "as if" nature has a purpose.

A Distinction: Human has choices but not animal. This fact is, captured by artists, e.g., in The Animals in War Memorial, which is situated at London's Hyde Park. This sculpture by David Backhouse depicts all the animals that have been used by troops in wartime, from horses and mules to dogs, elephants, camels, canaries and even glowworms.

## How the Mind Works: From Deciding to Action

The many debates over mind and matter cover much of the history of human thoughts. The main engaging question, prior to the age of Enlightenment was how a nonphysical (i.e., mind) causes a physical (e.g., movements)?

Behavioural and Brain Sciences: It is a fact that humankind use crude information, such as colours, sounds, etc., in the environment in order to behave in a certain way. When forms of energy we call "stimuli" impinge on us our response begins. Creating an inner copy of the information, which is a representation of reality, does this. However this representation is at the service of the "will" in determining our behaviour.

In recent years there have been more interesting studies on the static geometry, i.e., the anatomy of the brain, leading to important testable predictions. However, the valuable progress in the brain/ mind problem should be a comparative study in discovering relations between the physical dynamical structures generated by brain activity and the mental/conceptual structures. This includes the topology of subjective time and its alterations in psychopathology.

The brain is made up of billions of nerve cells. The portion of the brain responsible for thought and memory consists primarily of nerve cells, or neurons. Each neuron has three parts, dendrites (inputs), a cell body, and an axon (output) as shown below:

The dendrites connect to the axons of other neurons. When these other neurons are stimulated, the dendrites convey the signal to the cell body via a synapse or connection, which either excites or inhibits the neuron with a different strength for each synapse:

When the excitation sufficiently outweighs inhibition, the neuron "fires". This sends a signal down its axon, which in turn excites or inhibits other neurons, and perhaps causes a muscle to move. For at least three reasons, we are interested in knowing how our mind works:

1. Better decisions are made by knowing the mechanism of our mind.
2. Happiness or unhappiness are the states of mind.
3. A better understanding of the mind can lead to setting new priorities as to what is taught/learned.

Mind is what your brain does consciously, recall the often used phrases such as: never mind!, mind the gap, or mind your own business. A strategic thinking process is a neural network process inside our brains through many functional layers.

The focal point of practical reasoning is action, as the focal point of empirical reasoning is observation. Perceptual takings or 'judgments' are the thoughts which typically arise from the impact of the world on our mind through our sensory capacities.

Consciousness thinking is self-knowledge, that is, knowing what you know. Moreover, the process of becoming conscious distributes what you know throughout your brain via the brain neural network branches, i.e., chains of thought. Unlike the connectivity between only two nodes of the network (what we call memorizing), the availability, and therefore expansion, of what you know throughout your neural network branches makes the information processing of your brain accurate. Thus, you possess a reflective, brilliant mental model of reality. However, one must be cautioned that the way we choose to see the world (i.e., modelling) creates the world we see.

It is necessity to integrate your observations, your experiences, and your knowledge into a mental model. Your duty is whether the model is true or false, whether it represents reality rationally. Unfortunately, it might be a grab-bag of notions snatched at random, whose sources, validity, context and consequences you do not know, notions which, more often than not, you would drop like a hot potato if you knew.

Human beings are basically electrochemically driven membrane processes. We take in oxidant and fuel, we change the form of it, things move through membranes, and we oxygenate our blood-that's how nature works. The brain at very early times in development, and at first they are present in an immature pattern of wiring that only grossly approximates the adult precision. In order for the adult pattern of connections to form, neural function is necessary. The adult brain consists of about 1 trillion ($10^{12}$)-nerve cells, each connected to at least 20,000 other cells. The possible combinations are greater than the number of molecules in the known universe. Each neuron makes a very stereotyped set of connections with specific partner neurons. Unlike common belief that our mind works like a computer, a useful analogy is to think of nerve cells as rather like a telephone system. Our brains employ a mixture of chemical and electrical signals to send and receive phone calls within the brain. Each nerve cell sends a long process, an axon-like a phone line-to connect itself to other cells that can be located the equivalent of hundreds of miles away. The brain contains well over 1,000 trillion connections.

Learning can be defined as: The process of connectivity of the nodes within your neural network of the brain. The mind is like the stomach. It's not how much you put into it, but how much it digests. Knowledge is the only instrument of production that is not subject to diminishing returns. During brain connectivity development (i.e., education), all these connections have to be formed from scratch-nerve cells are made in different places in the brain by undergoing many successive cell divisions. Then each cell has to spin out its long process towards the appropriate target neurons.

The process is much like stringing phone lines from one city to another-between New York and Philadelphia, for instance. First, trunk lines between the two cities must be laid down. Then, phones at specific addresses within each city need to be wired so that when a specific phone number is dialed, only that phone rings and not the wrong numbers.

The brain first sets down a basic framework of circuits-rather like trunk lines according to strict circuit diagrams determined by a genetic blueprint. Then, long before the adult precise circuits are formed, the "switch" is turned on: brain function itself completes the wiring process by running test patterns on the circuits, thereby selecting correct connections and eliminating errors. Using the phone analogy, it is as if, once the trunk lines are strung between two cities, the first set of phone calls to be placed cause many phones to ring because many connections, including the correct ones, are formed initially. Then, a process of error-correction occurs, in which phoning it eliminates the incorrect connections and strengthens the correct ones.

Special early cell types in the brain place these molecules in specific combinations and locations, and they are sensed molecularly by the growing axon tips of "pioneer" neurons as they spin out the first connections. Once these early connections are formed, neural function begins and neurons signal to each other by sending chemical-electrical signals over their long distance connections. In the phoning process itself, the frequent use of connections strengthens them with rewards of special nerve growth factors and other signaling molecules. The inappropriate use of wrong connections causes their elimination. It is in this second phase of wiring where experience of the world can have a profound influence on the selection and maintenance of connections.

This observation forms the basis for the classic model of the critical period for brain development. Because different parts of the brain mature at different rates and times, neuroscientists believe there are different critical periods for different functions. A challenge for the future is to learn exactly what those periods are in terms of the specific development of brain circuits, for instance, for language acquisition, or reading.

An initial activity-independent step in which the basic framework of connections is constructed strictly according to the genetic blueprint, followed by a step in which brain function selects and refines from a wealth of possible connections. This second step is a prolonged period that experience can profoundly influence the important details of brain circuitry.

There are just not enough genes to account for the incredible precision of connectivity present in the adult brains (over 1,000 trillion connections). An elegant solution is to "hard wire" the trunk lines with specific molecular guidance clues, but then flip the switch to "on" early and let neural function make the final decisions. And this flexibility in final decision-making, after all, is what lets us adapt to our environment. For example, the brain does not know if it is going to have to learn English, Spanish, or Japanese after birth. An elegant solution to the wiring problem is to establish the fundamental framework of language circuitry using strict molecular mechanisms and then sculpt out the details depending on specific experiences after birth. Without this superb flexibility, we could not learn or remember or adapt to our environment-in short, those properties that make us uniquely human. Not much useful theory has been developed to explain how "reason for decision" and "cause for action" are related. A primary reason for this lack of knowledge is that reason for decision is treated as a multifaceted and rich construct, while cause for action is an external manifestation which is subject to interpretation.

***Categorization Process of the Memory:*** Categorization is the cognitive process by which distinct entities are treated as equivalent. It allows us to understand and make predictions about objects and events in our world. The categorization process is based on criteria to group together entities in the same category. These criteria include perceptual or structural similarity, and the commonalties of their elements that provide homogeneity about the entities that belong to them.

The categorization of objects and concepts facilitate a common goal and serve the similar function. As we deepen our understanding of the external world, the representation of concepts and objects changes. Therefore, the categorization process is intimately tied to our new criteria, and the context in which the entities influence the way they are classified.

***Persistence of a Model:*** Mind retains a thought process of a model of an external world for limited duration, unless a new thought replaces it. For example, when someone is talking to you, his/her voice echos in your mind, till you replace it with new thought. It is evident that the mind retains vision for a split second. This accounts for the fact that when a motion picture flashes a series of progressive images, instead of the mind seeing the flashing of a series of images, it sees the illusion of motion.

***Motivation in Making Decisions:*** The mind is generally unwilling to allocate energy to decisions whose value it is not convinced. The unspoken and even unconscious questions "what is it good for?" and "will I be able to do that?" can frequently stymie our efforts to take in a decision.

***Information versus Knowledge:*** Information is a commodity capable of yielding knowledge. Knowledge is information-produced by self. Information possesses a meaning which can only be interpreted in the light of knowledge. Purposeful action is based, not on information, but on knowledge. There are two types of knowledge: knowing that, and know how. We all know that 12X12 = 144. "Knowing how" is more critical since it captures "knowledge about" rather than "knowledge of" which belongs to memory. "Knowing how" requires systematic study and reflection, judgement, proposition, testing, and its integration with some other relevant forms of know-how. "Knowing how" is an ultimate source of strategic advantage within the organizational systems of the firm. Simply knowing how is not enough, because there might be other ways of achieving the same goal. For example, Nissan's plants in Japan, Mexico and the US use different mixes of technology and labour to create the same cars with almost similar overall productivity.

Knowledge base which is a set of facts and rules (such as, if-then-else) obtained from experience and stored in our memory. Knowledge isn't how much you have committed to memory. It's being able to differentiate between what you do know and what you don't. It's the correct connectivity of the brain neural networks and how wide these networks are.

As we age, we use different parts of the brain for memory tasks. Recent studies have found that older adults use their frontal cortex for simple short-term memory tasks. Younger people use that area for complex short-term memory tasks. Older adults also activate both hemispheres for spatial memory; younger people use the left hemisphere.

Inference is a part of neural network of our brains that analyzes available data and the facts and rules stored in the knowledge base of the brain.

Understanding is the integrated mind that is able to span the relevant functional areas across the brain by the neural network connectivity. What is it indeed that gives us the feeling of elegance in understanding? It is the harmony of the diverse parts, their symmetry, their happy balance; in a word it is all that introduces order, all that gives unity, that permits us to see clearly and to comprehend at once both the ensemble and the details.

Non-sensory experiences represent almost all context information in consciousness. They condition most aspects of conscious cognition including voluntary retrieval, perception, monitoring, problem solving, emotion, and evaluation, meaning recognition. Many peculiar aspects of non-sensory qualitative context that resist being 'grasped' by an act of attention, are explained as adaptations shaped by the cognitive functions they serve. The most important non-sensory experience is coherence or "rightness." Rightness represents degrees of context fit among contents in consciousness, and between conscious and non-conscious processes. Rightness (not familiarity) is the feeling-of-knowing in implicit cognition. The experience of rightness suggests that neural mechanisms "compute" signals indicating the global dynamics of the neural network integration.

Understanding is the ability to give meaning. In other words, understanding is possible only by an anticipation of meaning which it constitutes interconnectivity of a specific and limited neural networks. The interconnectivity exhausts itself to a resourceful finite thought called understanding. This implies that, if it takes a lot of words to say what you have in mind, give it more thought. Consecutive strategic thinking is a process which does not allow you to go out of the boundary of the subject of your thought. This focusing process should be taught at an early education. For example, a student in the class can be called upon to talk for five minutes about his/her uncle, when he/she goes out of the boundary and talks about uncles' neighbor for too long the class will shout "you are out of focus"

Focusing on one-thing-at-a-time The prefrontal cortex and other key areas of the brain handle tasks like a browser. When doing two things, those parts of the brain repeatedly switch from one task to another. Therefore, it's better to do one thing at a time rather than three things at once. Otherwise, your lost time when moving from one task to another increases even more with the complexity of the problem. Since activating the rules for each task takes several tenths of a second, therefore multitasking, in the end, takes more time than doing one thing at a time.

Why do we need to analyse? We need analysis because our minds think about specific and limited ways, one thing at a time. Then, after the analysis process, we synthesize what belongs together to see the whole or to solve the problem. There are different moods of knowledge such as: symbolic knowledge, declarative knowledge, representation, and procedural knowledge. For example, symbolic knowledge is needed for development of mathematical and statistical thinking.

Experiences and feelings are inherently conscious states. There is something it is like to feel pain, to have an itch, to experience bright red. Philosophers call this sort of consciousness "phenomenal consciousness." Even though phenomenal consciousness seems to be a relatively primitive matter, something more widespread in nature than higher-order or reflective consciousness, it is deeply puzzling.

Why are people different? We are all different because we all have different history. Thoughts and emotions give us a sense of continuity, our identities, create our conscious selves, our personalities which are not "localized" components of the brain, but are a function of the organism's life-history, cumulative experience, the totality of memories stored, recollected, analysed, modified, and retained in the physical configurations of the network-connectivity in the brain.

Experience includes the collection of all the mistakes we have made in the past. Recently, a manager was asked if he was going to fire an employee who made a mistake that cost the company $600,000.

No, the manager replied, "I just spent $600,000 training him. Why would I want somebody to hire his experience."

***Roots of decision-making:*** The West was born 500 years ago when Europe broke free of the centralized control of the Roman Catholic Church. Self and consciousness has diverse perspectives, including, Psychology, Sociology, Philosophy, Neuroscience, Cognitive Science, and Media Studies, etc. The active topics relevant to decision making in these areas are:

- Where we came from: Self and consciousness in pre-human species. Are humans really unique? and through human history is there something special about modern self and consciousness?
- Where we are now: Humans as biological beasts and cognitive creatures — The brain and mind as biological and cognitive systems underlying self and consciousness.
- Where we are now: Humans as social beings — The social underpinnings of self and consciousness, including how self and consciousness emerge in face-to-face interactions over the course of development and how societal belief systems impact and often disturb the self and consciousness of individuals.
- Where we might go: Where humans will likely go in the future, including how human selves and consciousness might be changed by interacting with computers and related electronic media.

Perception of color, sounds and their physical reality: We see colours for a purpose and the act of seeing is part of what the later Wittgenstein called a language game. For instance, a good apple is an edible color, so it is wrong to reduce colours to waves, as their function is much wider. The same applies to sounds and airwaves; the growl of a bear is not really airwaves in the wider context of danger. Because they serve a functional purpose, sensible images cannot be reduced to isolated scientific facts but exist in their own right as primaries. Their perception is usually right because of evolution, whether we consider colours as wavelengths, or photon's states energy. The brain's perceived image and sound are a construct put together according to what we "expect" to see or hear.

***Deciding among Models:*** Suppose you decide to use a model for a particular process for making concrete decisions about your own life and those of others, who may be affected, directly or indirectly, by your decisions, that is the ultimate reason why we have models? We create some models de novo from our own experience, but most we learn from external sources, including formal education. Now, supposing one is presented with two apparently competing models of a process. One of them (A) has more objective evidence for its validity in the form of scientifically controlled studies, ability to be mathematically confirmed, reliable historical documentation, endorsement by experts in the field, and so forth. The other (B) is untested and perhaps un-testable, and is endorsed by people with less impressive pedigrees. However, based on your limited experience, applying model B in cases where the two differ in their recommendations produces a better result.

### *How to Distinguish among Rumor, Belief, Opinion, and Fact*

As a necessity the human rational strategic thinking has evolved to cope with his/her environment. The rational strategic thinking which we call reasoning is another means to make the world calculable, predictable, and more manageable for the utilitarian purposes. In constructing a model of reality, factual information is therefore needed to initiate any rational strategic thinking in the form of reasoning. However, we should not confuse facts with beliefs, opinions, or rumors. The following table helps to clarify the distinctions:

With respect to belief, Henri Poincaré said, "Doubt everything or believe everything: these are two equally convenient strategies. With either, we dispense with the need to think." Believing means not wanting to know what is fact. Human beings are most apt to believe what they least understand. Therefore, you may rather have a mind opened by wonder than one closed by belief. The greatest derangement of the mind is to believe in something because one wishes it to be so.

Religion is the most widely debated and least agreed upon phenomenon of human history. The history of humanity is filled with unsettling normative perspectives reflected in, for example, inquisitions, witch hunts, denunciations, and brainwashing techniques. The "sacred beliefs" are not only within religion, but also within ideologies, and could even include science. In much the same way that Thomas Kuhn observed that scientists trying to "save the theory." For example, the Freudian treatment is a kind of brainwashing by the therapist where the patient is in a suggestive mood completely and religiously believing in whatever the therapist is making of him/her and blaming himself/herself in all cases. The use of religion, psychoanalysis, or the mass media, as instruments by which people are helped to adjust to a dehumanizing social order without being challenged to change it, is essentially a betrayal of man. There is this huge lumbering momentum from the Cold War where thinking is still not appreciated. Nothing is so firmly believed as that which is least known. For example, many people do not believe the official spokesman from the government, however, they trust "an unidentified source". The fact of the matter is that there is no hip world and there is no straight world. There's a world, you see, which has people in it that believes in a variety of different things. Everybody believes in something and everybody, by virtue of the fact that they believe in something, uses that something to support their own existence.

Nothing is easier than self-deceit. For what each man wishes, that he also believes to be true.

Whoever believes in something will have an ever lasting-life. The cultural history is littered with discarded belief-models. However, this does not mean that someone who didn't understand what was going on invented the model nor had no utility or practical value. The main idea was the cultural values of any wrong model. The falseness of a belief is not necessarily an objection to a belief. The question is, to what extent is it life-promoting, and life enhancing for the believer? As an example, to attain happiness in another world we need only to believe something, while to secure it in this world we must make good decisions.

The natural right authorizes a person to do to others anything that does not in itself diminish what is theirs, so long as they do not want to accept it – such things as merely communicating his thoughts to them, telling or promising them something, whether what he says is true and sincere or untrue and insincere; for it is entirely up to them whether they want to believe him or not. As Stoic philosophy teaches us: It is beyond our control whether others choose to insult us or offend us in some way, but it is always in our control whether we choose to be insulted or offended. If we want to remain eudaimon and tranquil, it would be wise not to be easily insulted or offended.

Opinions (or feelings) are slightly less extreme than beliefs, however, they are dogmatic. An opinion means that a person has certain views that they think are right. Also, they know that others are entitled to their own opinions. People respect others' opinions and in turn expect the same. In forming one's opinion, the empirical observations are obviously strongly affected by attitude and perception. However, opinions that are well rooted should grow and change like a healthy tree. Fact is the only instructional material that can be presented in an entirely non-dogmatic way. Everyone has a right to his/her own opinion, but no one has a right to be wrong in his/her facts.

Opinions have vested interests just as everyone has. Public opinion is often a sort of religion, with the majority as its prophet. Moreover, the prophet has a short memory and does not provide consistent opinions over time.

An opinion, right or wrong can never constitute an offense, nor in itself an obligation. It may be mistaken, involve an absurdity, or be a contradiction. It is a truth or it is an error but it can never be a crime, or a virtue.

Rumors and gossip are even weaker than opinion. Now the question is who will believe these? For example, rumors and gossip about a person are those when you hear something you like, about someone you do not. Here is an example you might be familiar with: Why is there no Nobel Prize for mathematics? It is the *opinion* of many that Alfred Nobel caught his wife in an amorous situation with Mittag-Leffler, the foremost Swedish mathematician at the time. Therefore, Nobel was afraid that if he were to establish a mathematics prize, the first to get it would be M-L. The story persists, no matter how often one repeats the plain *fact* that Nobel was not married.

It is curious how much more interest can be evoked by a mixture of gossip, belief, and opinion than by facts.

To understand the difference between feeling and strategic thinking, consider carefully the following true statement: He that thinks himself the happiest man really is so; but he that thinks himself the wisest is generally the greatest fool. Most people do not ask for facts in making up their decisions. They would rather have one good, soul-satisfying emotion than a dozen facts. This does not mean that you should not feel anything. Notice your feelings. But do not think with them.

Facts are different than beliefs, rumors, and opinions. Facts are the basis of decisions. A fact is something that is right and one can prove to be true based on evidence and logical arguments. A fact can be used to convince yourself, your friends, and your enemies. Facts are always subject to change. Data becomes information when it becomes relevant to your decision problem. Information becomes fact when the data can support it. Fact becomes knowledge when it is used in the successful completion of a structured decision process. However, a fact becomes an opinion if it allows for different interpretations, i.e., different perspectives. Note that what happened in the past is fact, not truth. Truth is what we think about, what happened (i.e., a model).

Science and religion are profoundly different. Religion asks us to believe without question, even (or especially) in the absence of hard evidence. Indeed, this is essential for having a faith. Science asks us to take nothing on faith, to be wary of our penchant for self-deception, to reject anecdotal evidence. Science considers deep but healthy skepticism a prime feature. One of the reasons for its success is that science has built-in, error-correcting machinery at its very heart.

Learn how to approach information critically and discriminate in a principled way between beliefs, opinions, and facts. Critical thinking is needed to produce well-reasoned representation of reality in your modelling process. Analytical thinking demands clarity, consistency, evidence, and above all, a consecutive, focused-thinking.

Examples of belief, opinion, and facts can be found in religions, economics, and econophysics, respectively.

Management Science is built up with facts, as a house is with stones. But a collection of facts is no more a useful science for the manager than a heap of stones is a house. To meet the the essence for communication, judgment, and persuasion of knowledge, your model must include, among others:

- It must explain the phenomena of interest — which means, you must be able to derive or create the phenomena using the model.
- It must predict future phenomena.
- You must make a good case for ruling out alternative explanations.

For example, in order to rule out alternative explanations, you first need to know what your client would think of as plausible explanations (models). This means, you must get "subjective" with your clients and encourage them to provide their best shot at causal explanations before you build your model. And it means you also have to think very hard about what a harsh critic of your model will say — what alternative explanations they could use to discredit your efforts.

You score big if your model explains, and, even more dramatically, if it predicts, something that their formulations do not. You also score big if, with the deeper understanding provided by your model, it becomes evident that their explanation does not work.

***Consciousness and the Mind:*** Contrary to philosophical tradition, modern theorists of the mind have often downplayed the importance of consciousness. Instead, they have accounted for the mind in terms of phenomena like mechanisms, dispositions, abilities and even environmental features. One of many inspirations for this trend is that a variety of specific mental phenomena, like searching, comparing, understanding and reading are involved. These cases may exemplify any of the phenomena at issue without being in any particular type of conscious state however; consciousness may be a more important aspect of the mind than is supposed. In order to understand consciousness one would benefit from developing a more eclectic intellectual style. Consciousness is, as proposed by almost everyone except the reductionists, a truly mysterious concept. Its study and dissection merits a multidisciplinary approach. Waving this multidisciplinary flag has positively enlarged the discussion and neurologists, psychiatrists, mathematicians, and so on, have moved to the philosophy of mind arena, first with caution and now with a more powerful voice.

Identifying what we mean by consciousness is a first step and the link between consciousness and some other mental activity, e.g., awareness, memory, executive functioning, etc., is a logical step. Knowledge has four necessary conditions: It must be justifiable, It must be true, It must be believable, and It must rules out counter-examples.

***Conclusions:*** Thinking while attempting to find a model, i.e., to describe a domain of familiar objects behaving in familiar ways such that we can see how the phenomena to be explained would arise if they consisted of this sort of thing. Such a model is accompanied by a commentary, which qualifies or limits the analogy between the domain of familiar objects and those being posted by the thinking. The commentary distinguishes, in effect, between those aspects of the model that actually represent some aspect of the phenomena being modeled and those aspects of the model that are simply artifacts of the modelling process itself. This sense of model is mental model accounts of thinking in psychology or cognitive anthropology.

By definition, a lie is a dishonestly made statement. It is a willful misrepresentation, in one's statement, of one's beliefs. Both a truthful person and a liar could hold false beliefs. We should not uncritically regard an untruthfully made statement as an untrue statement, or a truthfully made statement as a true statement. The only instance when a lie is necessarily false is when the liar's corresponding belief that was distorted was true. In other instances, the lie could be either true or false. Therefore, a lie is not necessarily a false statement.

Should it be said that I am using a word whose meaning I don't know, and so am talking nonsense?--Say what you choose, so long as it does not prevent you from seeing the facts, and when you see them there is a good deal that you will not say. I then thought: what is the use of studying while not thinking for yourself; if all that it does for you is to enable you to talk with some plausibility about some abstruse questions of logic etc., and if it does not improve your thinking about the important questions of everyday life, if it does not make you more conscientious than any, that is like journalist in the use of the dangerous phrases such people use for their own ends.

You see, I know that it's difficult to think well about 'certainty', 'probability', 'perception' etc. but it is, if possible, still more difficult to think, or try to think, really honestly about your life and other people's lives.

### *Leadership versus Managerial's Duties and Styles*

There is a distinction between the intelligence of the hedgehog which knows one big thing and the intelligence of the fox which knows many little things. Hedgehogs fit what they learn into a world view. Foxes improvise explanations case by case.

Leadership is the ability to inspire confidence and support among the people who are needed to achieve organizational goals. Leadership has been defined in many ways. Several other representative definitions of leadership are as follows:

- Interpersonal influence, directed through communication towards goal attainment.
- The influential increment over and above mechanical compliance with direction and orders.
- An act that causes others to act or respond in a shared direction.
- The art of influencing people by persuasion or example to follow a line of action.
- The principal of dynamic force that motivates and co-ordinates the organization in the accomplishment of its objectives.
- A willingness to take responsibilities and accountabilities.

A major point about leadership is that it is not found only among people in high level positions. Leadership is needed at all levels in an organization and can be practiced to some extent even by a person not assigned to a formal leadership position.

To understand leadership it is important to grasp the difference between leadership and management. We get a clue from the standard conceptualization of the functions of management: planning, organizing, directing, and controlling.

Leading is a major part of a manager's job, yet a manager must also plan, organize, and control. Broadly speaking, leadership deals with interpersonal aspects of manager's job, whereas planning, organizing, and controlling deal with the administrative aspects. Leadership deals with the change, inspiration, motivation, and influence.

The following set contains a stereotype of the difference between management and leadership as is the case with most stereotypes, the differences tend to be exaggerated: {(Leader, Manager)} = { (Does the right things, Does things right), (Visionary, Rational), (Passionate, Business like), (Creative, Persistent), (Inspiring Innovative, Tough Minded), (Courageous, Analytical Structured), (Imaginative, Deliberative), (Experimental, Stabilizing), (Shares Knowledge, Centralizes Knowledge), (Trusting, Guarded), (Warm and Radiant, Cool and Reserved), (Expresses Humility, Rarely admits to being wrong), (Initiator, Implementer)}

Following are several key distinctions between management and leadership:

- Management is more formal and scientific than leadership. It relies on universal skills such as planning, budgeting and controlling. Management is an explicit set of tools and techniques, based reasoning and testing, that can be used in a variety of situations.
- Leadership in contrast to management involves having a vision of what the organization can become and mobilizing people to accomplish it.
- Leadership requires eliciting cooperation from and teamwork from a large network of people and keeping the people in that network motivated, using every manner of persuasion.
- Leadership produces change, often to a dramatic degree, such as spearheading the launch of a new product or opening a new market for an old product. Management is more likely to produce a degree of predictability and order.

- Top level leaders are likely to transform their organizations, whereas top level managers just manage (or maintain organizations.)
- A leader creates a vision (i.e., a loft goal) to direct the organization. In contrast the key function of the manager is to implement the vision. The manager and his or her team thus choose the means to achieve the end that the leader formulates.

If these views are to be taken to their extreme, the leader is an inspirational figure and the manager is a stodgy bureaucrat mired in the status quo. But we must be careful not to downplay the importance of management. Effective leaders have to be good managers themselves, or be supported by effective managers. A germane example is the inspirational entrepreneur who is preoccupied with motivating employees and captivating customers that the internal administration is neglected. As a results costs sky rocket beyond income, and such matters as funding the employee pension plan and paying bills and taxes on time are overlooked. In short the difference between leadership and management is one of emphasis. Effective leaders also manage, effective managers also lead.

Satisfatction of Leaders: The type of satisfactions that you might obtain from being a formal leader depends on your particular leadership position. Factors such as the amount of money you are paid and the type of people in your group influences your satisfaction. There are seven sources of satisfaction that leaders often experience.

1. A feeling of power and prestige: Being a leader automatically grants you some power. Prestige is forthcoming because many people think highly of people who are leaders. In many organizations, top-level leaders are addressed as Mr., Mrs., or Ms., whereas lower-ranking people are referred to by their surnames.
2. A chance to help others grow and develop: A leader works directly with people, often teaching them job skills, serving as a mentor, and listening to personal problems. Part of a leader's job is to help other people become managers and leaders. A leader often feels as much of a "people helper" as does a human resources manager or a counsellor.
3. High income: Leaders, in general, receive higher pay than team members, and executive leaders in major business corporations typically earn several million dollars per year. A handful of business executives receive compensation of over

$100 million per year. If money is an important motivator or satisfier, being a leader has a built-in satisfaction. In some situations a team leader earns virtually the same amount of money as other team members. Occupying a leadership position, however, is a starting point on the path to high-paying leadership positions.

4. Respect and status: A leader frequently receives respect from group members. He or she also enjoys a higher status than people who are not occupying a leadership role. Status accompanies being appointed to a leadership position on or off the job. When an individual's personal qualifications match the position, his or her status is even higher.
5. Good opportunities for advancement: Once you become a leader, your advancement opportunities increase. Obtaining a leadership position is a vital first step for career advancement in many organizations. Staff or individual contributor positions help broaden a person's professional experience, but most executives rise through a managerial path.
6. A feeling of "being in on" things: A side benefit of being a leader is that you receive more inside information. For instance, as a manager you are invited to attend management meetings. In those meetings you are given information not passed along to individual contributors. One such tidbit might be plans for expansion or downsizing.
7. An opportunity to control money and other resources: A leader is often in the position of helping to prepare a department budget and authorize expenses. Even though you cannot spend this money personally, knowing that your judgment on financial matters is trusted does provide some satisfaction. Many leaders in both private and public organizations control annual budgets of several million dollars.

Dissatisfaction and Frustrations of Leaders: About one out of ten people in the work force is classified as a supervisor, administrator, or manager. Not every one of these people is a true leader. Yet the problems these people experience often stem from the leadership portions of their job. Many individual contributors refuse to accept a leadership role because of the frustrations they have seen leaders endure. The frustrations experienced by a wide range of people in leadership roles revolve around the problems described next.

1. Too much uncompensated overtime: People in leadership jobs are usually 'expected to work longer hours than other employees. Such unpaid hours are called casual overtime. People in organizational leadership positions typically spend about fifty-five hours per week working. During peak periods of peak demands, this figure can surge to eighty hours per week.
2. Too many "headaches.": It would take several pages to list all the potential problems leaders face. Being a leader is a good way to discover the validity of Murphy's Law: "If anything can go wrong, it will." A leader is subject to a batch of problems involving people and things. Many people find that a leadership position is a source of stress, and many managers experience burnout.
3. Not enough authority to carry out responsibility: People in managerial positions complain repeatedly that they are held responsible for things over which they have little control. As a leader, you might be expected to work with an ill-performing team member, yet you lack the power to fire him or her. Or you might be expected to produce high-quality service with too small a staff and no authority to become fully staffed.
4. Loneliness: As Secretary of State and former five-star general Colin Powell says, "Command is lonely." The higher you rise as a leader, the lonelier you will be in a certain sense. Leadership limits the number of people in whom you can confide. It is awkward to confide negative feelings about your employer to a team member. It is equally awkward to complain about one group member to another. Some people in leadership positions feel lonely because they miss being "one of the gang."
5. Too many problems involving people: A major frustration facing a leader is the number of human resources problems requiring action. The lower your Leadership position, the more such problems you face. For example, the office supervisor spends more time dealing with problem employees than does the chief information officer.
6. Too much organizational politics: People at all levels of an organization, from the office assistant to the chairperson of the board, must be aware of political factors. Yet you can avoid politics more easily as an individual contributor than you can as a leader. As a leader you have to engage in political byplay from three directions: below, sideways, and upward. Political

tactics such as forming alliances and coalitions are a necessary part of a leader's role. Another troublesome aspect of organizational politics is that there are people lurking to take you out of the game, particularly if you are changing the status quo. These enemies within might attack you directly in an attempt to shift the issue to your character and style and avoid discussing the changes you are attempting to implement.

7. The pursuit of conflicting goals: A major challenge leader's face is to navigate among conflicting goals. The central theme of these dilemmas is attempting to grant others the authority to act independently, yet still getting them aligned or pulling together for a common purpose.

***Skill Development in Leadership:*** Leader characteristics and traits refers to the inner qualities, such as self-confidence and problem-solving ability, that help a leader function effectively in many situations. Leader behaviour and style refers to the activities engaged in by the leader, including his or her characteristic approach, that relate to his or her effectiveness. A leader who frequently coaches group members and practices participative leadership, for example, might be effective in many circumstances.

***Creative Thinking:*** Many effective leaders are creative in the sense that they arrive at imaginative and original solutions to complex solutions. Creative ability lies on a continuum, with some leaders being more creative than others. At one end the creative continuum are business leaders who think of innovative products and services. At the middle of the creativity continuum are leaders who explore imaginative-but not break through-solutions to organizational problems. At the low end of creativity continuum are leaders who inspire group members to push forward with standard solutions to organizational problems.

Creativity is such an important aspect of the leaders role in the modern organization that the development of creative-problem solving skills. An important part of becoming more creative involves understanding the stages involved in creativity, which is generally defined as the production of novel and useful ideas. An attempt has been made to understand creativity more specifically as it pertains to the workplace. Organizational creativity is the creation of a valuable, useful new product, service, idea, procedure, or process by individuals working together in a complex social system.

***Opportunity or Problem Recognition:*** A person discovers that a new opportunity exists or a problem needs resolution. Thirty-five years ago an entrepreneurial leader, Robert Cowan, recognized a new opportunity and asked, "Why do business meetings have to be conducted in person? Why can't they connect through television images?"

***Immersion:*** The individual concentrates on the problem and becomes immersed in it. He or she will recall and collect information that seems relevant, dreaming up alternatives without refining or evaluating them.

***Incubation:*** The person keeps the assembled information in mind for: a while. He or she does not appear to be working on the problem actively; however, the subconscious mind is still engaged. While the information is simmering it is being arranged into meaningful new patterns.

***Insight:*** The problem-conquering solution flashes into the person's mind at an unexpected time, such as on the verge of sleep, during a shower, or while running. Insight is also called the Aha! experience: All of a sudden some-thing clicks. At one point Cowan suddenly thought of forming a teleconferencing business to exploit the potential of his idea.

***Verification and Application:*** The individual sets out to prove that the creative solution has merit. Verification procedures include gathering supporting evidence, using logical persuasion, and experimenting with new ideas. Businesspeople typically follow the same five steps of creative thought that inventors do. Even though creativity usually follows the same steps, it is not a mechanical process that can be turned on and off. Much of creativity is intricately woven into a person's intellect and personality. Furthermore, creativity varies among individuals, and creative people themselves have peaks and valleys in their creativity. Overcoming traditional sequential thinking is so important to creative thinking that the process has been characterized in several different ways. Listed next are five concepts of creative thinking. These concepts have much in common and can be considered variations of the same theme. Distinguishing among them is not nearly as important as recognizing that they all carry the same message: Creative thinking requires nontraditional thinking.

- A creative person thinks outside the box: A box in this sense is a category that confines and restricts thinking. Because you are confined to a box, you do not see opportunities outside the box. For example, if an insurance executive thinks that health insurance is only for people, he or she might miss out on the growing market for domestic animal health insurance. Inside the accompanying box insert, you will find several business examples of thinking outside the box.

- People who are not creative suffer from "hardening of the categories.": A low-creativity individual thinks categorically: "Only men can drive bulldozers"; "Only women can work in child care Centres as caregivers"; "Passenger vehicles can only be sold by having potential customers visit a dealer showroom or outdoor lot.
- To be creative one must develop new paradigms: A paradigm is a model or framework. An example of a quality-inhibiting paradigm is that suppliers should be treated shabbily because they need the company more than the company needs them. In reality, creative companies form partnerships of mutual respect with suppliers. Developing a new paradigm can also benefit an organization by giving a business a new twist, thus leading to a new source of revenues. eBay established a new paradigm for a retailer because it functions as a broker, thereby eliminating the expense of inventory, handling, and shipping.
- Creativity requires overcoming traditional mental sets: A traditional mental set is a conventional way of looking at things and placing them in familiar categories. Overcoming traditional wisdom refers to the same idea. One traditional mental set is that the only way for people to obtain the death benefit on their life insurance policy is to die. Several years ago an investor initiated the concept of viatical settlement, in which a person with a terminal illness sells his or her policy to an investor for about 80 percent of the policy value. When the person dies, the investor receives the death benefit from the insurance company. The sooner the person dies the better the return on the investment, for the person who buys the policy from the ailing or aging person.

Viatical settlements grew out of the AIDS epidemic, as many young people with no dependents and meager savings were faced with overwhelming medical bills.

Today the concept has been extended to cancer patients and missing home residents who prefer to cash in life insurance policies rather than cash in other assets. In the present form of viatical settlements, sellers and buyers are matched by a "living benefits" broker.

- Creative people engage in lateral thinking in addition to vertical thinking: Vertical thinking is an analytical, logical process that results in few answers. The vertical, or critical, thinker is looking for the one best solution to a problem, much like solving an equation. In contrast, lateral thinking spreads out to find many different solutions to a problem. The vertical-thinking leader attempts to find the best possible return on investment strictly in financial terms. The lateral-, or creative-thinking, leader might say, "A financial return on investment is desirable. But let's not restrict our thinking. Customer loyalty, quality, being a good corporate citizen and job satisfaction are also important returns on investment."

A good example of such lateral thinking in solving both a scientific and business problem took place in the communications industry. A problem with many communications satellites is that the satellite is so far away. Also, buildings and terrain block many of the signals from tower-based systems.

As with other types of personal development, leadership development requires considerable self-discipline. In the present context, self-discipline is mobilizing one's effort and energy to stay focused on attaining an important goal. Self-discipline is required for most forms of leadership development. Assume, for example, that a leader is convinced that active listening is an important leadership behaviour. The leader reads about active listening and also attends a workshop on the subject. After the reading and workshop are completed, the leader will need to concentrate diligently in order to remember to listen actively. Self-discipline is particularly necessary because the pressures of everyday activities often divert a person's attention from personal development.

Self-discipline plays an important role in the continuous monitoring of one's behaviour to ensure that needed self-development occurs. After one identifies a developmental need, it is necessary to periodically review whether one is making the necessary improvements. Assume that a person recognizes the developmental need to become a more colourful communicator as a way of enhancing charisma. The person would need self-discipline to make the conscious effort to communicate more colourfully when placed in an appropriate situation. People with dynamic personalities will rise to the top. These leaders will make institutions even flatter, simpler, and faster moving, but they will not hunger for the perks of leadership.

A basic principle of learning is that practice is necessary to develop and improve skills.

## Cognitive Decision Making

Recognition is an understanding by the "similarity process" of mind in the behavioural and cognitive decision process. Decision-making is the central activity for both leaders and managers. Managing and leading are not the same. The manager's responsibility is "To Do the Things Right", and the leader's responsibility is "To Do the Right Things". Leaders have a goal of creating an innovative environment that will of necessity produce mistakes, and managers have a goal of honing their craft to reduce and eliminate mistakes and waste. The assumption that cognition can be studied by looking exclusively at what goes on in the brain has undergone considerable criticism.

A diverse and growing number of researchers claim that an organism's cognitive abilities are partly constituted by prior and posterior conception, action, environmental manipulation and intricate couplings that spread the causality across organisms and structures in their physical, social, and technological environments. Research in this area is interdisciplinary in nature, drawing on fields such as philosophy, cognitive science, developmental studies, neuroscience, artificial intelligence, simulation science and robotics. Much of it is inspired by or complemented by the insights of thinkers in the phenomenological (i.e., subjectivity rather than objectivity) area that emphasize the ways in which experience and thought are structured by bodily constraints and environmental interaction.

***Cognitive decision theory:*** This is an empirical, descriptive, non-statistical, context related process theory and considers a "decision" as a decision making process very similar to a problem solving process, which is a special, time consuming, context dependent information processing process. The human decision maker is considered in analogy to a computer system, i.e. data and knowledge has to be fed into the system. This and the type of information processing performed determine the outcome.

***The connectionist paradigm:*** Neural nets also model living (human) information processing, but on a more physical and not so functional level. Information is processed from input via hidden to output layers of artificial neurons. One of the differences between the "cognitive" and the "neural" decision model is, that the latter includes explicitly and even concentrates on learning and on topological features, while the former does not exclude learning but does not consider it as one of the points of major interest.

The most important issue for the strategic decision maker is the outcome of decisions. Clearly, what we think or feel is not relevant to the physical world, however they influence on our value judgment in our goal setting. The decision maker's model is based one readily measurable — either from actual decisions or from surveys polls, or interactive simulations. Statistical techniques deal with the validity, applicability, and scalability of such information. This information can then be used to rigorously model the decisions as a function of perceived conditions and personal tastes, values, and preferences. Qualitative Choice Theory is one of the more popular approaches in that it is easily calibrated and parameterized, is robust, and has the feature that allows "analogous" decision data to be applied to new situations.

The OR/MS/DS/SS modelling process aims at structuring complex problems, exploring different perspectives and facilitating participation and engagement of the decision maker with the OR/MS/DS/SS analyst. The success in OR/MS/DS/SS modelling requires both quantitative (hard) and qualitative (soft) data together in a single engagement. The real-world decision problems exist within a complex organizational context that has both social and personal dimensions. Moreover various stages of the OR/MS/DS/SS modelling process, from the initial stage of understanding the problem, to the final stage of implementing a good strategy, require a different and appropriate method and technique for a particular decision problem. Unfortunately, the devolution of OR/MS/DS/SS has been from a concern with real-world problems to one with applications of mathematical techniques. Much published research in OR/MS/DS/SS is unengaged and focused on decision mathematics or optimization. That is, most papers published in leading OR/MS/DS/SS journals take little or no account of how their finding might be used in practice, nor do they express much concern about this issue.

The management scientist is not the decision maker. The decision maker must incorporate other necessary perspectives including the organizational, environmental, conflicting, historical, political, dynamic, and psychological aspects of the problem into the management scientist's analytical model. For example, he/she must know how to remove any "invisible" barriers (also called "Chinese walls"), between departments in an organization.

One must be cautioned that the way we choose to see the world (i.e., modelling) creates the world we see. When describing reality, you must be careful not to weave in your own wishful views. For example, describing nature as if it has human traits is a modelling process called the "pathetic fallacy." It has been found that, so far as we can discover, nature is indifferent to our values and can only be understood by ignoring our notions of good and bad. The Universe may have a purpose, but nothing we know suggests that this purpose has any similarity to ours.

For example, history does not have any purpose, as Hegel's metaphysics claimed it has. However, the purpose of studying history is to predict the future. The following figure illustrates the two extreme worldviews painted so far by the organized religions, morality, culture, and metaphysics which are collections of linguistic, and other kinds of logical fallacies. The Pythagorean' view of the world was to study the world as an external entity. This gave rise to the Western scientific and analytical tradition. However, the mysticism view of Eastern world, as expressed, e.g., by I Ching (i.e., Book of Changes), is based on the attitude that man is inseparable from the world.

We deplete nature's natural resources by using or even abusing them up to their limits. This reality must constantly remind us that there is a place for man somewhere between these extreme views. In abusing nature, Wally Hickel, a former governor of Alaska, defended and justified his decisions by believing that "you can't just let nature run wild." Sustainability requires living within the regenerative capacity of the biosphere. However, human demands have already exceeded the biosphere's regenerative capacity.

***Man can be programmed:*** Anyone who has read Étienne de la Boétie, Margaret Mead, or John Dewey will recognize that we are all programmed by our cultures. We accept as unfailing truisms that are not really truths but leading us into folly. The "Dominator Paradigm" recognized the dominants and domineering world view by the power of the sword (Arm force), the flag (Nationalism), and the cross (Religion).

The procedure for domination invariably followed the three steps:

1. Learn the dominant myths of the target people and, in the process, gain their trust.
2. Find the gaps or superstitions in their beliefs.
3. Either replace the superstitions or augment them with facts that redirect the target group's perceptions and allegiance.

The program started with the Jewish Creation Myth that the universe was created for man. The Greeks extended the concept with the dictum that "man is the measure of all things." The Inquisition made heresy to think otherwise and burned over a million witches at the stake (mostly beautiful young women) to impress it on society. Columbus started the spread of the Dominator Paradigm world wide during the age of "discovery" and colonization.

Adam Smith started the trend to make it the ethical base of our Euro-American culture with his concept that by "self-interest" and an "unseen hand" economics would solve all of our social and ethical problems. USA has achieved its commercial and financial supremacy under a regime of private ownership. It conquered the wilderness, built our railroads, our factories, our public utilities, gave us the telegraph, the telephone, the electric light, the automobile, the airplane, the radio and a higher standard of living for all the people than obtains anywhere else in the world. Not many great inventions ever came from a government-owned industry.

As Friedrich Nietzsche has said, "The task is to rediscover beneath all flattering colours and make-up the frightful prototext *homo natura*, which means to translate man back into nature; to become master over the many vain and overly enthusiastic interpretations and connotations that have so far been scrawled and painted over that eternal basic text of *homo natura*."

At the basis of the whole modern view of the world lies the illusion that the so-called laws of nature are the interpretations of natural phenomena. This does not take a lawgiver into discount.

Any general statements such as "everyone will have some kind of middle life crisis, such as depression, during their middle-age or at a later stage in his/her life time" may not be correct. Humans have no nature to be discovered, but they do have history. It was necessary for humans to abandon all instincts to become a member of society by following its norms and customs.

It is impossible to overlook the extent to which civilization is built upon a renunciation of instinct. Almost nothing is left in humans to be called instinct, common sense, or other similar names. For example, common sense is the collection of prejudices acquired usually by age 18. Unfortunately, there have been many useless axiomatic models of human nature in the Western culture, including the works of Locke, Berkeley, Hume, Mill, Malthus, Quesnay and, of course, Jeremy Bentham and its Felicific Calculus.

With regard to the pathetic fallacy process, I think it can only be expected that humans will describe nature "as-if" it has human traits. As humans, we are limited to viewing the world from our own perspective based on experiences, knowledge, language, etc. When we don't actually know how to describe something that we don't fully understand (nature being an example), we express an idea/thought in terms that are familiar to us. The danger comes in an individual's interpretation of the word. For example, the word aggressive may have either a negative connotation (pushy, overbearing) or a positive connotation (powerful, ambitious). Second, with regard to common sense, instinct, and intuition, I do not believe that science should be used in an attempt to explain how these "skills" are applied by people in understanding something. I believe these "skills" are positively non-scientific. Isn't that the point? Even though I will not attempt to classify or define these concepts, I believe that they exist on an emotional level and therefore cannot be explained by science.

***Social Cognitive:*** Social Cognitive (SC) is the property of a systems whereby the collective behaviours of entities interacting locally with their environment cause coherent functional global patterns to emerge. SC provides a basis with which it is possible to explore collective and distributed decision making without centralized control or the provision of a global model. To tackle the formation of a coherent social collective intelligence from individual behaviours, it must consider concepts related to self-organization, and the social bounds. It also includes the role played not only by the environmental media as a driving force for societal learning, but also by positive and negative feedback produced by the interactions among agents. The results will be the collective adaptation of a social community to its dynamic cultural environment.

***Intuition is a mode of fast thinking:*** Intuitive state is a rapid selective cycling and recycling gathering information and ideas from one's memory and applying value to them. This is done so fast that one cannot have a clear record of what is happening. Intuition may not always help you in finding the right answer to even a simple question. Suppose you are filling two ice cube trays with water, boiling hot in one, cold in the other, and placing both in a freezer. The question is: Which tray turns to ice quicker?" If your answer is the tray with boiling hot water, then you are right. Why? How could you resolve this apparent isolation of the laws of thermodynamics.

Why do different managers make different decisions for a given problem? Why are we all different? Because we all have different experiences and unique backgrounds. Every experience in life shapes our mind in a unique way. Knowledge is a biological phenomenon. Humans experience the world in their own ways. Through their internal processes, each human engages in a creative relationship with the external world, bringing forth a myriad of different models.

The history of science shows how weak common sense, instinct, and intuition can be taken as guides to our understanding. For example, intuition is a truncated logic and it is never clearly justified on a scientific ground.

***Do not Take a "Model" as the "Reality":*** A model is not a property of the reality, but of its description. Models are useful but they all certainly come with their own baggage of simplification, and theorization of reality, however, the price for not modelling is eternal obfuscation. A model could be as good as "virtual reality", however, it is never the "real reality." Unfortunately, in many cases, modelling becomes an end rather than a means. The modeler spends so much time in creating the model that he/she falls in love with the model: the model becomes the reality. Do not take a "model" as the "reality." Unfortunately, many do. There are much more models in the world than realities. For a successful decision, reality must take precedence over the decision model, for reality cannot be fooled.

For example, the above image is only a model of a particular type of pipe from a particular point of view. You cannot put tobacco in it. The Pooh's Little Instruction Book says "When you are a Bear of Very Little Brain, and Think of Things, you find sometimes that a Thing which seemed very Thingish inside you is quite different when it gets out into the open and has other people looking at it."

***Effective Communication Skills:*** The management scientist must know that his/her success depends on effective communication skills (i.e., making common what is individually experienced). Proper focus on communicating the results and recommended course of action obtained by the modeler is needed. This helps to achieve a consensus concerning an acceptable course of action. Finally, be aware that in many historical cases humans invented some models of reality in order to discard the reality itself. For example, in some religious models, a better world after death is created to discard this world.

***Human Performance and New Technology:*** Human performance is the key to unlocking markets and organizations. New technologies open many options for what we do and how and where we do it. They allow new processes, new structures, new strategies.

But the good decision makers will build their plans on a simple platform. Human performance is at the core of business performance. They will put the human issues front and centre of their strategies and their execution plans, and they will bring rigor, discipline, and mathematical modelling to match the way they develop and apply technology.

Qualitative considerations such as re-organization and refinements are as important as quantitative factors in an effective strategic decision-making process. The main question is How to merge different mental models within an organization a shared mental model? The progression in that direction might be one of the following two possibilities:

1. if the organization contains conflicting mental models it will not move far, resulting in political infighting.
2. if the organization contains a single mental model (i.e., consensus) it can move in that direction until it comes up against the reality when it requires an adaptation.

Over time, however, the organization whose mental models most closely match the reality will survive, while others fail.

***Cognitive Decision Science:*** The cognitive decision science concerns the nature of the decision maker intentions. Often intentions are entities of thinking, which are introspectively accessible to the conscious mind, and causally efficacious in the production of implementation of the decision, i.e., intentional realism of the decision. However, intentions might be conceived of as abstract patterns discernable in the behaviour of organisms, which are ascribed as instruments of prediction, without much awareness of internal representational machinery responsible for the implantation of our decisions. The third model of cognitive decision science rightly considers both processes: our choices and the subjectivity of re-evaluation of all values as the measure of intentional and our final decision.

Cognitive Impairments Factors: The following factors may impair our decision making process performance including speed, reasoning, planning, judgment, impulse control, temper control, perception, awareness, attention, language, learning, memory and timing.

- Disorganization: Difficulties in planning, organization, sequencing and prioritizing.
- Lack of Initiation: The initiation or starting of an activity, conversation or behaviour is often compromised.

- Fixed Mindedness: Perseverance or being fixed on a specific thought or action can occur when behaviours are inadequately regulated by the brain.
- Impulsivity: Some persons experience difficulties with impulse control and may develop problem behaviours such as irritability, temper outbursts, and acting without thinking.

### Behavioural Decision Making

Physical sciences are in general based on the cause-and-effect logic. Human's behaviours are, however based on motives. There is always a motivation force generated by some causes and purposes that can tell why a person makes a particular decision, i.e., the Emotivisim School of thought.

Managers wish to motivate workers to exert effort. For example, there is large literature on the use of wages and monetary incentives for this purpose, but in practice the "honor" or "prestige" of an award can be a significant motivator as well, unless the award is given so often that its prestige is diluted. The main focus must be on management of the reputation of an award that may or may not have a fixed monetary component but how to manage the award over time.

The cardinal aim of modelling human behaviour is to model a business process that increases workforce enthusiasm considering all aspects of human behaviour including group dynamics, project work climate, and organizational culture.

A Behavioural Decision Making Classification: Decision making types may allows for only three unique systems of making decisions:

1. Individualism — which access inequity, relishes competition and identifies with the rights and power of the individual.
2. Collaboration — which treats all men as equally important, exalts collaborative efforts and identifies with unlimited democracy.
3. Power and authority — which respects power and identifies with controlling authority.

An organizational system based upon the "nature of man" blends the three possible systems into a harmonious unity, accepting that any one of the systems standing alone is both unstable and ineffective.

The universality of the three decision-making processes seems obvious. Everyone wants to be free to make his or her own decisions. At the same time, everyone needs the companionship and the sense of belonging that comes with being part of a group, and everyone fears the absolute solitude of unrestricted freedom. Finally, everyone wants to believe in something or someone, to conform his or her behaviour to some kind of authority, whether that authority comes internally from religious, political, or cultural values or externally from a leader in a hierarchy.

While it may seem obvious that everyone relies upon these three types of decision making, our political conversations often polarize into conflicts of two decision-making types, a battle of group consensus versus individual freedom. We have dogmas of the "left" and "right" or of "liberals" and "conservatives." Conforming to these dogmas is a serious blunder. Dogmas of the left or right fail to recognize the role that authority plays in balancing the interests of the group and the individual. Without a balance of all three types, organizations can quickly become unstable and ineffective. Organizations use decision-making processes that vary from elaborate designs with numerous decision points to relatively simple procedures. In each case, the process relies on a mix of the three types of decision making inherent in human thinking:

- Individual decision making based upon self interest,
- Group decision making based upon consensus, and
- Authoritative decision making based upon values, rules and hierarchies. The organizations that succeed during both good times and bad times are those that maintain an effective balance between these three ways of choosing a course of action. In fact, what we regard as a "civil" society is one that balances the three decision-making methods in a constant tug of war. As a result, modern "civil" societies facilitate the creation of balanced organizations.

There have been two extreme approaches to modelling human behaviour. The simple models emphasis on "rational persons," while other's emphasis is on the fact that people have much more complex motivations, both individually and collectively, especially in herd-instinct, or malicious-intent situations.

An integrative descriptive model for human behaviour must consider all aspects of decision-making factors including use the economic, sociology, law, and social psychology. This might be achieved at three levels: the individual, the organization, and the society, with interactions among the three. The interactions among these three levels include flows of information, and resources, and within each system of values and decision structures. These two kinds of flows shape the interactions between these three levels.

Facing Unfavorable Outcome of a Good Decision: Often an unfavorable outcome of a good decision leads individuals to switch away from that decision due to negative emotional responses to the outcome. Negative emotional reactions led many to abandon the option that they recalled as having been more successful in the past and which they expected to perform better in the future. They focus on their affective reactions rather than beliefs about the earlier disappointing outcome. Those individuals with a general tendency to focus on their needed cognition are less likely to switch away from the better option following a disappointing outcome. It is also likely that an emotional reaction to a negative outcome lead people to switch away from the options that they believe might be successful on the next occasion.

***Feeling versus Being:*** Feeling is different form being. Feeling is the mind response while being is the bodily manifestation of the same thing. For example, feeling of being sad is an emotion, which is not measurable, however, being sad, is a bodily response and therefore, the degree of being sadness is measurable on numerical scales by the appropriate psychometric instruments.

***Conflict Is a Part of Life:*** People and businesses suffer when conflict is ignored and not managed properly. Relationships are strained, productivity diminishes, and destruction can be the ultimate result. Many of us are so averse to conflict that we practice appeasement at any price, while others cling to adversarial approaches, which can escalate all the costs of settling differences. These behaviours are often the spawning ground for further conflict. They occur because we do not know about how to effectively use the array of possibilities that exist for successful conflict management. The OR/MS/DS/SS use of conflict modelling is in model-based decision support systems, i.e., the use of flexible, user-friendly software to build up systems of decision makers, set of options, and preferences. This facilitates rapid change in one's assumptions, and conditions among the participants.

Behavioural decision-making is to understand how people make decisions and how they can make the decision-making process more effective and efficient. A person could be very conservative, or perpetual in making any decision. The behaviour sciences are applicable to decision processes from both quantitative and qualitative viewpoints to improve a stronger foundation for making better decisions. The decision-maker's style and characteristics can be classified as: the thinker, the cowboy (snap and uncompromising), Machiavellian (ends justifies the means), the historian (how others did it), the cautious (even nervous), etc.

***Decision-Making versus Habits:*** Decision-making involves reaching a conclusion, which implies deliberation and thought and suggests a conscious act. While a natural reaction or unconscious act would be labeled as habit, reflex act, or impulsive act, or habit which is, unfortunately the Centre of gravity when we want to start the decision-making process. The Manager versus the Leader: A manager is defined, as a person who decides on "how to do the things right" while a leader is concerned with "how to do the right things.

***Power and the Leadership:*** Strategy implementation is a political process that involves bargaining, persuasion, and confrontation among actors who divide power.

People in power usually want to stay there. And one way they think they can do this is by enforcing rigid adherence to a set of principles that they believe are responsible for their organization's success. By requiring employees to abide by these superstitions — better known as company policies — rather than examining the facts, they build organizations that appear streamlined. In fact, they are doomed.

There is no such thing as "organizational behaviour;" it is the behaviour of the people in the organization. It is impossible to understand the decision-maker's behaviour in organizational situations where conflict exists without considering the role of power. Power has a major impact on information, uncertainty, and resource dependency since there is competition among organization's members for scarce resources. There is a big difference between management and leadership: while management works in the system, leadership works on the system. If one is able enough to accurately define all three of these parameters; Task, Time, and Resources, then one is able to deal with the decision-making modelling process. The very essence of leadership is that you have to have vision for these parameters. You can't blow an uncertain trumpet.

Leadership is defined as, "the quality of a leader, and the capacity to lead." It can also be defined as setting the example. Whether they realize it or not, a given staff will look to the leader to set the trend in the workplace. So what trend are you setting? There is a reason the CEO of a multi-billion dollar international soft drink company spends one day a month delivering cases of soda via delivery truck and wheeled dolly. Because he's smart and successful, and his staff is watching him like a hawk. They can't help but copy and respect the CEO's sense of enthusiasm and commitment to what the business is really all about—getting product into customer's hands. The Challenge of Leadership is mainly its human-side. The leader is to be strong, but not rude; kind, but not weak; bold, but not a bully; thoughtful, but not lazy; humble, but not timid; proud, but not arrogant; and have a sense of humor, without folly.

Before the leaders can inspire with emotion, they must be swamped with it themselves. Before they can move the tears of others, their own must flow. To convince others, they must themselves believe.

***Evil and Unethical Decisions:*** One must certainly be aware of the big difference between unethical and evil decisions. The CEO for an internationally known tire company signs off on the production of tires that he knows are likely to disintegrate under certain conditions. Even with such knowledge, he makes it clear that this information is not to be publicized and approves production and sales of the tires. Decide whether such a decision is an evil or unethical one? What about this scenario? An administrator in a fascist country followed the orders of his superior and signed off on the death of thousands of innocent men, women and children. He never personally killed any of those people himself nor would he. Without integrity, no company can have positive word of mouth.

***Reason Is Not the Supreme Judge:*** The critical and postmodern organization theorists have already built their case against Reason. They see reason as "disciplinary knowledge" in modern organizations because it constrains the natural autonomy of the individual. This view, all of the social sciences are seen as knowledge structures used in domination. Sociology, social work, law, psychology, and most certainly management and organization theory are implicated. Just as psychology is used to persuade the individual to adjust to (thus accept) the external world, theories of leadership and organization are used to develop discourses and classification schemes that reproduce systems of power. By rejecting Western cultural history, positioning the "naturalness" of the individual, and assuming all discipline is oppressive power generated by knowledge, critical organization theory and postmodern organization theory elevate individualism, although only implicitly, to the role of their supreme value.

Instrumental reasoning has been used successfully in science to make our world manageable. For its utilitarian characteristic, the instrumental reasoning is the supreme judge in any scientific field. It is possible to use reason to describe everything scientifically, but it would make no sense; it would be without meaning, as if you described a Beethoven ninth symphony as a variation of wave pressure.

***Dealing with People:*** While senior management formulate clear strategies to achieve the essential fit between internal strengths and weaknesses and external threats and opportunities. However, strategy implementation is a social process rooted in culture, involving common interest and integration. People react and adapt to environmental changes and constraints.

There are two ways to persuade people. The first is by using conventional rhetoric, which is what most managers are trained in. The other way to persuade people and ultimately a much more powerful way is by uniting an idea with an emotional appeal.

In any organization, it is a must for everyone to learn the ability to work with other people. Henry Ford used to say:

Coming together is a beginning;

Keeping together is progress;

Working together is success.

There are two different types of relationships among people namely the Frequent and Infrequent relationships. Negotiation is an effective tool for dealing with infrequent relationships. To have an effective negotiation one must separate the people from the problem, focus on interest (not taking positions), generate a variety of possibilities, and insist that the results be based on some objective numerable and measurable scales. For the ongoing relationships the strategies vary. The classical tactics are: carrots and sticks, tit-for-tat, and live-and-let-live.

Human abuse does not stem from a wanton exercise of power, rather, hurting people is a sign that we are still lacking power. Or it shows a sense of frustration in the face of this poverty. The blockage of self-developments is what lie behind abusive behaviour. Since whoever is dissatisfied with himself is continually ready for revenge and we others will be his victims. An eye for an eye will make the whole world go blind.

***Progressive Approach to Modelling:*** Modelling for decision making involves two distinct parties, one is the decision-maker and the other is the model-builder known as the analyst. The analyst is to assist the decision-maker in his/her decision-making process.

Therefore, the analyst must be equipped with more than a set of analytical methods.

Specialists in model building are often tempted to study a problem, and then go off in isolation to develop an elaborate mathematical model for use by the manager (i.e., the decision-maker). Unfortunately the manager may not understand this model and may either use it blindly or reject it entirely. The specialist may feel that the manager is too ignorant and unsophisticated to appreciate the model, while the manager may feel that the specialist lives in a dream world of unrealistic assumptions and irrelevant mathematical language.

Such miscommunication can be avoided if the manager works with the specialist to develop first a simple model that provides a crude but understandable analysis. After the manager has built up confidence in this model, additional detail and sophistication can be added, perhaps progressively only a bit at a time.

This process requires an investment of time on the part of the manager and sincere interest on the part of the specialist in solving the manager's real problem, rather than in creating and trying to explain sophisticated models. This progressive model building is often referred to as the bootstrapping approach and is the most important factor in determining successful implementation of a decision model. Moreover the bootstrapping approach simplifies otherwise the difficult task of model validating and verification processes.

***Resistance to Decisions:*** Progress is a nice word. But change is its motivator and change has its enemies. It is not so much that we are afraid of change or so in love with the old ways, but it is that place in between that we fear. It's like being between trapezes, there's nothing to hold on to. Any change, even a change for the better, is always accompanied by drawbacks and discomforts. Change is not made without inconvenience, even from worse to better. The most universal difficulties arise from people's fear of planned change.

People often oppose a proposed model merely because they have participated in planning it, or because it may have been planned by those whom they dislike. People resist changes. More accurately, they resist being changed by other people. Resistance can take the form of either open hostility or covert sabotage of decision-makers' efforts. Even the best designed strategy always fails if those who must carry it out refuse to do so. As Machiavelli wrote in The Prince "It must be remembered that there is nothing more difficult to plan, more uncertain of success, nor more dangerous to manage than the creation of a new order of things. For the initiator has the enmity of all who would profit by the preservation of the old institutions, and merely lukewarm defenders in those who would gain by the new ones."

***Incremental versus Optimal Changes:*** Optimal (i.e., the best) decisions are often used to justify sweeping organizational changes that may disrupt individual routines. One important value is the cooperation and morale that can develop when the members of the organization know that they are respected members of a productive organization. Noting this human-side of decision-making, many organizations use the goal-seeking approach rather than optimal decisions. This suggests that changes at any time be limited to a goal, which needs minor deviations from the current situation. This approach to decision-making is known as incrementalism, or the goal-seeking approach. For example, instead of maximizing profit, one may set the goal of achieving 10% increase in profit.

***Copping with the Major Changes: A Transitional Process :*** The responses of individuals will vary considerably not only from person to person, but also over time. By this we mean that a person will respond negatively to a change at one point, but perhaps have a different attitude to it at a later stage. However, there is a pattern in the response of an individual to change over a period of time. Obviously the more traumatic the change, the more pronounced will be the effect. The major changes at work can resemble other major changes, such as bereavement or marriage, in their effect on individuals. Often people going through such change progress through the following process, stage-by-stage:

- Immobilization
- Denial of change
- Incompetence
- Acceptance of reality
- Testing possibilities
- Search for meaning
- Integration.

The time taken to accept major changes fully can be as much as say, 18 months or even longer. However, an understanding of what is happening can often reduce the time needed to come to terms with change, and to fully adopt new ways of behaving. A leader's support and concern through the stages will also be critical for the individual team member faced with major change. Understanding of the process will also help the leader to deal with the individual in a way appropriate to the stage they are at.

### Leadership in a Diverse and Multicultural Environment

One must have a good sense of the importance of being multiculturally aware, knowledgeable, and skillful since demographic changes will continue at a rapid pace, making the need for these competencies more critical than ever.

These are prerequisites for top-level CEOs, and for all employees who influence others in the workplace, whether this influence is based on formal authority or informal norms. Being multiculturally competent can help every employee to get more out of every relationship in the workplace. Understanding both diversity and multiculturalism must focus on the complexity of culture, which plays a large role in both diversity and multiculturalism efforts. The development of multicultural awareness begins with an awareness of culturally learned conditions. The conditions include the following:

- Multicultural perspectives emphasize each group's similarities and differences at the same time.
- Multicultural perspectives are necessarily complex.
- Multicultural perspectives are dynamic for each person, place and time.

The inclusive multicultural perspective of emphasizing both similarities and differences has becoming the main focus on multicultural aspects of leading because of the inherent difficulties of measures of culture. It is easier to ignore culture or to limit the cultural perspective to either similarities or differences. Breaking this first rule of multiculturalism has resulted in false and inadequate/ incomplete choices.

The controversy over "political correctness" reflects the inadequate of this false dichotomy where both sides of the argument are wrong. The argument supporting an objectively "correct" view of each culture rightly protects the unique and different perspectives of each cultural group against insult but wrongly presumes that culture is defined by these objective guidelines.

The argument against political correctness rightly emphasizes the need to find common ground across cultures but wrongly presumes that cultural differences are unimportant. In order to escape from cultural encapsulation, leaders need to challenge the cultural bias of their own untested criteria. To leave our conditions untested or, worse yet, to be unaware of our culturally learned conditions, is not consistent with the standards of effective leadership.

The numbers of different country and cultural classifications available may create an overwhelming feeling of confusion about which one is "right". Instead of feeling overwhelmed, leaders who know that culture influences the conditions that individuals have as to what makes an effective leader should embrace the various aspects of culture as opportunities to educate themselves on the many dimensions of culture and what they mean for leaders in a multicultural environment. Multicultural development is a continuous learning process based on the following three stages of development:

1. The awareness includes conditions about cultural differences and similarities in behaviour, attitude, and values. Increased awareness provides more freedom of choice to those who become more aware of their own multiculturalism.
2. The knowledge expands the amount of facts and information about culturally learned conditions.
3. The skills apply effective and efficient action with people of different cultures based on the participants' clarified conditions and accurate knowledge.

Leaders need to be trained in awareness, knowledge, and skills to develop multicultural competency.

People differ in many ways. Ethnics and racial identity models provide a framework for understanding how people may differ in terms of their racial identity and the implications of those identifications. Leaders who are familiar with both their own identity and that of others will benefit in their interactions with others. Individuals also differ in terms of their intelligences and preferred learning style. Leaders who are more emotionally intelligent are more likely to find developing multicultural skills easier compared to leaders who score lower on emotional intelligence. Also, leaders who are more aware of their own learning style can better attend to the choices they make during the learning process. This information can also be used to help leaders step outside of the comfort zone of their learning style to help them see situations from other perspectives.

To help in exploring and understanding the formation of personal identity, one must consider the tripartite framework made up of three concentric circles representing universal, group, and individual levels of personal identity. Because we are all members of the human race, and belong to the species Homo sapiens, we share many similarities, and the universal level can be summed up with the statement, "All individuals are, in some respects, like all other individuals." Because all of us are born into a cultural matrix of beliefs, values, rules, and social practices, group-level factors influence us.

The group level of identity could be summarized by the following statement: "All individuals are, in some respects, like some other individuals." Some of the group-level factors are fixed and unchanging, e.g., race, gender, ability, age, while others are relatively non-fixed, e.g., education, socioeconomic status, marital status, geographic location. Moreover, individuals can belong to more than one cultural group, i.e., race, gender, and disability, some group identity can shift from one to the other depending on the situation.

The individual level of identity can best be summed up with the following statement: "All individuals are, in some way, like no other individuals." A holistic approach to understanding personal identity requires that we recognize all three levels: individual, group, and universal. Although the concentric circles may suggest a clear boundary, each level of identity must be viewed as permeable and ever changing in salience. In addition, even within a level of identity, multiple forces may be at work.

Conditions of Practice: "Practice makes perfect" has long been an accepted universal principle of learning. However, all practice may not be considered equal. Many issues have been researched that relate to conditions of pre-practice, practice, and post-practice and how they all relate to learning. Pre-practice conditions include attention advice which is providing information, independent of performance content, about the process or strategy that can be used to achieve an optimal learning outcome during training.

Providing intentional advice is like giving trainees a problem-solving, task-related strategy or schema to apply across similar task. It allows the trainees to know where to focus their attention during training. The intentional advice contributes to transfer of learning. This is likely because the type of learning encouraged by intentional advice leads to general strategies and rules that can be applied across a variety of job situations.

There is much preparatory work that must be done before training begins. The effectiveness of all training programs depends on a thorough needs assessment. All three levels: organizational, task, and individual are important either directly or indirectly to the development of leaders' multicultural awareness, knowledge, and skills. Training that does not transfer is wasted. Focusing on trainee characteristics, training design, and the work environment will not ensure the desired training results, but not considering these three factors will almost ensure that multicultural and diversity training fails.

Just as culture is complex but not chaotic, so should multicultural training be guided by a sequence of learning objectives that reflect the needs of both the leader and the multicultural context. Teaching multicultural leadership and communication should include any and all methods relevant to the multicultural context from the viewpoint of the culture that is being taught. Training designs needs to be comprehensive enough to include both culture-general and culture-specific perspectives. The developmental sequence from awareness to knowledge to skill provides an eclectic framework for organizing the content of multicultural training and a rationale for leader development in multicultural settings.

Regardless of whether conflict is the result of personal factors or organizational factors, and whether it results in positive or negative outcomes, it must be managed or it might likely lead to unintended consequences. The handling of conflict has been part of the management literature discussing five ways of dealing with conflict: domination, compromise, integration, avoidance, and suppression. A framework for classifying styles for handling interpersonal conflicts can be grouped into five types: forcing, withdrawing, smoothing, compromising, problem solving and the intentions and assertiveness.

Avoiding is a style low on both cooperativeness and assertiveness. It is a decision to take no action or to stay out of conflict. This style is often considered to be withdrawal or indifference.

The Accommodating style reflects concern for the other party in meeting its goals, but a relative lack of concern about your own goals. The result is a cooperative but unassertive style.

The Competing style is characterized by assertiveness and uncooperative behaviour. Your own concerns take precedence over the other party's concerns. Compromising is a style that is intermediate in both cooperativeness and assertiveness because each party must give something up to resolve the conflict. This is not seen as the optimal solution to conflict due to each party surrendering part of its position for the sake of agreement.

Collaborating is seen as a win-win situation that is high on both cooperativeness and assertiveness. This solution to conflict is satisfactory to both parties and is usually obtained after much discussion.

By reframing conflict between people into cultural categories, it becomes possible for two persons to disagree without either of them being wrong based on their different culturally learned conditions. One must describe the advantages of reframing conflict into cultural categories for constructive conflict management.

It is necessary for leaders to understand how conflict is understood and managed in non-Western cultures, not only because individuals from those countries are increasingly employed in organizations in the United States, but also because Western can learn a great deal from non-Western cultures about constructive conflict management. Conflict is managed quite differently in a high-context culture compared to a low-context culture, and each perspective has its advantages and disadvantages. The skilled conflict manager will need to understand both perspectives and know when either may be more appropriate.

Asian and Pacific cultures in particular offer a perspective for managing conflict in harmony, where conflict between people is often described in a cosmic context with spiritual implications. The goal in Asian and Pacific cultures is often to prevent overt conflict from occurring at all, which while the Western perspective is more often about resolving conflict once it has occurred.

Constructive conflict management may become the first priority of leaders, especially when conflict is between culturally different people. Leaders need to find common ground without losing their integrity. It will become important for leaders to understand interpersonal and intrapersonal conflict in the cultural context in which those behaviours are learned and displayed.

### Ethics and Decision Making

We have learned that a "good decision is never an accident" but this brings up a couple of other interesting issues such as – is an ethical decision never an accident or perhaps more intriguing is a good decision by necessity an ethical decision? The second question brings up numerous concerns many of which are debated in the newspapers on a daily basis thanks to the folks at Enron. Ethics and morality is rarely as obvious as the case at Enron, but on a higher level where does an individual's ultimate responsibility lie? Some would say with family, others with country and yet others with religion just to name a few. Trying to determine a common moral code is not easy task as the history of theology has taught us on countless occasions. Quantitative analysis is a key piece of effective decision-making but this is simply the execution and what numbers you choose to evaluate and how you choose to evaluate the results is highly subjective. The tools provide empirical information to utilize when making a decision but they do not provide the decision itself. This is true whether or not you are including ethics as part of the process or not.

Of particular interest to this paper is whether ethics and morality are a further step in the decision-making process or does it become an element of each step in the process. To determine this each of the stages in the decision-making process will be evaluated in the context of ethics and morality. Questions of interest are whether ethics and morality play a role in each stage and if so to what extent. The next section of the paper will provide some real world examples and finish up with the conclusions that can be drawn.

***Concept of Ethics and Morality:*** What is this concept we are trying to understand? "Morality is a system of rules that modifies our behaviour in social situations. It's about the doing of good instead of harm, and it sets some standard of virtuous conduct." Evaluating the difference of doing well versus harm and to what extent is subjective but this does not preclude us from attempting to find common ground. Please note that for the purposes of this paper I will use the terms ethics and morality interchangeably from this point forward. Often one identifies five principles in common morality:

- Autonomy: This relates to the question of exploitation of others and impacting their freedoms. Almost every decision has impacts on multiple persons and taking these impacts into not only consideration but engraining them in the process is not easy but necessary.
- Non-malfeasance:Will we be creating harm towards others? In government almost every regulation benefits one group while hurting another. The same holds true in the majority of business decisions – action creates a situation that by its very nature benefits some while does not for others. Doe this create harm? I would argue that something that is not beneficial to you does not mean it creates harm. Every challenge is an opportunity.
- Beneficence: Can this create good? A generic statement but worth considering and in essence all one needs to ask is can we solve the identified problem in a way that creates the most good.

- Justice: Is the process fair itself and is the resulting implementation fair. Essentially both the means and the end must be considered. The world is not equal nor should it be as all people are not created equal and what a boring place it would be if we were. There is all the difference in the world between treating people equally and attempting to make them equal.
- Fidelity: Does this follow our professional, corporate or governance roles as defined. Often this involves looking at the bigger picture and understanding the spirit of your role beyond straightforward results.

As you will have no doubt noticed these definitions are far from concrete or straightforward principles to apply. Every person potentially will have different perspectives or degrees of agreement in each case. However, great strides will have been made if each person is evaluating their concept of ethics. One of the greatest dangers in this field is people ignoring the concept due to the ambiguity.

The Impact on Decision Making: There are six key stages identified in the decision making process which include in order:

1. Identification of the Problem: Although this is the first stage this may be where morality can have the greatest impact. This is often the most difficult stage for the researcher and if it is not completed properly the results will be unsatisfactory regardless of the quality (or morality) of the work that follows. The framework that is built here constrains or sets the scope of the project. From an ethical perspective the first question of importance may be – is this really a problem at all? More times than not the focus of problems relates to the reduction of costs or increase in revenue (or that may be my business bias). At this point the problem needs to be resolved by a choice of means, which many find unfavorable. Some proponents of ethical decision-making challenge decision makers to evaluate whether the perceived problem truly is a problem. It sounds simple but in reality the process of considering all the potential alternatives, including do nothing, is not common. Business leaders are engrained with the belief that flexibility, change and adaptation are the answers.
2. What is the Goal: The dilemma here is whether the goal is to solve the problem in an ethical manner or simply determine the most ethical goal. The conflict here is do you select a goal

and then try to implement it in an effective matter later or do you choose your goals based on ethics. In a perfect world it would be optimal to choose a goal with ethics in mind, but in reality the maximized business goal is optimized by considering ethics in only a very general sense at this stage. Eliminate the few obvious options that are unlikely to have any ethical implementation and proceed forward.

3. Possible Actions: Pending your theory on determining the goal will have a huge influence on the types of actions that make sense. Actions are primarily determined by the goal you wish to achieve. Nevertheless ethics should influence the actions you are willing to take within the scope of your goal.
4. Predict Outcome: This may be the one stage in which ethics requires no change. Quantitative techniques are straightforward and merely calculate the results based on your inputs. The age-old computer theory of 'garbage in – garbage' out applies.
5. Pick the best alternative: Is the best alternative simply the predicted outcome which maximizes goals or does it merely provide empirical results for comparison (with which you can rid the outliers). Formulate the choice as a maxim for all similar cases is a concept those in favour of ethics will promote. This is a recurring theme which involves looking outside any particular situation and seeing the forest for the trees.
6. Implement Decision: In many cases this is an area where morality already plays a significant role in current business practice. Unions and significant regulations exist to ensure change is 'ethical'. However, I would submit that real influence is found long before implementation. At this point you are just trying to minimize or trivialize perceived problems in the selected decision. Nonetheless for that reason it is important that decision makers consider the impacts of implementation. Hopefully if no satisfactory implementation can be found than the problem will be revisited rather than selecting the best of a group of bad choices, which is widespread..

An Application: Medical and Health-Care decision-making have been around since the time when Hippocrates developed his famous hippocritical oath for healers. This ancient philosopher wrote an oath that addressed the professional and ethical issues faced by physicians in their pursuit of healing individuals. The age-old problem has been how does a human being make such an important decision without any rhyme or reason?

Throughout time mistakes have led to the death of sick people. These mistakes have been made because of bad Medical and Health-Care decisions. The practice of making decisions related to the treatment of a condition or person in order to make them healthy is the primary focus of this literature (Web site) review. There has never been any formal body of knowledge that can assist a practitioner in choosing the appropriate course of action. Most of the major medical schools educate their students through a series of didactic methods and practical experience. The instructors have always taught using research and examples, yet there has not been a formalized mathematical approach to making Medical and Health-Care decisions due to the high subjectivity to these kinds of decisions.

Scientific research can eliminate definitively wrong decisions. However, with the fact that humans are the most complex entities in the world, decisions can not be a "one-size-fits-all".

***Another Application:*** Lobby groups and labour unions are very interesting examples that potentially compromise ethics even though in many circumstances they have good intentions. By promoting the needs of a few over those of many can be considered unethical. This relates to David Ricardo's comparative advantage of the nation. These groups also have a direct negative impact on people who are not a part of these groups. Yet it seems strange at first glance that promoting the interests of workers could in fact be immoral. The problems lies in the fact that the benefits do not extend to all workers despite the fact that decades ago these strides did in fact help all. However, now legislation exists to cover the most basic protections. One must also consider the fact that we will never know what market corrections may have remedied these issues on its own.

For a decision maker the impact of lobby groups and labour unions represent an area of misconduct on either side. Resources and funds that could be used in production are now allocated to tasks, which do not further a country's growth. Some will argue that if business leaders had used ethical decision making then the need for unions would not have been required. You could also argue that getting involved in busting a union is making the ethical decision to improve the economy of the nation. What can be learned from this example? Other than the fact that ethics is not straightforward and that every situation is subjective this leads to the reality that

Government has a role to ensure the few common standards are legislated. Beyond that the ultimate guide for a decision lies in the individuals hands.

The morally best course of action in any situation takes matters of economic and technical appropriateness into account, but is not overridden by these. Although this sounds noble I would take issue with the tendency to leans toward morality as the key decision influence.

I feel that the economic and technical nature of a problem are the key determinants in decision making. Having said that I feel that ethics play a role in the majority of the stages of decision-making. Good process and analysis is not a barrier to morality. The key starts at the first stages of the decision process with problem identification and involves trying to ensure that one looks at the bigger picture and truly understanding what the goals are.

As stated earlier government plays a role to ensure basic protections are available to the entire population. For a business you have to expect people to be true to themselves. By our nature humans are self-interested and it's a corporation's responsibility to align the self-interest of its employees in the right direction. Corporate culture helps define this direction and can create an environment of ethical decisions.

Once the company culture is entrenched it is then necessary to hire the right people. Individuals make decisions and therefore employees will determine whether ethics are executed or become a problem. Once you have hired the right people it is necessary to have communication throughout the organization. Dialogue which includes the exploration of new meaning through discourse will facilitate ethical decisions. This gives the individual decision maker multiple inputs and a better grasp of the big picture.

Finally organizations must be extremely careful to monitor potential situations of conflict of interest. In this environment individuals will identify the problems, set goals and make decisions within the standard framework, which are both successful and ethical. The decision making process outlined earlier does not need to be modified but rather an organization needs to hire ethical people and provide them with an ethical environment. Effective decision-making and ethics are not mutually exclusive. In fact the utilization of an analytical decision making process will often flush out immoral decisions based on merit without any specific intent to do so.

## Personal and Public Views of Rationality

Consider the following example for the personal and public views of rationality. It is perfectly rational for an office worker to take his/her car heading home at the end of (around 5 PM, in US) a hard workday. However the outcome is very irrational for every one because it creates unbearable congestion on the major roads in the major cities. As another case, consider an arrested criminal who thought very rationally about his action prior to committing the crime, however, the law and order punish the criminal rationally according the nature of the crime.

Psychological issues such as ambivalence, inner conflict, and the constraints imposed upon decision-makers by connections to others, reveal that our strategic thinking is often more subtle than standard theories of rationality allow.

The OR/MS/DS/SS decision-making process deals with complex problems by decomposing them into a list of strategic objectives. Then, it focuses on each individual objective to plan for a tactical solution. Good models make explicit the objectives, interactions among the inputs, and properties in a situation, and then structures them for inference and decision. When a problem cannot be solved using that information alone, the set of models must be 'flushed out' so that a new search for a possible model can be constructed. Most people use their beliefs in the attainment of their goals rather than a rational view. Rational strategic thinking is an issue for everyone. It is said that rational strategic thinking yields three essential statements:

1. Whether a person can ever be said to have committed an error in reasoning.
2. Whether some deductive problems are beyond the capacity of reasoners who are untrained in logic.
3. Whether rationality is relative to culture.

Cognitive theory deals with the following questions:

- What is the mind computing?
- How is the mind doing it?
- What people are really doing the reasoning and strategic thinking ?

These are unresolved questions. For example, with respect to the last question, cognitive theory does not try to test whether an inference is valid or a rule is true or false, but rather, searches for relevant information to update their beliefs. Relevant information is determined through a rational strategy. Rational analysis is based on the assumption that recognition will be optimally adapted to the structure of the environment. Rationality behaviour is adaptive rational if it is optimized to an organism's environment, i.e. if it helps to achieve its goals and it is consistent with logical rules. How did the idea of reasoning as a means to attain one's goals come about? Humans have a demonstrated capacity for highly intelligent action in achieving goals and thereby promoting the specie's survival and, for some, prosperity. However, at the same time, they embarrass themselves when they have their reasoning and decision processes tested. So, we appear rational from one angle, and irrational from another.

The term "rational" can be used to mean two fundamentally different things: Personal Rationality and Public Rationality. However, both are goal directed. Difficulties often arise when these two meanings are glossed over or confused.

***Personal Rationality:*** Making a decision in a way that is generally reliable and efficient for achieving one's personal goals effectively. This kind of rationality, is 'Purpose-based Rationality'. It implies that the ends always rationalize the means. This is a version of the Machiavellian rationality, where individuals must overcome their social training and traditional ideas to seek their own way of making decisions. You may remember the song titles: "I Gotta Be Me" or "I Did It My Way."

Rational people make decisions that are best for them. This may be in terms of either psychological satisfaction or material gain. If a person carries out all the steps in the decision process and arrives at the resolution stage by the evaluation of the alternatives and predicting the outcomes, that person is regarded as rational if he/she acts upon the best action selected by the process. The process of internal balancing behaviour in our rational strategic thinking is shown in the following diagram:

***Public Rationality:*** Making a decision sanctioned by the law which requires evidence. This kind of rationality is 'Process-based Rationality' which means that the means must justify the ends. Within the domain of relevant law, it has to be a responsible and defensible decision.

Unfortunately, there are other isolated rationality types, such as the 'proof by pleasure principle' as opposed to the 'proof by contradiction principle'. However, failure to distinguish between these two distinct types of rationality can lead to empty or misleading judgment about human rationality.

***Here is a question for you:*** The debate on abortion belongs to which of these two categories of rationality? Abortion is a "premeditated decision to murder." Or, as a leading feminist declared, "don't put your law into my body." It's a hard decision to make.

***Global Social Decisions:*** In an increasingly globalize world, it is inevitable that many of the social problems which have so far been seen as national in character will assume a global character. Global social problems are those which cannot be confined within national boundaries and which need both national and international attention if they are to be ameliorated. Pollution of the atmosphere is a stark example of this process. Global Social Decisions must begin with an understanding of the contested concept of globalization and exploring the global social policies to the most important global social problems: Environmental Degradation, International Poverty, Crime, AIDS, Drugs, Family Violence, Racism and Migration.

***Knowledge and Information Are Different:*** Thinking of them as similar or synonymous distorts the entire concept of managing intangible assets. When we speak or write, we use language to articulate some of our tactic knowledge in an attempt to pass it on to others, it is called information. Knowledge and information are often confused with each other. In the information technology industry, they are used as synonyms. Thus, the word information is usually associated with both facts and the communication of facts. Information is in many ways ideal for communicating explicit knowledge. It is fast, independent of the originator, and secure. All three of these features are of vital importance in the information technology era because the computer is designed to handle information.

So it is tempting and seems commonsensical for the sender or speaker to attribute information with some sort of meaning. The trouble is people know more than they are conscious of or can put into words. For example, try to explain in words how to drive a golf ball or serve a tennis ball. These concepts are too complex to express fully in words. Attempts to do so are often ridiculous and almost always incomprehensible. The receiver of information – not the sender – gives it meaning. Information, as such, is meaningless. Information is perfect for broadcasting articulated knowledge but is unreliable an inefficient for transferring knowledge from person to person. It is best not to write but to talk when we wish to transfer knowledge.

Clearly such a distinction between knowledge and information is critical when discussing the contemporary challenge of knowledge management. It is valuable to further delineate different kinds of knowledge, and, more important, to better understand the appropriate means of transferring knowledge to others.

***Kinds of Knowledge:*** One of the basic distinctions is the difference between information and knowledge and second to that is the related distinction between explicit and tacit knowledge. When we record what we know, we are making that knowledge explicit in the form of documents, graphics, or other concrete media, this is converting knowledge to information.

Any form of knowledge that is made explicit is no longer knowledge but information. A well-used, but nevertheless important, metaphor uses an iceberg to show the relationship between explicit and tacit knowledge.

Tacit knowledge is knowledge that enters into the production of behaviours and/or the constitution of mental states but is not ordinarily accessible to consciousness and is represented by the submerged portion of the iceberg. The part that is exposed above the water is explicit knowledge. The beauty of this analogy is that both the exposed and the submerged are parts of the same chunk of ice. If all you have explicit knowledge, you can't do anything. Tacit knowledge makes explicit knowledge usable.

The three kinds of intellectual capital then are related to this model, with human capital represented by the submerged portion of the iceberg and structural capital by what is above the water. The management of structural knowledge involves raising the iceberg such that what was once human capital is now available to the organization in explicit form. Obviously, raising an iceberg is not an easy task and the analogy seems appropriate as the mass of tacit knowledge retained by the people in an organization will never surface. To better represent the portion of knowledge represented by the iceberg that is just below the surface of the water, I prefer to add a third distinction: implicit. Implicit knowledge is knowledge that can be codified but has not yet been made explicit.

This model then gives clarity to three distinctly different approaches to the management of intellectual capital, and each is further addressed in the following sections.

***Explicit Knowledge:*** An organization can best capitalize on the exposed explicit knowledge by providing the technology and business processes necessary to make this codified content easily accessible to those who need it within the company and to principal customers and suppliers. A significant portion of the resources and effort around knowledge management involves the design, development, and deployment of effective knowledge repositories and document management systems that organize and catalogue, thus providing easy and rapid access to the massive amounts of explicit material (paper correspondence, electronic mail, specifications, procedures, patents, training, presentations, manuals, whitepapers, etc.) that can be generated by a company.

Unfortunately, many of the existing approaches to management of these explicit knowledge assets resemble the way most of us organize our attics. This problem cab be describe using the metaphor of a small used book store where the books are distributed around the room in the cardboard boxes in which the originally arrived. The process for locating what we are looking for involves an exhaustive search through every one of the boxes since no effort was made to organize the content in any meaningful way.

***Implicit Knowledge:*** Assuming there is an adequate system in place for handling the explicit knowledge of an organization, a second management approach involves capturing implicit knowledge by recording it in a structured way and thus converting it into information. This can involve the straightforward documentation of core business processes, procedures, and best-known methods in document form, but can also be the collection of video recordings from key customer or management presentations and conference addresses. The development of most forms of training and education programs involves the process of translating valuable expert knowledge into information. The results can be in the form of classroom, computer-based, or on-line training, or reference material utilizing streaming audio, video, or a combination of various media.

***Tacit Knowledge:*** By definition, tacit knowledge cannot be codified and remains with the individual who developed it through a combination of formal learning and experience. The means for managing this kind of knowledge are not much different from those for managing human resources in general. Competitive processes need to be designed for the effective selection of knowledgeable hires, as well as the development of all employees, plus effective compensation and benefits programs to retain the talented and knowledgeable people on whom the organization depends for innovation and decision making. Specific focus should be on mentoring and apprenticeship opportunities that are the most effective means for transfer of tacit knowledge. In addition, the norms and culture of the organization should be shaped and developed to support and encourage the sharing of knowledge and the importance of innovation and risk taking.

***Knowledge and a Culture of Learning:*** The explicit culture can be understood and at one level managed by the physical artifacts or documented mission, vision, values, operating philosophies, and policies of the organization that lie above the surface of the water. The implied culture is simply the actual culture as experienced by the people in the organization and can be made explicit through observations of the actions, espoused values, attitudes, and decisions that people make. However, at the root, and the most difficult to expose, are the tacit knowledge, basic assumptions, or mental models held by people that give rise to their felt values and ultimately observable behaviour.

Five elements comprise the core learning message to make it compelling in engaging people's passion. They are: a positive vision of the future; inspiring core values; engaging and inclusive leadership style; emotional intelligence competencies; and leadership courage.

***Assessing the Motivating Potential of Jobs:*** Any job can be designed, or assessed and redesigned, to be more compelling. That is, any job can be inherently motivating for an employee to perform. It is all a matter of holistic engagement. Only jobs that engage the hands, mind, heart, and spirit of an employee are truly holistically engaging, and thus inherently motivating for employees. And each of these levels of employee engagement does not afford equal motivational impact. Arguably, only by engaging the heart and the spirit of an employee does an organization ever access half of that employee's motivation, this paints a sobering picture for most leaders, especially when they accurately recognize that most jobs continue to be designed and staffed with only hands and mind engagement, and too often only hands engagement, as design factors that are intentionally considered.

By assigning subscores of one to ten to each of the four design components (hands, mind, heart, spirit), and then multiplying these subscores by the factors assigned to each design component (hand = 10 percent, mind = 40 percent, heart = 20 percent, and spirit = 30 percent), and overall assessment of the level of holistic engagement and related employee motivation afforded by a particular job can be determined. Thus, the formula for determining the holistic Engagement Score (ES) associated with a job is as follows:

ES = 0.1HandsScore + 0.4MindScore + 0.2HeartScore + 0.3SpiritScore,

The range for ES is the lowest possible ES being 1 and the highest being 10.

## Human Understanding in a Historical Context

In this section we are interested in a historical development view of knowledge; that is how we came to know recently as Modelling-Knowledge:

Knowledge-Modelling Categories and Their Principles

Factual Knowledge: It is based on universal reasoning that includes hypothesis testing, and mathematics, it required intellectual thinking

Cognitive Knowledge: It is based on empirical facts that includes know-how, and object knowledge, it required training

Principal Knowledge: It is based on conjecture such as metaphysics, it belong to realm of appearances

Subjective Knowledge: It is based on belief, it belong to realm of deceptions

During the Renaissance art and literature flourished. In the Medieval era, people only believed what the authorities told them to believe. During the Enlightenment, freedom of thought allowed mankind to think and to question authority. When you have questions, you need answers. The neck represents the logic needed to support the thought. The head represents the quantitative era. The quantitative era was started by Newton who developed a scientfic method:

Newton's finding turn upside down the Aristotelian view. For example Newton shows that everything wants to move. The reason something is at rest is because of resistance. For example, the table rests on the floor.

Newton was very important because the Aristotelian view dominated human thought in all areas for twenty centuries. With Newton, Aristotelian view faded. From the time of Newton not only all things in external nature, but the subtlest mysteries of life and organization, and even of the intellect and moral being, were conjured within the language of mathematics and the tools of mathematical modelling process. Traditionally, logic and mathematics have been considered exemplary cases of fields in which our knowledge is a priori. Consequently, questions about the epistemological status and ontological import of logical and mathematical truths have recurred throughout the intellectual history. Of interest are: the nature of logic and mathematics, the nature of logical and mathematical knowledge, the relationship of logic to ontology, and the question of how our minds are able to think about and come to know logical and mathematical truths.

The decision can be either personal or public; however both required the same decision-making process. The field of decision-making is growing as a measuring tool and process for helping people to make good decisions. However, there are many tools that either fail to properly integrate, or simply lack an analysis of showing how emotions help or hinder decision making and the role of creative and critical thinking together with working out what values are at issue in making decisions.

The main question is how the decision process must be carried out adequately? The answer is the realization of the fact that decision-making is the heart of being human and requires a multidisciplinary approach. For example, the role and core of emotions are judgment through revaluation of all values. This realization allows us to make sense of both the rationalist view that emotions are a hindrance, and the individual notion that emotions are major considerations. Decision-making involves unpacking emotions to see what they can reliably tell us about the situation, our values, and potential options and how they can motivate us. However, critical thinking needs to be employed throughout the decision-making process so that we adequately understand the situation and assess potential values and creative options. The driving force of making a decision is the values we wish to realize with our decision.

One must explore the skills and knowledge necessary to facilitate a decision making process. There are four categories of insights and methods, which we have learnt to be of key significance to decision-making

Aristotle's Ideas About Practical Knowledge: In the Nicomachean Ethics, Aristotle makes a distinction on two kinds of knowledge that is of the greatest relevance to the practical decision consultant and the decision maker. By theoretical knowledge he means knowledge of things that do not change, which in ethics means the general, universal things we can say about what is really right and wrong, and what is living well and living badly. For Aristotle, the moral virtue is a state of character in which we are disposed to feel things in accordance with the means, that is, to feel them in the right way, to the right person, at the right time, for the right reason. However, theoretical knowledge on its own is not enough to lead a flourishing human life. We also need practical knowledge, which for Aristotle means knowing the right thing to do in a particular circumstance through understanding the circumstance rightly, knowing what matters, and effective means-end reasoning to bring about what matters. One can know the right thing to do in general, and what is required, as theoretical knowledge, but this is of little use if one fails to apply this knowledge to this situation. Therefore, developing Aristotle's insights, the decision consultant and the decision maker need both theoretical knowledge and practical knowledge. These conditions can be understood as a series of stages in decision-making:

***Understanding the situation and decision:*** The decision-maker needs to understand the decision being faced, and the situation it is located in, as accurately, open-mindedly and fully as is reasonable.

***Understanding what matters:*** the decision-maker needs to understand what really his/her ultimate objective is. What values are at stake? Aristotle emphasized the archer is more likely to hit the target if they are aware of what that are aiming at. The important values are the target, so without an awareness of what matters the decision-maker does not know what they are aiming at, and have no criterion on which to make the decision.

***Searching for options:*** Even if the decision-maker understands the situation and appreciate what matters, they still need to be aware of the possible options. If they mistakenly think they are limited to two options, when a third option, not thought of, and actually would fulfil more of what matters, then they would not have made as wise decision a decision as they could have.

***Choosing the best option:*** Each option needs to be assessed in a logical manner, choosing that option which, given a sound understanding of the situation, satisfies as much as possible of what matters. If we lack the critical powers to assess these options, then we will still fail to make wise decisions.

***Implementing the decision:*** Finally, the decision-maker prepares for implementing the decision, armed with a fallback plan and follow-up activities to check on the implementation. Once the decision-maker has made a selection of the best option, they need to make a final check on it, and work out how to implement and monitor it. We will now explore in turn the ways in which the emotions, creative and critical thinking and ethics can be used to help wise decision-making.

***Spinoza on the Emotions:*** Unpacking the emotional core of a decision is, we believe, and will illustrate below, vital. There are various philosophers we have found to be of most use in helping dealing us towards wise decision-making.

Spinosa's idea that the emotions contain their own logic; and their own reason by arguing that emotions are very much like a sense which helps us to detect value. Emotions, although they have their own logic, are not necessarily reliable. Indeed, not only are they often motivated by our needs, but they also distort our picture of the world. Given the cognitive content of the emotion we can see that emotional knowledge lies in making sound judgments about the significance of an event, and an appropriate reaction to it. As For decision-making we must not ignore the emotions – else we risk both missing out their informational value and allowing them to distort our view of the situation, the problem, what matters, our options and our ability to implement the decision.

The decision-making consultant can help in a number of ways, both in dealing with the particular decision being faced by asking the decision-makers about their emotions. What do they feel – is it anger, anxiety, excitement, or being overwhelmed? Next, we need to question them what this emotion is about. If they are angry what is this anger directed towards, if they are feeling overwhelmed what about the problem seems overwhelming to them, if they are excited what about the decision excites them. Thirdly, we need to ask – and here the greatest skill and tack is required-whether, on reflection, this emotion is appropriate.

***Nietzsche's Critical and Creative Thinking:*** Creative thinking is the generation of thoughts, ideas, decisions and actions, often by novel and unexpected means. Such thinking is useful at different stages in the process of decision-making.

How the situation is framed can be crucially important to determining how the decision-maker proceeds. Revaluation of all values is Nietzsche's phrase for creative thinking, which involves 'pattern-switching within a patterning system' as a way to get multi-perspectives on understanding the problem being faced. What is needed is overcoming rather than suffering. Critical thinking is a process, the goal of which is to think for yourself in order to make reasonable decisions about what to believe and what to do. The decision consultant's role is not just to help the decision makers to think skillfully, but also to care about how their thinking is being used. Critical thinking needs to be applied throughout the decision-making process, in gaining an accurate understanding the situation, in assessing values, in assessing options and in carrying out and monitoring the chosen option.

***The Ethics of Right and Wrong:***When making decisions that are mainly of a prudential nature, we can draw on ideas from thinkers like Nozick about states of mind and states of the world. In considering the ethical dimensions of a decision, we can in addition learn from Hume and other utilitarian about considering the interests of other parties, the deontologists about their rights and our corresponding duties, and Kant about what should happen, regardless of the role we have in the decision.

Nozick suggests that our conclusion should not be that states of mind do not matter, but that states of the world matter as well as states of mind. In general, people do think that their experiences matter; but what also matters is the relationship of their experiences to reality, and things that are happening in the world outside their experiences.

These insights are of direct relevance to the decision-making consultant when they are helping the decision-maker to think about what matters in a specific situation. The decision-maker will normally be asked first to list the things that seem to matter in the situation. Utilitarian' ideas about consequences and other parties are useful, e.g., when a consultant asks the decision makers to list the other parties affected by their decision and what their interests are. Whilst the utilitarian alert us to the interests of other parties, Kant remind us that, regardless of the consequences, their might be some rights that other people have in this situation, and corresponding to these rights, duties on our parts.

The above multi-perspectives provide a rich range of skill for both consultant and the decision maker. It is important therefore that the decision consultant chooses which of these seem relevant, and offers each tentatively as something the client may want to consider, rather than dogmatically insisting upon a viewpoint. On the other hand, the consultant should not accept the answers given as final, the tools of critical thinking are particularly useful ways of checking that the client is considering long-term consequences and other parties.

The introduction of zero into the decimal system was the most significant achievement in the development of a number system in which calculation with large numbers become feasible. Without the notion of zero modelling process in astronomy, physics, and chemistry would have been unthinkable. The lack of such a symbol is one of the serious drawbacks in Roman numeral system, beside being difficult to use in any arithmetic operations such as multiplication. The above timeline table indicates the major historical events relevant to the developments of the modelling process as we know it today. Thus, the quantitative modelling process of our knowledge has a short history of about 300 years. So, from a historical perspective, our management knowledge is even younger, however it is growing very fast and much stronger. The quantitative processing approach to knowing is spreading in almost all fields to make the world calculable and, therefore more manageable.

The most effective model includes personality dynamics that are strong in the emotional, physical and mental principles. The results will be a microworld model for representing reality and a boundary object model, for example, for negotiating for a social order.

### *Transactional and Transformational Theories*

Eric Berne first analysed the relations between a group and its leadership in terms of Transactional Analysis.

The transactional leader (Burns, 1978) is given power to perform certain tasks and reward or punish for the team's performance.

It gives the opportunity to the manager to lead the group and the group agrees to follow his lead to accomplish a predetermined goal in exchange for something else. Power is given to the leader to evaluate, correct and train subordinates when productivity is not up to the desired level and reward effectiveness when expected outcome is reached.

The transformational leader (Burns, 1978) motivates its team to be effective and efficient. Communication is the base for goal achievement focusing the group on the final desired outcome or goal attainment. This leader is highly visible and uses chain of command to get the job done. Transformational leaders focus on the big picture, needing to be surrounded by people who take care of the details. The leader is always looking for ideas that move the organization to reach the company's vision.

### *Emotions*

Leadership can be perceived as a particularly emotion-laden process, with emotions entwined with the social influence process. In an organization, the leader's mood has some effects on his/her group. These effects can be described in 3 levels:

1. The mood of individual group members. Group members with leaders in a positive mood experience more positive mood than do group members with leaders in a negative mood. The leaders transmit their moods to other group members through the mechanism of emotional contagion. Mood contagion may be one of the psychological mechanisms by which charismatic leaders influence followers.
2. The affective tone of the group. Group affective tone represents the consistent or homogeneous affective reactions within a group. Group affective tone is an aggregate of the moods of the individual members of the group and refers to mood at the group level of analysis. Groups with leaders in a positive mood have a more positive affective tone than do groups with leaders in a negative mood.
3. Group processes like coordination, effort expenditure, and task strategy. Public expressions of mood impact how group members think and act. When people experience and express mood, they send signals to others. Leaders signal their goals, intentions, and attitudes through their expressions of moods. For example, expressions of positive moods by leaders signal that leaders deem progress toward goals to be good. The group members respond to those signals cognitively and behaviorally in ways that are reflected in the group processes.

In research about client service, it was found that expressions of positive mood by the leader improve the performance of the group, although in other sectors there were other findings.

Beyond the leader's mood, her/his behaviour is a source for employee positive and negative emotions at work. The leader creates situations and events that lead to emotional response. Certain leader behaviours displayed during interactions with their employees are the sources of these affective events. Leaders shape workplace affective events. Examples – feedback giving, allocating tasks, resource distribution. Since employee behaviour and productivity are directly affected by their emotional states, it is imperative to consider employee emotional responses to organizational leaders. Emotional intelligence, the ability to understand and manage moods and emotions in the self and others, contributes to effective leadership in organizations.

### Neo-emergent Theory

The Neo-emergent leadership theory (from the Oxford school of leadership) espouses that leadership is created through the emergence of information by the leader or other stakeholders, not through the true actions of the leader himself. In other words, the reproduction of information or stories form the basis of the perception of leadership by the majority.

It is well known that the great naval hero Lord Nelson often wrote his own versions of battles he was involved in, so that when he arrived home in England he would receive a true hero's welcome. In modern society, the press, blogs and other sources report their own views of a leader, which may be based on reality, but may also be based on a political command, a payment, or an inherent interest of the author, media or leader. Therefore, it can be contended that the perception of all leaders is created and in fact does not reflect their true leadership qualities at all.

### Styles

Leadership style refers to a leader's behaviour. It is the result of the philosophy, personality and experience of the leader.

### Autocratic or Authoritarian Style

Under the autocratic leadership style, all decision-making powers are centralized in the leader, as with dictator leaders.

They do not entertain any suggestions or initiatives from subordinates. The autocratic management has been successful as it provides strong motivation to the manager. It permits quick decision-making, as only one person decides for the whole group and keeps each decision to himself until he feels it is needed to be shared with the rest of the group.

### Participative or Democratic Style

The democratic leadership style favours decision-making by the group as shown, such as leader gives instruction after consulting the group.

They can win the co-operation of their group and can motivate them effectively and positively. The decisions of the democratic leader are not unilateral as with the autocrat because they arise from consultation with the group members and participation by them.

### Laissez-faire or Free Rein Style

A free-rein leader does not lead, but leaves the group entirely to itself as shown; such a leader allows maximum freedom to subordinates, i.e., they are given a free hand in deciding their own policies and methods.

Different situations call for different leadership styles. In an emergency when there is little time to converge on an agreement and where a designated authority has significantly more experience or expertise than the rest of the team, an autocratic leadership style may be most effective; however, in a highly motivated and aligned team with a homogeneous level of expertise, a more democratic or laissez-faire style may be more effective. The style adopted should be the one that most effectively achieves the objectives of the group while balancing the interests of its individual members.

### *Narcissistic Leadership*

Various academics such as Kets de Vries, Maccoby and Thomas have identified narcissistic leadership as an important and common leadership style.

### *Toxic Leadership*

A toxic leader is someone who has responsibility over a group of people or an organization, and who abuses the leader-follower relationship by leaving the group or organization in a worse-off condition than when s/he first found them.

## Performance

In the past, some researchers have argued that the actual influence of leaders on organizational outcomes is overrated and romanticized as a result of biased attributions about leaders. Despite these assertions however, it is largely recognized and accepted by practitioners and researchers that leadership is important, and research supports the notion that leaders do contribute to key organizational outcomes . To facilitate successful performance it is important to understand and accurately measure leadership performance.

Job performance generally refers to behaviour that is expected to contribute to organizational success (Campbell, 1990). Campbell identified a number of specific types of performance dimensions; leadership was one of the dimensions that he identified. There is no consistent, overall definition of leadership performance (Yukl, 2006). Many distinct conceptualizations are often lumped together under the umbrella of leadership performance, including outcomes such as leader effectiveness, leader advancement, and leader emergence (Kaiser et al., 2008).

For instance, leadership performance may be used to refer to the career success of the individual leader, performance of the group or organization, or even leader emergence. Each of these measures can be considered conceptually distinct. While these aspects may be related, they are different outcomes and their inclusion should depend on the applied/research focus.

## Contexts

### *Organizations*

An organization that is established as an instrument or means for achieving defined objectives has been referred to as a formal organization. Its design specifies how goals are subdivided and reflected in subdivisions of the organization. Divisions, departments, sections, positions, jobs, and tasks make up this work structure. Thus, the formal organization is expected to behave impersonally in regard to relationships with clients or with its members. According to Weber's definition, entry and subsequent advancement is by merit or seniority.

Each employee receives a salary and enjoys a degree of tenure that safeguards her/him from the arbitrary influence of superiors or of powerful clients. The higher his position in the hierarchy, the greater his presumed expertise in adjudicating problems that may arise in the course of the work carried out at lower levels of the organization. It is this bureaucratic structure that forms the basis for the appointment of heads or chiefs of administrative subdivisions in the organization and endows them with the authority attached to their position.

In contrast to the appointed head or chief of an administrative unit, a leader emerges within the context of the informal organization that underlies the formal structure. The informal organization expresses the personal objectives and goals of the individual membership. Their objectives and goals may or may not coincide with those of the formal organization. The informal organization represents an extension of the social structures that generally characterize human life — the spontaneous emergence of groups and organizations as ends in themselves.

In prehistoric times, humanity was preoccupied with personal security, maintenance, protection, and survival. Now humanity spends a major portion of waking hours working for organizations. Her/His need to identify with a community that provides security, protection, maintenance, and a feeling of belonging continues unchanged from prehistoric times. This need is met by the informal organization and its emergent, or unofficial, leaders.

Leaders emerge from within the structure of the informal organization. Their personal qualities, the demands of the situation, or a combination of these and other factors attract followers who accept their leadership within one or several overlay structures. Instead of the authority of position held by an appointed head or chief, the emergent leader wields influence or power. Influence is the ability of a person to gain co-operation from others by means of persuasion or control over rewards. Power is a stronger form of influence because it reflects a person's ability to enforce action through the control of a means of punishment.

A leader is a person who influences a group of people towards a specific result. It is not dependent on title or formal authority. (elevos, paraphrased from Leaders, Bennis, and Leadership Presence, Halpern & Lubar). Ogbonnia (2007) defines an effective leader "as an individual with the capacity to consistently succeed in a given condition and be viewed as meeting the expectations of an organization or society." Leaders are recognized by their capacity for caring for others, clear communication, and a commitment to persist. An individual who is appointed to a managerial position has the right to command and enforce obedience by virtue of the authority of his position. However, she or he must possess adequate personal attributes to match his authority, because authority is only potentially available to him. In the absence of sufficient personal competence, a manager may be confronted by an emergent leader who can challenge her/his role in the organization and reduce it to that of a figurehead. However, only authority of position has the backing of formal sanctions. It follows that whoever wields personal influence and power can legitimize this only by gaining a formal position in the hierarchy, with commensurate authority. Leadership can be defined as one's ability to get others to willingly follow. Every organization needs leaders at every level.

### Management

Over the years the philosophical terminology of "management" and "leadership" have, in the organisational context, been used both as synonyms and with clearly differentiated meanings. Debate is fairly common about whether the use of these terms should be restricted, and generally reflects an awareness of the distinction made by Burns (1978) between "transactional" leadership (characterised by e.g. emphasis on procedures, contingent reward, management by exception) and "transformational" leadership (characterised by e.g. charisma, personal relationships, creativity).

## Group Leadership

In contrast to individual leadership, some organizations have adopted group leadership. In this situation, more than one person provides direction to the group as a whole. Some organizations have taken this approach in hopes of increasing creativity, reducing costs, or downsizing. Others may see the traditional leadership of a boss as costing too much in team performance. In some situations, the main the team member(s) best able to handle any given phase of the project become(s) the temporary leader(s). Additionally, as each team member has the opportunity to experience the elevated level of empowerment, it energizes staff and feeds the cycle of success. Leaders who demonstrate persistence, tenacity, determination and synergistic communication skills will bring out the same qualities in their groups. Good leaders use their own inner mentors to energize their team and organizations and lead a team to achieve success.

*According to the National School Boards Association (USA)*

These Group Leadership or Leadership Teams have specific characteristics:

Characteristics of a Team:

- There must be an awareness of unity on the part of all its members.
- There must be interpersonal relationship. Members must have a chance to contribute, learn from and work with others.
- The member must have the ability to act together toward a common goal.

Ten characteristics of well-functioning teams:

- Purpose: Members proudly share a sense of why the team exists and are invested in accomplishing its mission and goals.
- Priorities: Members know what needs to be done next, by whom, and by when to achieve team goals.
- Roles: Members know their roles in getting tasks done and when to allow a more skillful member to do a certain task.
- Decisions: Authority and decision-making lines are clearly understood.
- Conflict: Conflict is dealt with openly and is considered important to decision-making and personal growth.
- Personal traits: members feel their unique personalities are appreciated and well utilized.

- Norms: Group norms for working together are set and seen as standards for every one in the groups.
- Effectiveness: Members find team meetings efficient and productive and look forward to this time together.
- Success: Members know clearly when the team has met with success and share in this equally and proudly.
- Training: Opportunities for feedback and updating skills are provided and taken advantage of by team members.

### *Primates*

Mark van Vugt and Anjana Ahuja in Naturally Selected: The Evolutionary Science of Leadership present evidence of leadership in nonhuman animals, from leadership in ants and bees to baboons and chimpanzees. They suggest that leadership has a long evolutionary history and that the same mechanisms underpinning leadership in humans can be found in other social species too. Richard Wrangham and Dale Peterson, in *Demonic Males: Apes and the Origins of Human Violence* present evidence that only humans and chimpanzees, among all the animals living on earth, share a similar tendency for a cluster of behaviours: violence, territoriality, and competition for uniting behind the one chief male of the land. This position is contentious. Many animals beyond apes are territorial, compete, exhibit violence, and have a social structure controlled by a dominant male (lions, wolves, etc.), suggesting Wrangham and Peterson's evidence is not empirical. However, we must examine other species as well, including elephants (which are matriarchal and follow an alpha female), meerkats (who are likewise matriarchal), and many others.

It would be beneficial, to examine that most accounts of leadership over the past few millennia (since the creation of Christian religions) are through the perspective of a patriarchal society, founded on Christian literature. If one looks before these times, it is noticed that Pagan and Earth-based tribes in fact had female leaders. It is important also to note that the peculiarities of one tribe cannot necessarily be ascribed to another, as even our modern-day customs differ.

The current day patrilineal custom is only a recent invention in human history and our original method of familial practices were matrilineal. The fundamental assumption that has been built into 90% of the world's countries is that patriarchy is the 'natural' biological predisposition of homo sapiens. Unfortunately, this belief has led to the widespread oppression of women in all of those countries, but in varying degrees. The Iroquoian First Nations tribes are an example of a matrilineal tribe, along with Mayan tribes, and also the society of Meghalaya, India.

By comparison, bonobos, the second-closest species-relatives of man, do *not* unite behind the chief male of the land. The bonobos show deference to an alpha or top-ranking female that, with the support of her coalition of other females, can prove as strong as the strongest male in the land. Thus, if leadership amounts to getting the greatest number of followers, then among the bonobos, a female almost always exerts the strongest and most effective leadership. However, not all scientists agree on the allegedly "peaceful" nature of the bonobo or its reputation as a "hippie chimp".

## Historical Views

Sanskrit literature identifies ten types of leaders. Defining characteristics of the ten types of leaders are explained with examples from history and mythology. Aristocratic thinkers have postulated that leadership depends on one's blue blood or genes: monarchy takes an extreme view of the same idea, and may prop up its assertions against the claims of mere aristocrats by invoking divine sanction: see the divine right of kings. Contrariwise, more democratically-inclined theorists have pointed to examples of meritocratic leaders, such as the Napoleonic marshals profiting from careers open to talent.

In the autocratic/paternalistic strain of thought, traditionalists recall the role of leadership of the Roman *pater familias*. Feminist thinking, on the other hand, may object to such models as patriarchal and posit against them emotionally-attuned, responsive, and consensual empathetic guidance, which is sometimes associated with matriarchies. Comparable to the Roman tradition, the views of Confucianism on "right living" relate very much to the ideal of the (male) scholar-leader and his benevolent rule, buttressed by a tradition of filial piety.

Leadership is a matter of intelligence, trustworthiness, humaneness, courage, and discipline... Reliance on intelligence alone results in rebelliousness. Exercise of humaneness alone results in weakness. Fixation on trust results in folly. Dependence on the strength of courage results in violence. Excessive discipline and sternness in command result in cruelty. When one has all five virtues together, each appropriate to its function, then one can be a leader. — Sun Tzu In the 19th century, the elaboration of anarchist thought called the whole concept of leadership into question. (Note that the *Oxford English Dictionary* traces the word "leadership" in English only as far back as the 19th century.) One response to this denial of élitism came with Leninism, which demanded an élite group of disciplined cadres to act as the vanguard of a socialist revolution, bringing into existence the dictatorship of the proletariat.

Other historical views of leadership have addressed the seeming contrasts between secular and religious leadership. The doctrines of Caesaro-papism have recurred and had their detractors over several centuries. Christian thinking on leadership has often emphasized stewardship of divinely-provided resources-human and material-and their deployment in accordance with a Divine plan. Compare servant leadership. For a more general take on leadership in politics, compare the concept of the statesman.

## Action Oriented Environments

This is a unique approach to team leadership that is aimed at action oriented environments where effective functional leadership is required to achieve critical or reactive tasks by small teams deployed into the field. In other words leadership of small groups often created to respond to a situation or critical incident.

In most cases these teams are tasked to operate in remote and changeable environments with limited support or backup (action environments). Leadership of people in these environments requires a different set of skills to that of front line management. These leaders must effectively operate remotely and negotiate both the needs of the individual, team and task within a changeable environment. This has been termed Action Oriented Leadership. Some example action oriented leadership is demonstrated in the following ways: extinguishing a rural fire, locating a missing person, leading a team on an outdoor expedition or rescuing a person from a potentially hazardous environment.

## Titles Emphasizing Authority

At certain stages in their development, the hierarchies of social ranks implied different degrees or ranks of leadership in society. Thus a knight led fewer men in general than did a duke; a baronet might in theory control less land than an earl.

In the course of the 18th and 20th centuries, several political operators took non-traditional paths to become dominant in their societies. They or their systems often expressed a belief in strong individual leadership, but existing titles and labels ("King", "Emperor", "President" and so on) often seemed inappropriate, insufficient or downright inaccurate in some circumstances. The formal or informal titles or descriptions they or their flunkies employ express and foster a general veneration for leadership of the inspired and autocratic variety. The definite article when used as part of the title (in languages that use definite articles) emphasizes the existence of a sole "true" leader.

### Critical Thought

Noam Chomsky and others have brought critical thinking to the very concept of leadership and have provided an analysis that asserts that people abrogate their responsibility to think and will actions for themselves. While the conventional view of leadership is rather satisfying to people who "want to be told what to do", these critics say that one should question why they are being subjected to a will or intellect other than their own if the leader is not a Subject Matter Expert (SME).

The fundamentally anti-democratic nature of the leadership principle is challenged by the introduction of concepts such as autogestion, employeeship, common civic virtue, etc., which stress individual responsibility and/or group authority in the work place and elsewhere by focusing on the skills and attitudes that a person needs in general rather than separating out leadership as the basis of a special class of individuals. Similarly, various historical calamities are attributed to a misplaced reliance on the principle of leadership.

### Varieties of Individual Power

According to Patrick J. Montana and Bruce H. Charnov, the ability to attain these unique powers is what enables leadership to influence subordinates and peers by controlling organizational resources. The successful leader effectively uses these power(s) to influence employees, and it is important for the leader to understand the uses of power to strengthen the leadership functioning.

The authors distinguish the following types of organizational power:

- Legitimate Power refers to the different types of professional positions within an organization structure that inherit such power (e.g. Manager, Vice President, Director, Supervisor, etc.). These levels of power correspond to the hierarchical executive levels within the organization itself. The higher position such as President of the company has a higher power than the rest of professional positions in the hierarchical executive levels.

- Reward Power is the power given to managers that attain administrative power over a range of rewards. Employees who work for managers desire the reward from the manager and will be influenced by receiving it as a result of work performance. The rewards may be pay raisse or promotions.
- Coercive Power is the manager's ability to punish an employee. Punishment can be a mild punishment such as a suspension or a serious punishment such as termination.
- Expert Power is attained by the manager due to his or her own talents such as skills, knowledge, abilities, or previous experience. A manager which has this power within the organization may be a very valuable and important manager in the company.
- Charisma Power A manager who has charisma will have a positive influence on workers, and create the opportunity for interpersonal influence. A person has charisma, and this will confer great power as a manager.
- Referent Power a power that is gained by association. A person who has power by association is often referred to assistant or deputy.
- Information Power a person who has possession of important information at an important time when such information is needed to organizational functioning. Someone who has this information knowledge has genuine power. For example, a manager's secretary would be in a powerful position if the secretary has information power.

Corporations are the most common form of business organization, and one which is chartered by a state and given many legal rights as an entity separate from its owners. This form of business is characterized by the limited liability of its owners, the issuance of shares of easily transferable stock, and existence as a going concern. The process of becoming a corporation, called incorporation, gives the company separate legal standing from its owners and protects those owners from being personally liable in the event that the company is sued (a condition known as limited liability). Incorporation also provides companies with a more flexible way to manage their ownership structure. In addition, there are different tax implications for corporations, although these can be both advantageous and disadvantageous. In these respects, corporations differ from sole proprietorships and limited partnership.

# 8

# Corporate Behaviour

Corporate behaviour is the behaviour of an organisation when considered as a single body. The behaviour of an organisation is influenced by the arrangements for its ownership and control. When the owner(s) appoint agents to manage the organisation, conflicts of interest arise which are studied as the principal-agent problem.

## Business Ethics

Business ethics (also known as corporate ethics) is a form of applied ethics or professional ethics that examines ethical principles and moral or ethical problems that arise in a business environment. It applies to all aspects of business conduct and is relevant to the conduct of individuals and entire organizations.

Business ethics has both normative and descriptive dimensions. As a corporate practice and a career specialization, the field is primarily normative. Academics attempting to understand business behaviour employ descriptive methods. The range and quantity of business ethical issues reflects the interaction of profit-maximizing behaviour with non-economic concerns. Interest in business ethics accelerated dramatically during the 1980s and 1990s, both within major corporations and within academia. For example, today most major corporations promote their commitment to non-economic values under headings such as ethics codes and social responsibility charters. Adam Smith said, "People of the same trade seldom meet together, even for merriment and diversion, but the conversation ends in a conspiracy against the public, or in some contrivance to raise prices." Governments use laws and regulations to point business behaviour in what they perceive to be beneficial directions. Ethics implicitly regulates areas and details of behaviour that lie beyond governmental control. The emergence of large corporations with limited relationships and sensitivity to the communities in which they operate accelerated the development of formal ethics regimes.

## Functional Business Areas

### *Finance*

Fundamentally, finance is a social science discipline. The discipline borders behavioural economics, sociology, economics, accounting and management. It concerns technical issues such as the mix of debt and equity, dividend policy, the evaluation of alternative investment projects, options, futures, swaps, and other derivatives, portfolio diversification and many others. It is often mistaken to be a discipline free from ethical burdens. The 2008 financial crisis caused critics to challenge the ethics of the executives in charge of U.S. and European financial institutions and financial regulatory bodies. Finance ethics is overlooked for another reason—issues in finance are often addressed as matters of law rather than ethics.

### *Finance Paradigm*

Aristotle said, "the end and purpose of the polis is the good life". Adam Smith characterized the good life in terms of material goods and intellectual and moral excellences of character. Smith in his *The Wealth of Nations* commented, "All for ourselves, and nothing for other people, seems, in every age of the world, to have been the vile maxim of the masters of mankind."

However, a section of economists influenced by the ideology of neoliberalism, interpreted the objective of economics to be maximization of economic growth through accelerated consumption and production of goods and services. Neoliberal ideology promoted finance from its position as a component of economics to its core.

Proponents of the ideology hold that unrestricted financial flows, if redeemed from the shackles of "financial repressions", best help impoverished nations to grow. The theory holds that open financial systems accelerate economic growth by encouraging foreign capital inûows, thereby enabling higher levels of savings, investment, employment, productivity and "welfare", along with containing corruption. Neoliberals recommended that governments open their financial systems to the global market with minimal regulation over capital flows. The recommendations however, met with criticisms from various schools of ethical philosophy. Some pragmatic ethicists, found these claims to unfalsifiable and a priori, although neither of these makes the recommendations false or unethical per se. Raising economic growth to the highest value necessarily means that welfare is subordinate, although advocates dispute this saying that economic growth provides more welfare than known alternatives. Since history shows that neither regulated nor unregulated firms always behave ethically, neither regime offers an ethical panacea.

Neoliberal recommendations to developing countries to unconditionally open up their economies to transnational finance corporations was fiercely contested by some ethicists. The claim that deregulation and the opening up of economies would reduce corruption was also contested. Dobson observes, "a rational agent is simply one who pursues personal material advantage ad infinitum. In essence, to be rational in finance is to be individualistic, materialistic, and competitive.

Business is a game played by individuals, as with all games the object is to win, and winning is measured in terms solely of material wealth. Within the discipline this rationality concept is never questioned, and has indeed become the theory-of-the-firm's sine qua non". Financial ethics is in this view a mathematical function of shareholder wealth. Such simplifying assumptions were once necessary for the construction of mathematically robust models. However signalling theory and agency theory extended the paradigm to greater realism.

### Human Resource Management

Human resource management occupies the sphere of activity of recruitment selection, orientation, performance appraisal, training and development, industrial relations and health and safety issues. Business Ethicists differ in their orientation towards labour ethics. Some assess human resource policies according to whether they support an egalitarian workplace and the dignity of labour.

Issues including employment itself, privacy, compensation in accord with comparable worth, collective bargaining (and/or its opposite) can be seen either as inalienable rights or as negotiable. Discrimination by age (preferring the young or the old), gender/sexual harassment, race, religion, disability, weight and attractiveness. A common approach to remedying discrimination is affirmative action.

PotentialEmployees have ethical obligations to employers, involving intellectual property protection and whistle-blowing.

Employers must consider workplace safety, which may involve modifying the workplace, or providing appropriate training or hazard disclosure.

Larger economic issues such as immigration, trade policy, globalization and trade unionism affect workplaces and have an ethical dimension, but are often beyond the purview of individual companies.

### *Trade Unions*

Unions for example, may push employers to establish due process for workers, but may also cost jobs by demanding unsustainable compensation and work rules.

Unionized workplaces may confront union busting and strike breaking and face the ethical implications of work rules that advantage some workers over others.

### *Management Strategy*

Among the many people management strategies that companies employ are a "soft" approach that regards employees as a source of creative energy and participants in workplace decision making, a "hard" version explicitly focused on control and Theory Z that emphasizes philosophy, culture and consensus.

None ensure ethical behaviour. Some studies claim that sustainable success requires a humanely treated and satisfied workforce.

### *Sales and Marketing*

Marketing Ethics came of age only as late as 1990s. Marketing ethics was approached from ethical perspectives of virtue or virtue ethics, deontology, consequentialism, pragmatism and relativism.

Ethics in marketing deals with the principles, values and/or ideals by which marketers (and marketing institutions) ought to act. Marketing ethics is also contested terrain, beyond the previously described issue of potential conflicts between profitability and other concerns. Ethical marketing issues include marketing redundant or dangerous products/services transparency about environmental risks, transparency about product ingredients such as genetically modified organisms possible health risks, financial risks, security risks, etc., respect for consumer privacy and autonomy, advertising truthfulness and fairness in pricing & distribution.

According to Borgerson, and Schroeder (2008), marketing can influence individuals' perceptions of and interactions with other people, implying an ethical responsibility to avoid distorting those perceptions and interactions.

Marketing ethics involves pricing practices, including illegal actions such as price fixing and legal actions including price discrimination and price skimming. Certain promotional activities have drawn fire, including greenwashing, bait and switch, shilling, viral marketing, spam (electronic), pyramid schemes and multi-level marketing. Advertising has raised objections about attack ads, subliminal messages, sex in advertising and marketing in schools.

### Production

This area of business ethics usually deals with the duties of a company to ensure that products and production processes do not needlessly cause harm. Since few goods and services can be produced and consumed with zero risk, determining the ethical course can be problematic. In some case consumers demand products that harm them, such as tobacco products. Production may have environmental impacts, including pollution, habitat destruction and urban sprawl. The downstream effects of technologies nuclear power, genetically modified food and mobile phones may not be well understood. While the precautionary principle may prohibit introducing new technology whose consequences are not fully understood, that principle would have prohibited most new technology introduced since the industrial revolution. Product testing protocols have been attacked for violating the rights of both humans and animals.

### Modern History of Property Rights

Modern discourse on property emerged by the turn of 17th century within theological discussions of that time. For instance, John Locke justified property rights saying that God had made "the earth, and all inferior creatures, [in] common to all men".

In 1802 Utilitarian Jeremy Bentham stated, "property and law are born together and die together".

One argument for property ownership is that it enhances individual liberty by extending the line of non-interference by the state or others around the person. Seen from this perspective, property right is absolute and property has a special and distinctive character that precedes its legal protection. Blackstone conceptualized property as the "sole and despotic dominion which one man claims and exercises over the external things of the world, in total exclusion of the right of any other individual in the universe".

### *Slaves as Property*

During the seventeenth and eighteenth centuries, slavery spread to European colonies including America, where colonial legislatures defined the legal status of slaves as a form of property. During this time settlers began the centuries-long process of dispossessing the natives of America of millions of acres of land. Ironically, the natives lost about 200,000 square miles (520,000 $km^2$) of land in the Louisiana Territory under the leadership of Thomas Jefferson, who championed property rights.

Combined with theological justification, property was taken to be essentially natural ordained by God. Property, which later gained meaning as ownership and appeared natural to Locke, Jefferson and to many of the 18th and 19th century intellectuals as land, labour or idea and property right over slaves had the same theological and essentialized justification It was even held that the property in slaves was a sacred right. Wiecek noted, "slavery was more clearly and explicitly established under the Constitution as it had been under the Articles". Accordingly, US Supreme Court Chief Justice Roger B. Taney in his 1857 judgment stated, "The right of property in a slave is distinctly and expressly affirmed in the Constitution".

### *Natural Right vs Social Construct*

Neoliberals hold that private property rights are a non-negotiable natural right. Davies counters with "property is no different from other legal categories in that it is simply a consequence of the significance attached by law to the relationships between legal persons." Singer claims, "Property is a form of power, and the distribution of power is a political problem of the highest order". Rose finds, "'Property' is only an effect, a construction, of relationships between people, meaning that its objective character is contestable. Persons and things, are 'constituted' or 'fabricated' by legal and other normative techniques.". Singer observes, "A private property regime is not, after all, a Hobbesian state of nature; it requires a working legal system that can define, allocate, and enforce property rights." Davis claims that common law theory generally favours the view that "property is not essentially a 'right to a thing', but rather a separable bundle of rights subsisting between persons which may vary according to the context and the object which is at stake".

In common parlance property rights involve a 'bundle of rights' including occupancy, use and enjoyment, and the right to sell, devise, give, or lease all or part of these rights. Custodians of property have obligations as well as rights. Michelman writes, "A property regime thus depends on a great deal of cooperation, trustworthiness, and self-restraint among the people who enjoy it." Menon claims that the autonomous individual, responsible for his/her own existence is a cultural construct moulded by Western culture rather than the truth about the human condition. Penner views property as an "illusion"—a "normative phantasm" without substance. In the neoliberal literature, property is part of the private side of a public/private dichotomy and acts a counterweight to state power. Davies counters that "any space may be subject to plural meanings or appropriations which do not necessarily come into conflict".

Private property has never been a universal doctrine, although since the end of the Cold War is it has become nearly so. Some societies, e.g., Native American bands, held land, if not all property, in common. When groups came into conflict, the victor often appropriated the loser's property. The rights paradigm tended to stabilize the distribution of property holdings on the presumption that title had been lawfully acquired.

Property does not exist in isolation, and so property rights too. Bryan claimed that property rights describe relations among people and not just relations between people and things Singer holds that the idea that owners have no legal obligations to others wrongly supposes that property rights hardly ever conflict with other legally protected interests. Singer continues implying that legal realists "did not take the character and structure of social relations as an important independent factor in choosing the rules that govern market life". Ethics of property rights begins with recognizing the vacuous nature of the notion of property.

### Intellectual Property

Intellectual property (IP) encompasses expressions of ideas, thoughts, codes and information. "Intellectual property rights" (IPR) treat IP as a kind of real property, subject to analogous protections, rather than as a reproducible good or service. Boldrin and Levine argue that "government does not ordinarily enforce monopolies for producers of other goods. This is because it is widely recognized that monopoly creates many social costs. Intellectual monopoly is no different in this respect. The question we address is whether it also creates social benefits commensurate with these social costs."

International standards relating to Intellectual Property Rights are enforced through Agreement on Trade Related Aspects of

Intellectual Property Rights (TRIPS). In the US, IP other than copyrights is regulated by the United States Patent and Trademark Office. The US Constitution included the power to protect intellectual property, empowering the Federal government "*to promote the progress of science and useful arts, by securing for limited times to authors and inventors the exclusive right to their respective writings and discoveries*". Boldrin and Levine see no value in such state-enforced monopolies stating, "we ordinarily think of innovative monopoly as an oxymoron. Further they comment, 'intellectual property' "is not like ordinary property at all, but constitutes a government grant of a costly and dangerous private monopoly over ideas.

We show through theory and example that intellectual monopoly is not necessary for innovation and as a practical matter is damaging to growth, prosperity, and liberty". Steelman defends patent monopolies, writing, "Consider prescription drugs, for instance. Such drugs have benefited millions of people, improving or extending their lives. Patent protection enables drug companies to recoup their development costs because for a specific period of time they have the sole right to manufacture and distribute the products they have invented." The court cases by 39 pharmaceutical companies against South Africa's 1997 Medicines and Related Substances Control Amendment Act, which intended to provide affordable HIV medicines has been cited as a harmful effect of patents.

One attack on IPR is moral rather than utilitarian, claiming that inventions are mostly a collective, cumulative, path dependent, social creation and therefore, no one person or ûrm should be able to monopolize them even for a limited period. The opposing argument is that the benefits of innovation arrive sooner when patents encourage innovators and their investors to increase their commitments. Roderick Long, a libertarian philosopher, observes, "Ethically, property rights of any kind have to be justified as extensions of the right of individuals to control their own lives.

Thus any alleged property rights that conflict with this moral basis—like the "right" to own slaves—are invalidated. In my judgment, intellectual property rights also fail to pass this test. To enforce copyright laws and the like is to prevent people from making peaceful use of the information they possess. If you have acquired the information legitimately (say, by buying a book), then on what grounds can you be prevented from using it, reproducing it, trading it? Is this not a violation of the freedom of speech and press? It may be objected that the person who originated the information deserves ownership rights over it. But information is not a concrete thing an individual can control; it is a universal, existing in other people's minds and other people's property, and over these the originator has no legitimate sovereignty.

You cannot own information without owning other people". Machlup concluded that patents do not have the intended effect of enhancing innovation. Self-declared anarchist Proudhon, in his 1847 seminal work noted, "Monopoly is the natural opposite of competition," and continued, "Competition is the vital force which animates the collective being: to destroy it, if such a supposition were possible, would be to kill society"

Mindeli and Pipiya hold that the knowledge economy is an economy of abundance because it relies on the "infinite potential" of knowledge and ideas rather than on the limited resources of natural resources, labour and capital. Allison envisioned an egalitarian distribution of knowledge. Kinsella claims that IPR create artificial scarcity and reduce equality. Bouckaert wrote, "Natural scarcity is that which follows from the relationship between man and nature.

Scarcity is natural when it is possible to conceive of it before any human, institutional, contractual arrangement. Artificial scarcity, on the other hand, is the outcome of such arrangements. Artificial scarcity can hardly serve as a justification for the legal framework that causes that scarcity. Such an argument would be completely circular. On the contrary, artificial scarcity itself needs a justification" Corporations fund much IP creation and can acquire IP they do not create, to which Menon and others object. Andersen claims that IPR has increasingly become an instrument in eroding public domain.

Ethical and legal issues include: Patent infringement, copyright infringement, trademark infringement, patent and copyright misuse. submarine patents, gene patents, patent, copyright and trademark trolling, Employee raiding and monopolizing talent, Bioprospecting, biopiracy and industrial espionage, digital rights management. Notable IP cases include Napster, Eldred v. Ashcroft and Air Pirates.

### Industry-specific Concerns

Health care is one of many industries that have specific ethical concerns. High costs limit access, and unproven therapeutic regimes offer complex trade-offs between access and safety. Patent law is intended to encourage innovation but may further limit access to needed therapies.

### *International Issues*

While business ethics emerged as a field in the 1970s, international business ethics did not emerge until the late 1990s, looking back on the international developments of that decade. Many new practical issues arose out of the international context of business. Theoretical issues such as cultural relativity of ethical values receive more emphasis in this field. Other, older issues can be grouped here as well. Issues and subfields include:

- The search for universal values as a basis for international commercial behaviour.
- Comparison of business ethical traditions in different countries. Also on the basis of their respective GDP and [Corruption rankings].
- Comparison of business ethical traditions from various religious perspectives.
- Ethical issues arising out of international business transactions; e.g., bioprospecting and biopiracy in the pharmaceutical industry; the fair trade movement; transfer pricing.
- Issues such as globalization and cultural imperialism.
- Varying global standards—e.g., the use of child labour.
- The way in which multinationals take advantage of international differences, such as outsourcing production (e.g. clothes) and services (e.g. call centres) to low-wage countries.
- The permissibility of international commerce with pariah states.

The success of any business depends on its financial performance. Financial accounting helps the management to report and also control the business performance.

The information regarding the financial performance of the company plays an important role in enabling people to take right decision about the company. Therefore, it becomes necessary to understand how to record based on accounting conventions and concepts ensure unambling and accurate records.

Foreign countries often use dumping as a competitive threat, selling products at prices lower than their normal value. This can lead to problems in domestic markets. It becomes difficult for these markets to compete with the pricing set by foreign markets. In 2009, the International Trade Commission has been researching anti-dumping laws. Dumping is often seen as an ethical issue, as larger companies are taking advantage of other less economically advanced companies.

### Economic Systems

Political economy and political philosophy have ethical implications, particularly regarding the distribution of economic benefits. John Rawls and Robert Nozick are both notable contributors.

### Law and Regulation

Very often it is held that business is not bound by any ethics other than abiding by the law. Milton Friedman is the pioneer of the view. He held that corporations have the obligation to make a profit within the framework of the legal system, nothing more.

Friedman made it explicit that the duty of the business leaders is, "to make as much money as possible while conforming to the basic rules of the society, both those embodied in the law and those embodied in ethical custom".

Ethics for Friedman is nothing more than abiding by 'customs' and 'laws'. The reduction of ethics to abidance to laws and customs however have drawn serious criticisms.

Counter to Friedman's logic it is observed that legal procedures are technocratic, bureaucratic, rigid and obligatory where as ethical act is conscientious, voluntary choice beyond normativity. Law is retroactive. Crime precedes law.

Law against a crime, to be passed, the crime must have happened. Laws are blind to the crimes undefined in it. Further, as per law, "conduct is not criminal unless forbidden by law which gives advance warning that such conduct is criminal. *Also, law presumes the accused is innocent until proven guilty and that the state must establish the guilt of the accused beyond reasonable doubt. As per liberal laws followed in most of the democracies, until the government prosecutor proves the firm guilty with the limited resources available to her, the accused is considered to be innocent. Though the liberal premises of law is necessary to protect individuals from being persecuted by Government, it is not a sufficient mechanism to make firms morally accountable.*

## Implementation

### Corporate Policies

As part of more comprehensive compliance and ethics programs, many companies have formulated internal policies pertaining to the ethical conduct of employees.

These policies can be simple exhortations in broad, highly generalized language (typically called a corporate ethics statement), or they can be more detailed policies, containing specific behavioural requirements (typically called corporate ethics codes). They are generally meant to identify the company's expectations of workers and to offer guidance on handling some of the more common ethical problems that might arise in the course of doing business. It is hoped that having such a policy will lead to greater ethical awareness, consistency in application, and the avoidance of ethical disasters.

An increasing number of companies also require employees to attend seminars regarding business conduct, which often include discussion of the company's policies, specific case studies, and legal requirements. Some companies even require their employees to sign agreements stating that they will abide by the company's rules of conduct.

Many companies are assessing the environmental factors that can lead employees to engage in unethical conduct. A competitive business environment may call for unethical behaviour. Lying has become expected in fields such as trading. An example of this are the issues surrounding the unethical actions of the Saloman Brothers.

Not everyone supports corporate policies that govern ethical conduct. Some claim that ethical problems are better dealt with by depending upon employees to use their own judgment.

Others believe that corporate ethics policies are primarily rooted in utilitarian concerns, and that they are mainly to limit the company's legal liability, or to curry public favour by giving the appearance of being a good corporate citizen. Ideally, the company will avoid a lawsuit because its employees will follow the rules. Should a lawsuit occur, the company can claim that the problem would not have arisen if the employee had only followed the code properly.

Sometimes there is disconnection between the company's code of ethics and the company's actual practices. Thus, whether or not such conduct is explicitly sanctioned by management, at worst, this makes the policy duplicitous, and, at best, it is merely a marketing tool.

Jones and Parker write, "Most of what we read under the name business ethics is either sentimental common sense, or a set of excuses for being unpleasant." Many manuals are procedural form filling exercises unconcerned about the real ethical dilemmas. For instance, US Department of Commerce ethics program treats business ethics as a set of instructions and procedures to be followed by 'ethics officers'., some others claim being ethical is just for the sake of being ethical. Business ethicists may trivialize the subject, offering standard answers that do not reflect the situation's complexity.

### Ethics Officers

Ethics officers (sometimes called "compliance" or "business conduct officers") have been appointed formally by organizations since the mid-1980s. One of the catalysts for the creation of this new role was a series of fraud, corruption, and abuse scandals that afflicted the U.S. defence industry at that time. This led to the creation of the Defence Industry Initiative (DII), a pan-industry initiative to promote and ensure ethical business practices.

The DII set an early benchmark for ethics management in corporations. In 1991, the Ethics & Compliance Officer Association (ECOA)—originally the Ethics Officer Association (EOA)—was founded at the Centre for Business Ethics (at Bentley College, Waltham, MA) as a professional association for those responsible for managing organizations' efforts to achieve ethical best practices. The membership grew rapidly (the ECOA now has over 1,200 members) and was soon established as an independent organization.

Another critical factor in the decisions of companies to appoint ethics/compliance officers was the passing of the Federal Sentencing Guidelines for Organizations in 1991, which set standards that organizations (large or small, commercial and non-commercial) had to follow to obtain a reduction in sentence if they should be convicted of a federal offense. Although intended to assist judges with sentencing, the influence in helping to establish best practices has been far-reaching.

In the wake of numerous corporate scandals between 2001–04 (affecting large corporations like Enron, WorldCom and Tyco), even small and medium-sized companies have begun to appoint ethics officers. They often report to the Chief Executive Officer and are responsible for assessing the ethical implications of the company's activities, making recommendations regarding the company's ethical policies, and disseminating information to employees. They are particularly interested in uncovering or preventing unethical and illegal actions. This trend is partly due to the Sarbanes-Oxley Act in the United States, which was enacted in reaction to the above scandals. A related trend is the introduction of risk assessment officers that monitor how shareholders' investments might be affected by the company's decisions.

The effectiveness of ethics officers is not clear. If the appointment is made primarily as a reaction to legislative requirements, one might expect little impact, at least over the short term. In part, this is because ethical business practices result from a corporate culture that consistently places value on ethical behaviour, a culture and climate that usually emanates from the top of the organization. The mere establishment of a position to oversee ethics will most likely be insufficient to inculcate ethical behaviour: a more systemic programme with consistent support from general management will be necessary.

The foundation for ethical behaviour goes well beyond corporate culture and the policies of any given company, for it also depends greatly upon an individual's early moral training, the other institutions that affect an individual, the competitive business environment the company is in and, indeed, society as a whole.

### Academic Discipline

As an academic discipline, business ethics emerged in the 1970s. Since no academic business ethics journals or conferences existed, researchers published in general management journals, and attended general conferences. Over time, specialized peer-reviewed journals appeared, and more researchers entered the field. Corporate scandals in the earlier 2000s increased the field's popularity. As of 2009, sixteen academic journals devoted to various business ethics issues existed, with Journal of Business Ethics and Business Ethics Quarterly considered the leaders.

The International Business Development Institute is a global non-profit organization that represents 217 nations and all 50 United States. It offers a Charter in Business Development (CBD) that focuses on ethical business practices and standards. The Charter is directed by Harvard, MIT, and Fulbright Scholars, and it includes graduate-level coursework in economics, politics, marketing, management, technology, and legal aspects of business development as it pertains to business ethics. IBDI also oversees the International Business Development Institute of Asia which provides individuals living in 20 Asian nations the opportunity to earn the Charter.

### Religious Views

The historical and global importance of religious views on business ethics is sometimes underestimated in standard introductions to business ethics according to Dr. Todd Albertson author of *The Gods of Business*. Particularly in Asia and the Middle East, religious and cultural perspectives have a strong influence on the conduct of business and the creation of business values. In Sharia law, followed by many Muslims, banking specifically prohibits charging interest on loans.

Traditional Confucian thought discourages profit-seeking. Christianity offers the Golden Rule command, "Therefore all things whatsoever ye would that men should do to you, do ye even so to them: for this is the law and the prophets."

### *Related Disciplines*

Business ethics is part of the philosophy of business, the branch of philosophy that deals with the philosophical, political, and ethical underpinnings of business and economics. Business ethics operates on the premise, for example, that the ethical operation of a private business is possible—those who dispute that premise, such as libertarian socialists, (who contend that "business ethics" is an oxymoron) do so by definition outside of the domain of business ethics proper.

The philosophy of business also deals with questions such as what, if any, are the social responsibilities of a business; business management theory; theories of individualism vs. collectivism; free will among participants in the marketplace; the role of self interest; invisible hand theories; the requirements of social justice; and natural rights, especially property rights, in relation to the business enterprise. Business ethics is also related to political economy, which is economic analysis from political and historical perspectives. Political economy deals with the distributive consequences of economic actions. It asks who gains and who loses from economic activity, and is the resultant distribution fair or just, which are central ethical issues.

## Corporate Crime

In criminology, corporate crime refers to crimes committed either by a corporation (i.e., a business entity having a separate legal personality from the natural persons that manage its activities), or by individuals that may be identified with a corporation or other business entity. Note that some forms of corporate corruption may not actually be criminal if they are not specifically illegal under a given system of laws. For example, some jurisdictions allow insider trading.

Corporate crime overlaps with:

- white-collar crime, because the majority of individuals who may act as or represent the interests of the corporation are employees or professionals of a higher social class;

- organized crime, because criminals can set up corporations either for the purposes of crime or as vehicles for laundering the proceeds of crime. Organized crime has become a branch of big business and is simply the illegal sector of major capital. It has been estimated that, by the middle of the 1990s, the "gross criminal product" of organized crime made it the twentieth richest organization in the world—richer than 150 sovereign states (Castells 1998: 169). The world's gross criminal product has been estimated at 20 percent of world trade. (de Brie 2000); and
- state-corporate crime because, in many contexts, the opportunity to commit crime emerges from the relationship between the corporation and the state.

## Definitional Issues

### Legal Person

An 1886 decision of the United States Supreme Court, in *Santa Clara County v. Southern Pacific Railroad* 118 U.S. 394 (1886), has been cited by various courts in the US as precedent to maintain that a corporation can be defined legally as a 'person', as described in the Fourteenth Amendment to the U.S. Constitution.

The Fourteenth Amendment stipulates that, "No State shall make or enforce any law which shall abridge the privileges or immunities of citizens of the United States; nor shall any State deprive any person of life, liberty, or property, without due process of law; nor deny to any person within its jurisdiction the equal protection of the laws."

In English law, this was matched by the decision in Salomon v Salomon & Co [1897] AC 22. In Australian law, under the *Corporations Act 2001 (Cth),* a corporation is legally a 'person'. This doctrine of corporate personhood has often impeded prosecution of corporate crime by allowing corporations to claim Bill of Rights protections in court, sometimes with success.

### Function of Law

History shows that laws have always served as instruments of regulation. Lea (2001) argues that whereas crime used to be the exceptional event, disrupting the otherwise normal socio-economic processes, as crime becomes more frequent it lost its status as an exceptional event and became "a standard, background feature of our lives—a taken for granted element of late modernity." (Garland 1996: 446)

### *Enforcement Policy*

Corporate crime has become politically sensitive in some countries. In the United Kingdom, for example, following a number of fatal disasters on the rail network and at sea, the term is commonly used in reference to corporate manslaughter and to involve a more general discussion about the technological hazards posed by business enterprises. Similar incidents of corporate crime, such as the 1985 Union Carbide accident in Bhopal, India (Pearce & Tombs: 1993) and the behaviour of the pharmaceutical industry (Braithwaite: 1984).

The Law Reform Commission of New South Wales offers an explanation of such criminal activities:

> *"Corporate crime poses a significant threat to the welfare of the community. Given the pervasive presence of corporations in a wide range of activities in our society, and the impact of their actions on a much wider group of people than are affected by individual action, the potential for both economic and physical harm caused by a corporation is great."*

Similarly, Russell Mokhiber and Robert Weissman (1999) assert:

"At one level, corporations develop new technologies and economies of scale. These may serve the economic interests of mass consumers by introducing new products and more efficient methods of mass production. On another level, given the absence of political control today, corporations serve to destroy the foundations of the civic community and the lives of people who reside in them."

### *Discussion: Criminalization*

Behaviour can be regulated by the civil law (including administrative law) or the criminal law. In deciding to criminalize particular behaviour, the legislature is making the political judgment that this behaviour is sufficiently culpable to deserve the stigma of being labelled as a crime. In law, corporations can commit the same offences as natural persons. Simpson (2002) avers that this process should be straightforward because a state should simply engage in victimology to identify which behaviour causes the most loss and damage to its citizens, and then represent the majority view that justice requires the intervention of the criminal law.

But states depend on the business sector to deliver a stable economy, so the politics of regulating the individuals and corporations that supply that stability become more complex. More specifically, the historical tradition of sovereign state control of prisons is ending through the process of privatisation. Corporate profitability in these areas therefore depends on building more prison facilities, managing their operations, and selling inmate labour. In turn, this requires a steady stream of prisoners able to work. (Kicenski: 2002)

The majority of crimes are committed because the offender has the 'right opportunity', i.e., where the offender simply sees the chance and thinks that he or she will be able to commit the crime and not be detected. For the most part, greed, rather than conceit, is the motive, and the rationalisation for choosing to break the law usually arises out of a form of contempt for the victim, namely that he, she or it will be powerless to prevent it, and has it coming for some reason. For these purposes, the corporation is the vehicle for the crime. This may be a short-term crime, i.e., the corporation is set up as a shell to open credit trading accounts with manufacturers and wholesalers, trades for a short period of time and then disappears with the revenue and without paying for the inventory.

Alternatively and most commonly, the primary purpose of the corporation is as a legitimate business, but criminal activity is secretly intermixed with legal activity to escape detection. To achieve a suitable level of secrecy, senior managers will usually be involved. The explanations and exculpations may therefore centre around rogue individuals who acted outside the organizational structures, or there may be a serious examination of the occupational and organisational structures (often hinged on the socio-economic system, gender, racism and/or age) that facilitated the criminal conduct of a corporation

Bribery and corruption are problems in the developed world, and the corruption of public officials is thought to be a large cause of crime in poor countries that have large IMF debts and IMF sovereign obligations.

### *Penalties*

In part, this will be a function of the public perception of the degrees of societal culpability involved. Weissman and Mokhiber (1999) catalog the silence and indifference of the major media in the face of the widespread corporate corruption. Only in part is this justifiable. The news media find it difficult to respond to corporate crime both because reporting may compromise the trial by tainting the jury's perceptions, or because of the danger of defamation proceedings. Further, major corporate crime is often complicated and more difficult to explain to the lay public, as against street or property crimes, which may provide graphic visual evidence of harm to victims injured, or of property that has been damaged or vandalized in spectacular fashion. But, more significantly, the news media are owned by large corporations which may also own prisons. Thus, the political decisions on the resources to allocate to investigate and prosecute will tend to match the electorate's understanding of the dangers posed by 'crime'. In sentencing, the fact that the convicted individuals may have had an impeccable character as presidents, CEOs, chairmen, directors and managers is likely to be a mitigating factor.

Examples of criminal behaviour in most jurisdictions include: insider trading, antitrust violations, fraud (usually involving the consumers), damage to the environment, exploitation of labour in violation of labour and health and safety laws, and the failure to maintain a fiduciary responsibility towards stockholders.

### Enforcement and Legal or Quasi-legal Corrupt Activities

One example, may be in the area of takeovers and top executive compensation:

> *It is fairly easy for a top executive to reduce the price of his/her company's stock—due to information asymmetry. The executive can accelerate accounting of expected expenses, delay accounting of expected revenue, engage in off balance sheet transactions to make the company's profitability appear temporarily poorer, or simply promote and report severely conservative (e.g. pessimistic) estimates of future earnings. Such seemingly adverse earnings news will be likely to (at least temporarily) reduce share price. (This is again due to information asymmetries since it is more common for top executives to do everything they can to window dress their company's earnings forecasts). There are typically very few legal risks to being 'too conservative' in one's accounting and earnings estimates.*

A reduced share price makes a company an easier takeover target. When the company gets bought out (or taken private)—at a dramatically lower price—the takeover artist gains a windfall from the former top executive's actions to surreptitiously reduce share price. This can represent 10s of billions of dollars (questionably) transferred from previous shareholders to the takeover artist. The former top executive is then rewarded with a golden handshake for presiding over the firesale that can sometimes be in the hundreds of millions of dollars for one or two years of work. (This is nevertheless an excellent bargain for the takeover artist, who will tend to benefit from developing a reputation of being very generous to parting top executives). Similar issues occur when a publicly held asset or non-profit organization undergoes privatization. Top executives often reap tremendous monetary benefits when a government owned or non-profit entity is sold to private hands. Just as in the example above, they can facilitate this process by making the entity appear to be in financial crisis—this reduces the sale price (to the profit of the purchaser), and makes non-profits and governments more likely to sell. Ironically, it can also contribute to a public perception that private entities are more efficiently run, reinforcing the political will to sell off public assets. Again, due to asymmetric information, policy makers and the general public see a government owned firm that was a financial 'disaster'—miraculously turned around by the private sector (and typically resold) within a few years.

### Accounting Scandals

Accounting scandals, or corporate accounting scandals, are political and business scandals which arise with the disclosure of misdeeds by trusted executives of large public corporations. Such misdeeds typically involve complex methods for misusing or misdirecting funds, overstating revenues, understating expenses, overstating the value of corporate assets or underreporting the existence of liabilities, sometimes with the cooperation of officials in other corporations or affiliates.

In public companies, this type of "creative accounting" can amount to fraud and investigations are typically launched by government oversight agencies, such as the Securities and Exchange Commission (SEC) in the United States. Scandals are often only the 'tip of the iceberg'. They represent the visible catastrophic failures. Note that much abuse can be completely legal or quasi legal. For example, in the domain of privatization and takeovers :

It is fairly easy for a top executive to reduce the price of his/her company's stock-due to information asymmetry. The executive can accelerate accounting of expected expenses, delay accounting of expected revenue, engage in off balance sheet transactions to make the company's profitability appear temporarily poorer, or simply promote and report severely conservative (eg. pessimistic) estimates of future earnings. Such seemingly adverse earnings news will be likely to (at least temporarily) reduce share price. (This is again due to information asymmetries since it is more common for top executives to do everything they can to window dress their company's earnings forecasts). There are typically very few legal risks to being 'too conservative' in one's accounting and earnings estimates.

A reduced share price makes a company an easier takeover target. When the company gets bought out (or taken private)-at a dramatically lower price-the takeover artist gains a windfall from the former top executive's actions to surreptitiously reduce share price. This can represent tens of billions of dollars (questionably) transferred from previous shareholders to the takeover artist.

The former top executive is then rewarded with a golden handshake for presiding over the firesale that can sometimes be in the hundreds of millions of dollars for one or two years of work. (This is nevertheless an excellent bargain for the takeover artist, who will tend to benefit from developing a reputation of being very generous to parting top executives).

Similar issues occur when a publicly held asset or non-profit organization undergoes privatization. Top executives often reap tremendous monetary benefits when a government owned or non-profit entity is sold to private hands. Just as in the example above, they can facilitate this process by making the entity appear to be in financial crisis-this reduces the sale price (to the profit of the purchaser), and makes non-profits and governments more likely to sell. It can also contribute to a public perception that private entities are more efficiently run reinforcing the political will to sell off public assets. Again, due to asymmetric information, policy makers and the general public see a government owned firm that was a financial 'disaster'-miraculously turned around by the private sector (and typically resold) within a few years.

## Notable Outcomes

The Enron scandal turned in the indictment and criminal conviction of one of the Big Five auditor Arthur Andersen on June 15, 2002. Although the conviction was overturned on May 31, 2005 by the Supreme Court of the United States, the firm ceased performing audits and is currently unwinding its business operations. On July 9, 2002 George W. Bush gave a speech about recent accounting scandals that had been uncovered. In spite of its stern tone, the speech did not focus on establishing new policy, but instead focused on actually enforcing current laws, which include holding CEOs and directors personally responsible for accountancy fraud.

In July, 2002, WorldCom filed for bankruptcy protection, in what was considered the largest corporate insolvency ever at the time.

These scandals reignited the debate over the relative merits of US GAAP, which takes a "rules-based" approach to accounting, versus International Accounting Standards and UK GAAP, which takes a "principles-based" approach. The Financial Accounting Standards Board announced that it intends to introduce more principles-based standards. More radical means of accounting reform have been proposed, but so far have very little support. The debate itself, however, overlooks the difficulties of classifying any system of knowledge, including accounting, as rules-based or principles-based.This also led to the establishment of Sarbanes-Oxley. On a lighter note, the 2002 Ig Nobel Prize in Economics went to the CEOs of those companies involved in the corporate accounting scandals of that year for "adapting the mathematical concept of imaginary numbers for use in the business world". In 2003, Nortel made a big contribution to this list of scandals by incorrectly reporting a one cent per share earnings directly after their massive layoff period.

They used this money to pay the top 43 managers of the company. The SEC and the Ontario securities commission eventually settled civil action with Nortel. However, a separate civil action will be taken up against top Nortel executives including Dunn, Beatty, Gollogly, Pahapill and Hamilton. These proceedings have been postponed pending criminal proceedings in Canada. In 2005, after a scandal on insurance and mutual funds the year before, AIG was investigated for accounting fraud. The company already lost over 45 billion US dollars worth of market capitalisation because of the scandal. Investigations also discovered over a billion US dollars worth of errors in accounting transactions. The New York Attorney General's investigation led to a $1.6 billion fine for AIG and criminal charges for some of its executives. CEO Maurice R. "Hank" Greenberg was forced to step down and is still fighting civil charges being pursued by New York state.

### *Corporate Law*

Corporate law (also "company" or "corporations" law) is the study of how shareholders, directors, employees, creditors, and other stakeholders such as consumers, the community and the environment interact with one another under the internal rules of the firm. Corporate law is a part of a broader companies law (or law of business associations). Other types of business associations can include partnerships (in the UK governed by the Partnership Act 1890), or trusts (like a pension fund), or companies limited by guarantee (like some universities or charities).

Corporate law is about big business, which has separate legal personality, with limited liability or unlimited liability for its members or shareholders, who buy and sell their stocks depending on the performance of the board of directors. It deals with the firms that are incorporated or registered under the corporate or company law of a sovereign state or their subnational states. The four defining characteristics of the modern corporation are:

- Separate Legal Personality of the corporation (the right to sue and be sued in its own name i.e. the law treats the company as a human being)
- Limited Liability of the shareholders (so that when the company is insolvent, they only owe the money that they subscribed for in shares)
- Shares (usually on a stock exchange, such as the London Stock Exchange, New York Stock Exchange or Euronext in Paris)
- Delegated Management, in other words, control of the company placed in the hands of a board of directors

In most developed countries outside of the English speaking world, company boards are appointed as representatives of both shareholders and employees to "codetermine" company strategy. Corporate law is often divided into corporate governance (which concerns the various power relations within a corporation) and corporate finance (which concerns the rules on how capital is used). A major contributor to company law in the UK is the Companies Act 2006.

## Corporate Law in Context

### *Definition*

The word "corporation" is generally synonymous with large publicly owned companies. In the United States, a company may or may not be a separate legal entity, and is often used synonymously with "firm" or "business." A corporation may accurately be called a company; however, a company should not necessarily be called a corporation, which has distinct characteristics. According to Black's Law Dictionary, in the U.S. a company means "a corporation — or, less commonly, an association, partnership or union—that carries on industrial enterprise."

The defining feature of a corporation is its legal independence from the people who create it. If a corporation fails, its shareholders will lose their money, and employees will lose their jobs, though disproportionately affecting its workers as opposed to its upper executives. Shareholders, however owning a part piece of the company, are not liable for debts that remain owing to the corporation's creditors. This rule is called limited liability, and it is why corporations end with "Ltd." (or some variant like "Inc." and "plc"). In the words of British judge, Walton J, a company is...

"...only a juristic figment of the imagination, lacking both a body to be kicked and a soul to be damned."

But despite this, corporations are recognized by the law to have rights and responsibilities like actual people. Corporations can exercise human rights against real individuals and the state, and they may be responsible for human rights violations. Just as they are "born" into existence through its members obtaining a certificate of incorporation, they can "die" when they lose money into insolvency. Corporations can even be convicted of criminal offences, such as fraud and manslaughter.

### Corporate Personality

One of the key legal features of corporations are their separate legal personality, also known as "personhood" or being "artificial persons". However, the separate legal personality was not confirmed under English law until 1895 by the House of Lords in *Salomon v. Salomon & Co.* Separate legal personality often has unintended consequences, particularly in relation to smaller, family companies. In *B v. B* [1978] Fam 181 it was held that a discovery order obtained by a wife against her husband was not effective against the husband's company as it was not named in the order and was separate and distinct from him. And in *Macaura v. Northern Assurance Co Ltd* a claim under an insurance policy failed where the insured had transferred timber from his name into the name of a company wholly owned by him, and it was subsequently destroyed in a fire; as the property now belonged to the company and not to him, he no longer had an "insurable interest" in it and his claim failed.

However, separate legal personality does allow corporate groups a great deal of flexibility in relation to tax planning, and also enables multinational companies to manage the liability of their overseas operations. For instance in *Adams v. Cape Industries plc* it was held that victims of asbestos poisoning at the hands of an American subsidiary could not sue the English parent in tort. There are certain specific situations where courts are generally prepared to "pierce the corporate veil", to look directly at, and impose liability directly on the individuals behind the company. The most commonly cited examples are:

- where the company is a mere façade
- where the company is effectively just the agent of its members or controllers
- where a representative of the company has taken some personal responsibility for a statement or action
- where the company is engaged in fraud or other criminal wrongdoing
- where the natural interpretation of a contract or statute is as a reference to the corporate group and not the individual company
- where permitted by statute (for example, many jurisdictions provide for shareholder liability where a company breaches environmental protection laws)
- in many jurisdictions, where a company continues to trade despite foreseeable bankruptcy, the directors can be forced to account for trading losses personally.

### Capacity and Powers

Historically, because companies are artificial persons created by operation of law, the law prescribed what the company could and could not do. Usually this was an expression of the commercial purpose which the company was formed for, and came to be referred to as the company's *objects*, and the extent of the objects are referred to as the company's capacity. If an activity fell outside of the company's capacity it was said to be *ultra vires* and void.

By way of distinction, the organs of the company were expressed to have various *corporate powers*. If the objects were the things that the company was able to do, then the powers were the means by which it could do them. Usually expressions of powers were limited to methods of raising capital, although from earlier times distinctions between objects and powers have caused lawyers difficulty. Most jurisdictions have now modified the position by statute, and companies generally have capacity to do all the things that a natural person could do, and power to do it in any way that a natural person could do it.

However, references to corporate capacity and powers have not quite been consigned to the dustbin of legal history. In many jurisdictions, directors can still be liable to their shareholders if they cause the company to engage in businesses outside of its objects, even if the transactions are still valid as between the company and the third party. And many jurisdictions also still permit transactions to be challenged for lack of "corporate benefit", where the relevant transaction has no prospect of being for the commercial benefit of the company or its shareholders. As artificial persons, companies can only act through human agents. The main agent who deals with the company's management and business is the board of directors, but in many jurisdictions other officers can be appointed too. The board of directors is normally elected by the members, and the other officers are normally appointed by the board. These agents enter into contracts on behalf of the company with third parties.

Although the company's agents owe duties to the company (and, indirectly, to the shareholders) to exercise those powers for a proper purpose, generally speaking third parties' rights are not impugned if it transpires that the officers were acting improperly. Third parties are entitled to rely on the ostensible authority of agents held out by the company to act on its behalf. A line of common law cases reaching back to *Royal British Bank v Turquand* established in common law that third parties were entitled to assume that the internal management of the company was being conducted properly, and the rule has now been codified into statute in most countries.

Accordingly, companies will normally be liable for all the act and omissions of their officers and agents. This will include almost all torts, but the law relating to crimes committed by companies is complex, and varies significantly between countries.

## Corporate Benefit

The interest of the company (sometimes "company benefit" or "commercial benefit") is a concept that the board of directors in corporations are in most legal systems required to use their power to promote. of the company for the commercial benefit of the company and its members. At common law, transactions which were not ostensibly beneficial to the company were set aside as being void as against the company.

An early illustration of this principle is to be found in *Hutton v West Cork Railway Co* (1883) 23 Ch D 654, where the English Court of Appeal held that the paying of a gratuity to employees prior to their dismissal was an improper exercise of the powers of the company, because the company was no longer a going concern, and thus stood to obtain no benefit (and no furtherance of its objects) through the payment of the gratuity; as Bowen LJ memorably remarked: "there are to be no cakes and ale except such as are required for the benefit of the company." (The decision itself is reversed by statute).

Any transaction which the directors enter into which is outside the powers of the company (and thus outside the scope of their authority) may nonetheless be ratified by the shareholders of the company, and will thereby be binding upon the company, see for example under English law, *Multinational Gas and Petrochemical Co v Multinational Gas and Petrochemical Services Ltd* [1983] Ch 258.

### Modern Developments

The rule is generally seen to be particularly harsh towards both third parties and against directors, who are regarded as being in breach of their duty only by acting with what others might regard as common human decency. Where the company's property could not be recovered from the third party, the directors would be personally liable to recompense the company.

There were also concerns that running companies ruthless for the financial benefit of the shareholders had a countervailing cost, making directors unwilling to participate in programmes that were beneficial to the community generally, or to the environment. It also meant that companies became much less willing to make donations to political parties, which may have had more impetus in bringing about legislative change than concern for communities or the environment.

Some legal systems have now abrogated by statute the rule that as against third parties the transaction may be void if it has insufficient commercial benefit to the company. In some countries, statutes now expressly provide for the directors to consider interests other than the pure financial interests of the shareholders.

However, in some jurisdictions there are proposals to make the power to act otherwise than for the financial benefit of the company even wider. For example, in the United Kingdom, the Companies Act 2006, when brought into force, will require that directors have to consider the impact of their actions on a much wider range of stakeholders. That Act would require a director "to promote the success of the company for the benefit of its members as a whole", but sets out six factors to which a director must have regards in fulfilling the duty to promote success. These are:

- the likely consequences of any decision in the long term
- the interests of the company's employees
- the need to foster the company's business relationships with suppliers, customers and others
- the impact of the company's operations on the community and the environment
- the desirability of the company maintaining a reputation for high standards of business conduct, and
- the need to act fairly as between members of a company.

The proposed new duties have been subject to some criticism, both from those who argue that the new duties do not have sufficient bite, and also from those who fear that it diverts directors' focus from what it is that they are meant to be doing (viz., generating profits), and there are fears of widespread litigation, and increase in director's insurance premiums.

However, because the new duties are expressed in non-imperative terms, and there is no sanction, the likelihood is that although they will empower the board of directors to take decisions that do not appear to directly financially benefit the company, they are unlikely to ever be required to do so.

### *Distinction from other Legal Concepts*

Conceptually, it is important to distinguish failure of a transaction for want of corporate benefit from other related legal concepts. These include:

- *Failure of consideration*: Under contract law in most common law legal systems, to be enforceable a contract requires both parties to provide consideration (i.e. something of value). However, the consideration does not need to be equal, and the gratuity given in *Hutton v West Cork Railway Co* would still have failed for want of corporate benefit if, for example, the company had allowed employees to purchase company property at a discount.
- *Transactions at an undervalue*: Although most examples of failure for want of corporate benefit involve transactions which were either a gift, or were made at a substantial undervalue, the concept is different in purpose and effect from provisions of insolvency law which prohibit undervalue transactions at a time when the company is insolvent.

## Corporate Governance

Corporate governance is primarily the study of the power relations between the board of directors and those who elect them (shareholders in the "general meeting" and employees). It also concerns other stakeholders, such as creditors, consumers, the environment and the community at large. One of the main differences between different countries in the internal form of companies is between a two-tier and a one tier board. The United Kingdom, the United States, and most Commonwealth countries have single unified boards of directors. In Germany, companies have two tiers, so that shareholders (and employees) elect a "supervisory board", and then the supervisory board chooses the "management board". There is the option to use two tiers in France, and in the new European Companies (Societas Europea).

Recent literature, especially from the United States, has begun to discuss corporate governance in the terms of management science. While post-war discourse centred on how to achieve effective "corporate democracy" for shareholders or other stakeholders, many scholars have shifted to discussing the law in terms of principal-agent problems. On this view, the basic issue of corporate law is that when a "principal" party delegates his property (usually the shareholder's capital, but also the employee's labour) into the control of an "agent" (i.e. the director of the company) there is the possibility that the agent will act in his own interests, be "opportunistic", rather than fulfil the wishes of the principal. Reducing the risks of this opportunism, or the "agency cost", is said to be central to the goal of corporate law.

## Corporate Constitution

The rules for corporations derive from two sources. These are the country's statutes (in the US, usually the Delaware General Corporation Law (DGCL); in the UK, the Companies Act 2006 (CA 2006); in Germany, the Aktiengesetz (AktG) and the Gesetz betreffend die Gesellschaften mit beschränkter Haftung (GmbH-Gesetz, GmbHG). The law will set out which rules are mandatory, and which rules can be derogated from. Examples of important rules which cannot be derogated from would usually include how to fire the board of directors, what duties directors owe to the company or when a company must be dissolved as it approaches bankruptcy. Examples of rules that members of a company would be allowed to change and choose could include, what kind of procedure general meetings should follow, when dividends get paid out, or how many members (beyond a minimum set out in the law) can amend the constitution. Usually, the statute will set out model articles, which the corporation's constitution will be assumed to have if it is silent on a bit of particular procedure.

The United States, and a few other common law countries, split the corporate constitution into two separate documents (the UK got rid of this in 2006). The memorandum of Association (or articles of incorporation) is the primary document, and will generally regulate the company's activities with the outside world. It states which objects the company is meant to follow (e.g. "this company makes automobiles") and specifies the authorised share capital of the company. The articles of association (or by-laws) is the secondary document, and will generally regulate the company's internal affairs and management, such as procedures for board meetings, dividend entitlements etc. In the event of any inconsistency, the memorandum prevails and in the United States only the memorandum is publicised. In civil law jurisdictions, the company's constitution is normally consolidated into a single document, often called the charter.

It is quite common for members of a company to supplement the corporate constitution with additional arrangements, such as *shareholders' agreements*, whereby they agree to exercise their membership rights in a certain way. Conceptually a shareholders' agreement fulfills many of the same functions as the corporate constitution, but because it is a contract, it will not normally bind new members of the company unless they accede to it somehow. One benefit of shareholders' agreement is that they will usually be confidential, as most jurisdictions do not require shareholders' agreements to be publicly filed. Another common method of supplementing the corporate constitution is by means of *voting trusts*, although these are relatively uncommon outside of the United States and certain offshore jurisdictions. Some jurisdictions consider the company seal to be a part of the "constitution" (in the loose sense of the word) of the company, but the requirement for a seal has been abrogated by legislation in most countries.

### Balance of Power

The most important rules for corporate governance are those concerning the balance of power between the board of directors and the members of the company. Authority is given or "delegated" to the board to manage the company for the success of the investors. Certain specific decision rights are often reserved for shareholders, where their interests could be fundamentally affected. There are necessarily rules on when directors can be removed from office and replaced. To do that, meetings need to be called to vote on the issues. How easily the constitution can be amended and by who necessarily affects the relations of power.

It is a principle of corporate law that the directors of a company have the right to manage. This is expressed in statute in the DGCL, where §141(a) states.

The business and affairs of every corporation organized under this chapter shall be managed by or under the direction of a board of directors, except as may be otherwise provided in this chapter or in its certificate of incorporation.

In Germany, §76 AktG says the same for the management board, while under §111 AktG the supervisory board's role is stated to be to "oversee" (*überwachen*). In the United Kingdom, the right to manage is not laid down in law, but is found in Art.2 of the Model Articles. This means it is a default rule, which companies can opt out of (s.20 CA 2006) by reserving powers to members, although companies rarely do. UK law specifically reserves shareholders right and duty to approve "substantial non cash asset transactions" (s.190 CA 2006), which means those over 10% of company value, with a minimum of £5,000 and a maximum of £100,000. Similar rules, though much less stringent, exist in §271 DGCL and through case law in Germany under the so called *Holzmüller-Doktrin*. Probably the must fundamental guarantee that directors will act in the members' interests is that they can easily be sacked.

During the Great Depression, two Harvard scholars, Adolf Berle and Gardiner Means wrote *The Modern Corporation and Private Property*, an attack on American law which failed to hold directors to account, and linked the growing power and autonomy of directors to the economic crisis. In the UK, the right of members to remove directors by a simple majority is assured under s.168 CA 2006 Moreover, Art.21 of the Model Articles requires a third of the board to put themselves up for re-election every year (in effect creating maximum three year terms). 10% of shareholders can demand a meeting any time, and 5% can if it has been a year since the last one (s.303 CA 2006). In Germany, where employee participation creates the need for greater boardroom stability, §84(3) AktG states that management board directors can only be removed by the supervisory board for an important reason (*ein wichtiger Grund*) though this can include a vote of no-confidence by the shareholders. Terms last for five years, unless

75% of shareholders vote otherwise. §122 AktG lets 10% of shareholders demand a meeting. In the US, Delaware lets directors enjoy considerable autonomy. §141(k) DGCL states that directors can be removed without any cause, unless the board is "classified", meaning that directors only come up for re-appointment on different years. If the board is classified, then directors cannot be removed unless there is gross misconduct. Director's autonomy from shareholders is seen further in §216 DGCL, which allows for plurality voting and §211(d) which states shareholder meetings can only be called if the constitution allows for it. The problem is that in America, directors usually choose where a company is incorporated and §242(b)(1) DGCL says any constitutional amendment requires a resolution by the directors. By contrast, constitutional amendments can be made at any time by 75% of shareholders in Germany (§179 AktG) and the UK (s.21 CA 2006).

### Director's Duties

In most jurisdictions, directors owe strict duties of good faith, as well as duties of care and skill, to safeguard the interests of the company and the members.

The standard of skill and care that a director owes is usually described as acquiring and maintaining sufficient knowledge and understanding of the company's business to enable him to properly discharge his duties. Directors are also strictly charged to exercise their powers only for a proper purpose. For instance, were a director to issue a large number of new shares, not for the purposes of raising capital but in order to defeat a potential takeover bid, that would be an improper purpose.

Directors have a duty to exercise reasonable skill care and diligence-This right enables the company to seek compensation from its director if it can be proved that he hasn't shown reasonable skill or care which in turn has caused the company to incur a loss. Directors also owe strict duties not to permit any conflict of interest or conflict with their duty to act in the best interests of the company. This rule is so strictly enforced that, even where the conflict of interest or conflict of duty is purely hypothetical, the directors can be forced to disgorge all personal gains arising from it. In *Aberdeen Ry v. Blaikie* (1854) 1 Macq HL 461 Lord Cranworth stated in his judgment that,

"A corporate body can only act by agents, and it is, of course, the duty of those agents so to act as best to promote the interests of the corporation whose affairs they are conducting. Such agents have duties to discharge of a fiduciary nature towards their principal. And it is a rule of universal application that no one, having such duties to discharge, shall be allowed to enter into engagements in which he has, *or can have*, a personal interest conflicting *or which possibly may conflict*, with the interests of those whom he is bound to protect... So strictly is this principle adhered to that no question is allowed to be raised as to the fairness or unfairness of the contract entered into..."

However, in many jurisdictions the members of the company are permitted to ratify transactions which would otherwise fall foul of this principle. It is also largely accepted in most jurisdictions that this principle should be capable of being abrogated in the company's constitution.

### *Corporate Litigation*

Members of a company generally have rights against each other and against the company, as framed under the company's constitution. In relation to the exercise of their rights, minority shareholders usually have to accept that, because of the limits of their voting rights, they cannot direct the overall control of the company and must accept the will of the majority (often expressed as *majority rule*). However, majority rule can be iniquitous, particularly where there is one controlling shareholder. Accordingly, a number of exceptions have developed in law in relation to the general principle of majority rule.

- Where the majority shareholder(s) are exercising their votes to perpetrate a fraud on the minority, the courts may permit the minority to sue
- members always retain the right to sue if the majority acts to invade their personal rights, e.g. where the company's affairs are not conducted in accordance with the company's constitution (this position has been debated because the extent of a personal right is not set in law). *Macdougall v Gardiner* and *Pender v Lushington* present irreconcilable differences in this area.
- in many jurisdictions it is possible for minority shareholders to take a *representative* or *derivative action* in the name of the company, where the company is controlled by the alleged wrongdoers.

## Corporate Finance

### *Shares and Share Capital*

Companies generally raise capital for their business ventures either by debt or equity. Capital raised by way of equity is usually raised by issued shares (sometimes called "stock" (not to be confused with stock-in-trade)) or warrants.

A share is an item of property, and can be sold or transferred. Holding a share makes the holder a member of the company, and entitles them to enforce the provisions of the company's constitution against the company and against other members. Shares also normally have a nominal or par value, which is the limit of the shareholder's liability to contribute to the debts of the company on an insolvent liquidation.

Shares usually confer a number of rights on the holder. These will normally include:

- voting rights
- rights to dividends (or payments made by companies to their shareholders) declared by the company
- rights to any return of capital either upon redemption of the share, or upon the liquidation of the company
- in some countries, shareholders have preemption rights, whereby they have a preferential right to participate in future share issues by the company.

Many companies have different classes of shares, offering different rights to the shareholders. For example, a company might issue both ordinary shares and preference shares, with the two types having different voting and/or economic rights. For example, a company might provide that preference shareholders shall each receive a cumulative preferred dividend of a certain amount per annum, but the ordinary shareholders shall receive everything else. The total number of issued shares in a company is said to represent its *capital*. Many jurisdictions regulate the minimum amount of capital which a company may have, although some countries only prescribe minimum amounts of capital for companies engaging in certain types of business (e.g. banking, insurance etc.).

Similarly, most jurisdictions regulate the maintenance of capital, and prevent companies returning funds to shareholders by way of distribution when this might leave the company financially exposed. In some jurisdictions this extends to prohibiting a company from providing financial assistance for the purchase of its own shares.

### Liquidations

Liquidation is the normal means by which a company's existence is brought to an end. It is also referred to (either alternatively or concurrently) in some jurisdictions as *winding up* or *dissolution*. Liquidations generally come in two forms, either *compulsory liquidations* (sometimes called *creditors' liquidations*) and *voluntary liquidations* (sometimes called *members' liquidations*, although a voluntary liquidation where the company is insolvent will also be controlled by the creditors, and is properly referred to as a *creditors' voluntary liquidation*). Where a company goes into liquidation, normally a liquidator is appointed to gather in all the company's assets and settle all claims against the company. If there is any surplus after paying off all the creditors of the company, this surplus is then distributed to the members.

As its names imply, applications for compulsory liquidation are normally made by creditors of the company when the company is unable to pay its debts. However, in some jurisdictions, regulators have the power to apply for the liquidation of the company on the grounds of public good, i.e. where the company is believed to have engaged in unlawful conduct, or conduct which is otherwise harmful to the public at large.

Voluntary liquidations occur when the company's members decide voluntarily to wind up the affairs of the company. This may be because they believe that the company will soon become insolvent, or it may be on economic grounds if they believe that the purpose for which the company was formed is now at an end, or that the company is not providing an adequate return on assets and should be broken up and sold off. Some jurisdictions also permit companies to be wound up on "just and equitable" grounds. Generally, applications for just and equitable winding-up are brought by a member of the company who alleges that the affairs of the company are being conducted in a prejudicial manner, and asking the court to bring an end to the company's existence. For obvious reasons, in most countries, the courts have been reluctant to wind up a company solely on the basis of the disappointment of one member, regardless of how well-founded that member's complaints are. Accordingly, most jurisdictions which permit just and equitable winding up also permit the court to impose other remedies, such as requiring the majority shareholder(s) to buy out the disappointed minority shareholder at a fair value.

### Insider Dealing

Insider trading is the trading of a corporation's stock or other securities (e.g. bonds or stock options) by individuals with potential access to non-public information about the company. In most countries, trading by corporate insiders such as officers, key employees, directors, and large shareholders may be legal, if this trading is done in a way that does not take advantage of non-public information. However, the term is frequently used to refer to a practice in which an insider or a related party trades based on material non-public information obtained during the performance of the insider's duties at the corporation, or otherwise in breach of a fiduciary or other relationship of trust and confidence or where the non-public information was misappropriated from the company. Illegal insider trading is believed to raise the cost of capital for securities issuers, thus decreasing overall economic growth.

In the United States and several other jurisdictions, trading conducted by corporate officers, key employees, directors, or significant shareholders (in the U.S., defined as beneficial owners of ten percent or more of the firm's equity securities) must be reported to the regulator or publicly disclosed, usually within a few business days of the trade.

Many investors follow the summaries of these insider trades in the hope that mimicking these trades will be profitable. While "legal" insider trading cannot be based on material non-public information, some investors believe corporate insiders nonetheless may have better insights into the health of a corporation (broadly speaking) and that their trades otherwise convey important information (e.g., about the pending retirement of an important officer selling shares, greater commitment to the corporation by officers purchasing shares, etc.)

### Corporate Liability

In criminal law, corporate liability determines the extent to which a corporation as a legal person can be liable for the acts and omissions of the natural persons it employs. It is sometimes regarded as an aspect of criminal vicarious liability, as distinct from the situation in which the wording of a statutory offence specifically attaches liability to the corporation as the principal or joint principal with a human agent.

### The Concepts

The imposition of criminal liability is only one means of regulating corporations. There are also civil law remedies such as injunction and the award of damages which may include a penal element. Generally, criminal sanctions include imprisonment, fines and community service orders. A company has no physical existence, so it can only act vicariously through the agency of the human beings it employs. While it is relatively uncontroversial that human beings may commit crimes for which punishment is a just desert, the extent to which the corporation should incur liability is less clear. Obviously, a company cannot be sent to jail, and if a fine is to be paid, this diminishes both the money available to pay the wages and salaries of all the remaining employees, and the profits available to pay all the existing shareholders. Thus, the effect of the only available punishment is deflected from the wrongdoer personally and distributed among all the innocent parties who supply the labour and the capital that keep the corporation solvent. Because, at a public policy level, the growth and prosperity of society depends on the business community, governments recognise limits on the extent to which each permitted form of business entity can be held liable (including general and limited partnerships which may also have separate legal personalities).

## The Act

### *The Offence*

The Act attempts to align the offence of corporate killing north and south of the border. An indictable offence is committed if the way in which an organisation's activities are managed or organised:

- Causes a person's death; and Amounts to a gross breach of a relevant duty of care owed by the organisation to the deceased; — and the way in which its activities are managed or organised by its senior management is a substantial element in the breach. Prosecution in England or Wales requires the permission of the Director of Public Prosecutions, and in Northern Ireland, the Director of Public Prosecutions for Northern Ireland and no natural person can be charged with aiding and abetting the offence. The common law offence of gross negligence manslaughter, as it applies to corporations, is abolished.

### *Organisations Liable*

The offence applies to:

- Corporations;
- Partnerships, trade unions and employers' associations, that are themselves employers.
- Police forces;
- Various, but not all, government departments.

### Relevant Duty of Care

A relevant duty of care is one of several duties of care owed by the organisation under the law of negligence and is a question of law for the judge. Various government policy decisions; policing, military and child protection activities; and emergency responses are excluded.

There are particular duties of care owed to persons in custody (s. 2(1)(d)) and, owing to the sensitivity and difficulty of such duties, implementation of this section was delayed. The Ministry of Justice published a report on progress towards implementation in July 2008.

### Gross Breach

A breach of a duty of care by an organisation is a gross breach if the alleged conduct amounts to a breach of that duty that falls far below what can reasonably be expected of the organisation in the circumstances. The jury must consider whether the evidence shows that the organisation failed to comply with any health and safety legislation that relates to the alleged breach, and if so:

- How serious that failure was; and
- How much of a risk of death it posed.

The jury may also:

- Consider the extent to which the evidence shows that there were attitudes, policies, systems or accepted practices within the organisation that were likely to have encouraged the failure, or to have produced tolerance of it; and
- Have regard to any health and safety guidance that relates to the alleged breach.

### Senior Management

Senior management means the persons who play significant roles in:

- The making of decisions about how the whole or a substantial part of its activities are to be managed or organised; or
- The actual managing or organising of the whole or a substantial part of those activities.

### Penalties

On conviction a corporation may be ordered to remedy any breach, or to publicise its failures, or be given an unlimited fine. Sentencing guidelines are expected in autumn 2008 but on 15 November 2007, the Sentencing Guidelines Council issued a consultative document recommending a starting point of a fine of 5% of company turnover for a first offence with a not guilty plea, rising to 10% of turnover.

## Mergers and Acquisitions

Mergers and acquisitions (abbreviated M&A) refers to the aspect of corporate strategy, corporate finance and management dealing with the buying, selling, dividing and combining of different companies and similar entities that can aid, finance, or help an enterprise grow rapidly in its sector or location of origin or a new field or new location without creating a subsidiary, other child entity or using a joint venture. The distinction between a "merger" and an "acquisition" has become increasingly blurred in various respects (particularly in terms of the ultimate economic outcome), although it has not completely disappeared in all situations.

# 9

# Key Concept: Competitive Advantage

Competitive advantage is often seen as the overall purpose of strategy. Some texts use the phrase *superior performance* to mean the same thing. Essentially, a business can be said to possess competitive advantage if it is able to return higher profits as a proportion of sales than its competitors.

The higher profits mean that it will be able to commit more retained profit to reinvestment in its strategy, thus maintaining its lead over its competitors in an industry. When this superiority is maintained successfully over time, a *sustainable* competitive advantage has been achieved. Competitive advantage can be lost when management fail to reinvest the superior profits in such a way that the advantage is not maintained.

## How Core Competences 'Work'

Core competences tend to be both complex and intangible so that it is necessary to explore the nature of resources and competences which underpin them before exploring the concept further. The purpose of such analysis is to allow managers to identify which resources and competences act as the foundation of existing or potential core competences. It is important to note that not all the competitors in an industry will possess core competences or distinctive capabilities (Kay, 1993).

It is only those organisations that are producing above average performance which can be considered as possessing core competences. Those with only average or below average performance possess competences and resources (without which they could not compete in the industry at all) but not core competences.

### *Made Simple*

Core competence (distinctive capability) = superior deployment of resources + superior application of 'general' competences. Core competence (distinctive capability) when applied in a market creates value for customers and this represents competitive advantage

## Resource Analysis

### Tangible and Intangible Resources

Resources can be either *tangible* or *intangible.* They are the inputs or assets which enable an organisation to carry out its activities. Tangible assets include stocks, materials machinery, buildings, human resources, finance and so on. Intangible assets include skills, knowledge, brand names and goodwill, patent rights, etc., but in a tourism context they also refer to what economists typically refer to as 'free resources'.

Tangible resources are obtained from outside organisations. Such resources are obtained in resource markets in competition with organisations from within and outside the industry. Intangible resources can often be developed within an organisation, but as with tangible resources, they have a value attached to them which, although sometimes difficult to quantify, can often be bought and sold in markets. Relationships with the suppliers of resources can form an important part of the organisation's core competence, as for example with its ability to attract the most appropriately skilled human resources in the job market.

Tourism is different from most other industries in that free resources are a vital part of the product. Free resources are those resources available in such abundance naturally, such as air, the sea, climate and culture, etc., that there is no need for an allocative mechanism (a market), in order to allocate them to users or consumers. Scarce resources on the other hand are the tangible and intangible resources, which are limited in their supply relative to the demand of consumers, and are therefore allocated in a market.

Bull (1995) argued that the basis for tourism lies in building upon free resources (or 'renewable resources' as they are sometimes termed), with a mixture of public sector and private sector resources. Free resources together with the scarce resources are combined to form what most tourists perceive as the tourist 'product'. It may be argued, as Bull (1995) pointed out, that in today's world there are few truly free resources since any human activity makes demands on the world's resources and, as a consequence, ultimately someone will have to pay a price. Indeed the concept of *sustainable tourism* largely rests upon the recognition of such a line of argument.

All resources have competing demands made upon them so that if they are used for one form of activity they cannot be used in other ways. For example, a large flat coastal area might be suitable for the development of a resort area for tourism or as a site for heavy industry. If tourism is chosen ahead of heavy industry an opportunity to develop heavy industry on this site has been lost. The cost of this choice is known as the *opportunity cost,* which represents the potential economic returns that are being given up in favour of the chosen option (in this example, developing tourism).

## Features of Tourism Resources

A number of points are pertinent to a consideration of tourism's use of resources and to their management in the industry. Particular challenges presented to tourism managers in the use of resources include the following.

### *Resource Immobility*

Many resources that are used cannot be moved either in terms of place or time. For example, a particular beach or mountain, the Empire State Building or the culture of Spain are geographically fixed. The Alpine shows of February cannot be replicated in May and the 'midnight sun', a tourist attraction in far northern latitudes, can be observed only during midsummer.

### *Resource Substitution*

It is often difficult to substitute one resource category with those of another. For example, in a car factory efficiency gains may be possible, and indeed have been achieved, through replacing employees by machines, *i.e.* the substitution of human resources with operational resources. In the case of a luxury hotel, an airline or a cruise ship, for instance, the quality of service is often perceived as being closely linked with the quality and number of staff. Consequently it is difficult to replace human resources with operational resources such as computers, and as a result tourism is usually viewed as a labour intensive industry.

### *Resource Conflict and Competition*

Tourism frequently makes extensive demands on the use of certain resource, which can be in serious conflict or competition with other uses. Such resource conflict or competition may be partially resolved through pricing mechanisms by which the activity that is able to pay the most is able to use the resources. Similarly, regulatory restrictions such as the geographical zoning of areas to permit specified activities only within a particular zone may resolve some conflicts. Some degree of conflict frequently remains. Thus the competing demands of the British army in using gunnery ranges in the Isle of Purbeck, Dorset (an Area of Outstanding Natural Beauty) and in the Northumberland National Park at Otterburn, Northumberland, are in conflict with tourist demands for unspoilt environments. In a local government setting, tourism has to compete for funding with other activities such as education and social services.

### Resource Ownership and Control

Tourism frequently has to utilise resources that are neither owned nor controlled by the companies operating within the sector. This results in a high degree of interdependence between tourism based business.

Thus airlines depend upon the physical resources provided by airports and the operating resources provided by air traffic control services. Although the airlines may have some influence over the way in which these resources are managed, they are rarely directly owned and managed. Projects aimed at regenerating decaying urban environments often have tourism at their heart. Such projects are often developed as public-private partnerships in which the public sector (local and national government) manage and control the overall redevelopment and provide limited funding (often termed 'pump, priming'). Private sector companies in such cases provide the major part of the financial resources. Examples of such public-private partnerships include the redevelopment of Cardiff Bay in the UK and of the Baltimore waterfront in the USA.

### Seasonality

Demand for most tourism resources and hence products, whether business or leisure based, is highly seasonal. This in turn is the result of factors such as climate, the distribution of holiday entitlements, the timing of events and festivals, and historic travel patterns. Consequently, the price that organisations have to pay for their resource inputs and the prices that consumers have to pay those organisations vary according to the season. For example long haul airline flights frequently have a low season, a high season and a 'shoulder' season with prices that reflect periods of relatively high, low and medium levels of demand respectively.

### Low Rewards

Tourism is often viewed as a low margin area of business. Whilst this is not necessarily the case, it is certainly true to say that the rewards from tourism are often slow to materialise and are susceptible to wide swings in cash flow and profitability. As Bull (1995) pointed out, rewards in tourism may be low for several reasons. The industry is often perceived as being relatively clean and pleasant both to invest in and to work in. Consequently, employees may be prepared to work for lower wages as they would rather work in such an attractive industry than elsewhere. Destinations are often situated in areas with few alternative land uses and employment opportunities and therefore little competition is provided for the use of resources. This puts an effective upper limit on rewards in terms of prices paid for land and development, and wages paid to employees. For example the development of tourism in the Yucatan Peninsula on the Caribbean coast of Mexico, has taken place over recent years in an area that is economically poorly developed and which is remote from major markets for goods and services. Hence the development of tourism in this beautiful region does not face strong competition from other industries for the use of resources and the costs of rewarding resources (in terms of land costs and wages) are relatively low.

### Capacity Constraints

The capacity of tourism resources is frequently constrained in some way. Thus in tourism the *carrying capacity* for a destination is often referred to. This refers to the ability of a site, resort, or a region to absorb tourism use without deteriorating. The notion of carrying capacity is central to the concept of sustainability. The rapid development of Spain's Costa del Sol for instance from the 1950s onwards demonstrates the need to constrain development. Extensive linear development along the coast to the west of Malaga led to overbuilding with poor planning controls. The relative popularity of the resort area subsequently diminished as consumers opted for more recent and better-planned resorts elsewhere. Thus the over use of resources led to the carrying capacity being exceeded and deterioration in the environment that had attracted tourists in the first place.

Similarly the capacity of physical and operational resources in tourism is often constrained, at least in the short to medium period. If a hotel (physical resource) is full or an airline flight (operational resource) is fully booked it is difficult to add capacity quickly whereas if additional demand is apparent for a manufactured product capacity can often be increased by overtime working, by putting on an extra shift of work or by running production lines at a faster rate. Thus in the tourism industry supply is often relatively fixed whereas demand fluctuates.

The managerial implication of this is that managers will often (in the short to medium term) try to influence demand rather than supply. Thus pricing measures and promotional activities will be altered in order to increase or reduce demand so that it matches the supply that is available. For example it has become common for UK tour operators to alter prices in a very active manner in the weeks immediately prior to the date of departure and hotels often make late alterations to their accommodation rates. This active management of prices (which can be moved upwards or downwards to inhibit or encourage demand respectively) is a way of managing the demand so that it matches the supply which has been previously fixed.

### Analysis by Specificity

Secondly, we can analyse resources according to their *specificity*. Resources can be specific or non-specific. For example, skilled workers tend to have specialised and industry-specific knowledge and skills. Some technology, for example computer software, is for general (non industry-specific) business use, like word-processing, database and spreadsheet software. Other computer software applications, like airline or hotel computer reservation systems, or yield management programme, are written for highly specialised uses. Whereas non-specific resources tend to be more flexible and form and basis of competences, industry-specific resources are more likely to act as the foundations of core competences (for example the specialised knowledge of procurement managers responsible for contracting accommodation in the tour operating sector).

### Analysis by Performance

Thirdly, resources can be evaluated on the basis of how they contribute to internal and external *measures of performance*. Internal measures include their contribution to:

- business objectives and targets—financial performance and output measures;
- historical comparisons—measures of performance over time (*e.g.* against previous years);
- business unit or divisional comparisons.

External measures can include:

- comparisons with competitors, particularly those who are industry leaders and those who are the closest competitors and are in its strategic grouping;
- comparisons with companies in other service based industries.

By employing these techniques of analysis, an organisation is able to internally and externally *benchmark* its performance as a stimulus to improving performance in the future. Performance, however, is based on more than resources, and competences must be similarly analysed and evaluated.

## Competences

Competences are attributes like skills, knowledge, technology and relationships that are common among the competitors in an industry. For example, all companies in the airline industry possess similar competences (basic abilities) in operations, marketing and distribution. They are less tangible than resources and are consequently more difficult to evaluate. Competences are more often developed internally but may also be acquired externally or by collaboration with suppliers, distributors or customers.

Competences are distinguished from core competences by the fact that they do not produce superior performance and by the fact that they are not distinctive when compared to the competences possessed by other companies in the industry. On the other hand, competences are essential for survival in a particular line of business. Competences also have the potential to be developed into core competences.

## Sustaining Core Competences—Club Med

In 1950, with Europe at peace, Frenchman Gillbert Trigano together with Gerard Blitz, a Belgian, bought some American army surplus tents and camp beds, set them up in a pinewood on the Spanish island of Majorca and called the enterprise Club Mediterranee.

The idea was a success from the start. Holiday camps were not new. In Britain Billy Butlin's camps had provided cheap refuges from rainy summers. But Club Med (as it became known) offered reliable sunshine and warm seas, along with what Gerard Blitz called 'an antidote to civilisation'. He saw no need for Club Med to make money, as long as they covered their costs. What mattered was that people could be liberated from their working lives for a week or two and live as the noble savage, do some cooking if they wanted to and help with the rudimentary washing-up. It was Trigano who turned Club Med into a profitable business. Tents were soon replaced by thatched huts. During Mr. Trigano's four decades with Club Med, bungalows and hotels were added with the soft comforts of home. Staff were hired to do the chores. There were Club Med establishments throughout the world from Tahiti to Bulgaria.

The romanticism that had made Club Med so appealing when Trigano and his early partner banged in the first tent pegs in Majorca was not discarded. Rather, Trigano made Club Med's hint of sensual pleasure a key part of its sales appeal. The partly Belgian idea, which had been launched in Spain with American equipment, became as French as Bardot. As a loyal Frenchman, Mr. Trigano made Club Med a messenger of his country's superiority in food, wine, language and indeed culture. Then, suddenly, it seemed that paradise was lost.

After Club Med had showed losses for three successive years in the 1990s, Harvard Business School chillingly used the firm as a study to illustrate 'the death of a brand'. Club Med, which a survey revealed that 77% of Americans and 88% of Europeans had heard of, had become Club Red. The young people who were once its customers were now middle-aged and less thrilled by its offer of organised, communal living, however comfortable. The next generation saw Club Med as just another big hotel chain.

After a revolt by shareholders of Club Med in 1997 Mr. Trigano and his son Serge, who had become chief executive, stood down from management. Philippe Bourgignon, who had revived Disney's sickly theme park near Paris, took over, with a promise to return Club Med back to health. Over the next three years the Group transformed its activities and staged a strong financial recovery. After being tested in the French market in 1998, the new group strategy was put into practice in 1999. Restoring the brand and distribution, regaining competitiveness and rationalizing management and organisation all contributed to strengthening the Club's market position.

The Club now enjoys an improved image, better product —client fit, a fair price policy, rising volumes and profitable product delivery. A new leisure concept Club Med World (a city based product) was successfully launched, the Club Med product range was broadened to include active wear, body care and sun creams, sunglasses, watches, water sports, etc. and Club Med.com was developed as a new distribution channel. With its transformation plan, strong growth has been achieved utilizing its three strategic assets: its employees, its members and its brand (a 'club'). In so doing the company is repositioning itself from being a hotel company to a service company based on the concept of a 'club' and on the strong sense of belonging which its members (750 000 in France alone) enjoy, enabling it to embody a lifestyle.

## Core Competences and Distinctive Capabilities

Kay (1993) presented a slightly different explanation arguing that competitive advantage is based upon what he termed *distinctive capability*. According to Kay (1993), distinctive capability can develop from four sources:

- *Architecture*—A network of relationships within or around the organisation. The relationships may be among employees (internal architecture), with suppliers and customers (external architecture) or among a group of organisations engaged in related activities (networks). For example, the strategic alliances that have been built up by the major international airlines in recent years are examples of using networks to strengthen the competitive position of individual airlines through shared activities and extending geographical scope.
- *Reputation*—In service markets reputation is an extremely important contributor to consumer choice of product, but given the intangibility of the product, reputation is usually built up slowly and at some cost as consumers gain experience. Given the high value and public profile of travel products, reputations can easily be damaged, for example, through disaster. A coach or aeroplane crash, a ferry sinking or a hotel fire quickly erodes the reputation of the affected organisation.
- *Strategic assets*—The strength of market position or dominance of a market is often based upon the possession of strategic assets. They can be of three types. First, an organisation may benefit from a monopoly position in a market, secondly, an organisation may have already incurred the costs of supplying a market which inhibits the ability of new entrants to compete effectively, and thirdly, some companies may benefit from the possession of licences or regulation that prevents competition. For example, the dominant position of major international airlines at their 'hub' airports (such as Lufthansa at Frankfurt, United at Chicago and American Airlines at Dallas/Fort Worth) is often the result of costs expended over many years and local

regulatory regimes that have allocated take-off and landing slots to these airlines over the years.

- *Innovation*—Through innovation companies are often capable of providing a distinctive product and/or reducing costs. However, innovations can often be copied (particularly in service industries) and the additional returns are often not forthcoming for the innovating company. For example, British Airways was the world's first airline to introduce flat beds for some of its business class passengers, but other airlines quickly followed its lead.

## British Airways' Core Competences

In the airline sector all airlines have the competences and resources required to operate flights between certain destinations. A company like British Airways (Kay, 1993) possesses core competences relating to its:

- Dominance of take off and landing slots at London's Heathrow airport.
- Licences it holds to operate certain routes to which access is denied for other airlines.
- Brand attributes which act as the basis of its reputation for high quality for other airlines.

These core competences, although initially identified by the author in the early 1990s, are still valid in the contemporary market. However, it could be argued that the web of cooperative partnerships with other airlines through the 'One World' strategic alliance in allowing for greater destination choice and flexibility of arrangements provides a further area of core competence for the airline.

Thus British Airways has distinctive capabilities in terms of strategic assets (Heathrow slots and licences), reputation (brand attributes) and architecture (strategic alliances).

The possession of these core competences enables the airline to charge premium prices for its products by targeting business travellers in particular and by altering aircraft seat configurations to accommodate a greater proportion of business and first class passengers. In this way, core competences are applied to the marketplace and in so doing form the basis of an organisation's competitive advantage.

## Outcomes of the Analysis

### *Aims of the Analysis*

The aims of an analysis of resources, competences and core competences (distinctive capabilities) are, therefore, to:

- understand the nature and sources of particular core competences;
- identify the need for and methods of adaptation of existing core competences;
- identify the need for new core competence building;
- identify potential sources of core competence based on resources and competences;
- ensure that core competences remain focused on customer needs.

Resources, competences and core competences are obviously closely related to the ways that a business organises and performs its value adding activities. It is therefore also necessary to analyse the way in which value adding activities are configured and co-ordinated.

## Competence Leveraging and Building

### *Competence Leveraging*

Competence leveraging refers to the ability of a business to exploit its core competences in new markets, thus meeting new customer needs. It can also refer to the ability of the business to modify and improve existing core competences.

### *Competence Building*

Competence building takes place when the business builds new core competences, based upon its resources and competences. It is often necessary to build new competences alongside existing ones when entering new markets as it is unlikely that existing competences will fully meet new customer needs.

### *From Distinctive Capability to Competitive Advantage*

According to Kay (1993), distinctive capability becomes a competitive advantage when it is applied in a relevant market. Each distinctive capability will have a market (or group of markets) in which the organisation can achieve a competitive advantage. Competitive advantage is a relative rather than an absolute notion and can be viewed in several ways.

Organisations can enjoy a competitive advantage relative to:

- other suppliers in the same market;
- other firms in the same industry; or,
- other competitors in the same strategic grouping.

In establishing competitive advantage therefore, it is important that activities are correctly matched up to the organisation's capabilities. It is also important that organisations are able to fully understand the inherent differences between: 'the market', 'the industry' and the 'strategic group'. The market refers to the needs of customers and potential customers, whereas the industry an organisation is in refers to a group of products linked by common technology, supply or distribution channels. The strategic group refers to those organisations that are identified as primary competitors.

### Markets, Industries and Strategic Groups

*The Market:*

- Defined by demand conditions;
- Based on consumer needs;
- Characterised by 'the law of one price'.

*The Industry:*

- Determined by supply conditions;
- Based on production or operations technology;
- Defined by the markets chosen by organisations.

*The Strategic Group:*

- Defined by the strategic choices of firms;
- Based on distinctive capabilities and market positioning;
- Subjective in determination.

During the 1980s Britain's largest brewer, Bass plc, viewed the market for beer as having unexciting growth prospects and redefined its core business as 'leisure'. Consequently the company bought Horizon Travel, a leading UK tour operator of the time. Bass was correct in its observation that pubs and holidays were alternative ways of spending leisure time and that they competed for the same share of consumer expenditure.

However, the skills involved in brewing beer and managing an estate of public houses were quite different from those required to run a tour operator. As a result, the tour operator was subsequently disposed of through a sale to the market leader, Thomson. Bass, perhaps failed fully to appreciate that there is a leisure market but that there is not a leisure industry. They did not possess the necessary operating skills (in the industry) to service the market effectively.

*Source:* Adapted from Kay (1993)

## Key Concept: Value Added

In simple terms, the value added to a good or service is the difference in the financial value of the finished product compared to the financial value of the inputs. As a sheet of metal passes through the various stages in car production, value is added so that a tonne of metal worth a few hundred pounds becomes a motor car worth several thousand pounds. The rate at which value is added is dependent upon how well the operations process is managed. If the car manufacturer suffers a cost disadvantage by, say, holding a high level of stock or working with out-of-date machinery, then the value added over the process will be lower.

Similarly, a tour operator gathers together various inputs in terms of transportation, accommodation, on-site services and ground handling arrangements and 'packages' them together and in so doing adds value to the customer. Efficiencies in procurement, for instance, achieved through the use of buying in bulk can be passed on to the customer. There are clear linkages between value adding activities, core competences, competences and resources. Resources form the inputs to the organisation's value adding activities while competences and core competences provide the skills and knowledge required to carry them out. The more that core competences can be integrated into value adding activities, the greater will be the value added.

### The Value Adding Process

Businesses can be regarded as systems that transform inputs (resources, materials, etc.) into outputs (goods and services). The activities inside the organisation *add value* to the inputs. The value of the products is equivalent to the price that a customer is willing to pay for them. The difference between the end value and the total costs is the *margin* (the quantity that accountants would refer to as the *profit margin*—before interest, taxation and extraordinary items). The rate at which value is added varies. If value is not being added as fast as it could be then *waste* is occurring and the organisation is not operating as efficiently as it might. Poor quality, low utilisation or occupancy and an under-skilled workforce are all examples of waste. Increased added value can be achieved through achieving a reduction in costs or increasing the price that the customer is willing to pay for the output.

## The Value Chain

The activities of the organisation can be broken down into a sequence of activities known as the *value chain* as described by Porter in 1985. Poon (1993) applied Porter's value chain to the travel and tourism industry. The activities within the chain may be classified into *primary* activities and *support* activities. Primary activities are those which directly add value to the final product. Support activities do not directly add value themselves but indirectly add value by supporting the effective execution of primary activities. Whilst the nature of the primary activities and the way in which they can add value vary greatly between differing types of tourism organisation according to the organisational context, the secondary activities are common in most organisational contexts.

## Analysis of the Value Chain

An organisation's value chain links into the value chains of other organisations, particularly those of suppliers and distributors. This 'chain' of value chains is sometimes called the *value system* or *total supply chain*. Linkages with suppliers are known as forward linkages while those with distributors and customers are backward linkages. Different types of organisation will have very different value chains. For example, the value chain of My Travel plc, a vertically integrated UK based tour operator, includes transportation of clients and retail distribution. In a smaller tour operator such as the independent tour operator Sunvil, however, the position is somewhat different. In the case of this company (which operates air holidays primarily to Greece and Cyprus), retail distribution and transportation are undertaken by other companies on a commercially agreed basis. Consequently these aspects do not form a part of the company's value chain but are important elements of the value system described above. Similarly, not all of an organisation's activities are of equal importance in adding value to its products. Those, which are of greatest importance can be considered as *core activities* and are often closely associated with core competences. Thus in an upscale hotel, clients are willing to pay premium prices because the level, type and consistency of customer service are of a high standard. Thus, this aspect may be of greatest importance in adding value and the organisation's core competences could be concentrated in this area.

A further point to stress is the importance of linkages between the component parts of the model. In some cases a key source of value added activity might lie in the way in which organisations link different parts of the value chain. For example for a tour operator it is important that demand and supply are closely coordinated so that excess capacity which cannot be sold is avoided and so that there is enough supply to meet customer demand.

This involves close linkages between the transportation, wholesaling and packaging, retail distribution and marketing and sales components. Analysis of value adding activities helps to identify where the most value is added and where there is potential to add greater value by changing the way in which activities are configured and by improving the way in which they are coordinated. It is important to note that an organisation's value chain is not analysed in isolation but that it is considered in conjunction with its external linkages to suppliers, distributors and customers. A value chain analysis would be expected to include:

- a breakdown of all the activities of the organizations;
- identification of core activities and their relationships to core competences and current organisational strategies;
- identification of the effectiveness and efficiency of the individual activities;
- examination of *linkages* between activities for additional added value;
- identification of *blockages* which reduce the organisation's competitive advantage.

A useful technique in value chain analysis involves comparison with the value chains of competitors to identify the benefits and drawbacks of alternative configurations.

The aim of value chain analysis is to identify ways in which the performance of the individual activities and the linkages between them can be improved. This may involve identification of improved configurations for activities or improved coordination of them. It is particularly important to consider the extent to which value chain activities support the current strategy of the organisation. For example, if the current strategy is based upon high quality then the activities must be configured so as to ensure the creation of high quality products. On the other hand, if the organisation competes largely on the basis of price then activities must be organised so as to minimize costs.

## The Service Profit Chain

During the 1990s an alternative framework was introduced by a team of researchers at Harvard University. The *service profit chain* (Heskett *et al.,* 1997) assesses the sources of profitability and growth in labour dominated service firms. Such companies are defined as those service companies where labour is both an important component of total cost and which are capable of differentiating the firm's service from that of competitors. The purpose of the service profit chain is to provide managers with a framework to help them manage such companies by enabling them to focus on (predominantly) quantifiable measures that lead to financial performance measures. In this regard it is similar in its approach to the 'balanced scorecard' approach to strategy developed by Kaplan and Norton (2001).

The Profit Impact of Market Strategy (PIMS) study initiated in the 1970s found, on examining thousands of companies in many industries, that one of the primary determinants of profitability was market share (Buzzell and Gale, 1992). However, other researchers (Reicheld and Sasser, 1990) questioned the findings in relation to service companies and concluded that customer loyalty is a more important determinant of profit in these companies. The service profit chain establishes links between profitability, customer loyalty and employee satisfaction, loyalty and productivity. The links in the chain (Heskett *et al.,* 1997) are as follows:

- Profit and growth are stimulated primarily by customer loyalty.
- Customer loyalty is a direct result of customer satisfaction.
- Customer satisfaction is largely influenced by the value of services provided to customers.
- Value is created by satisfied, loyal, and productive employees.
- Employee satisfaction results primarily from high quality support services and policies that enable employees to deliver results to customers.

# Bibliography


Ashworth, Greg and Larkham, P J: *Building a New Heritage: Tourism, Culture & Identity in the New Europe*, Routledge, London, 1994.

Benefice, Brian G, and Cooper, Chris: *Geography of Travel and Tourism*, Heinemann, London , 1987.

Bernthall, R.: *International Conference for Tourism Educators*, University of Surrey, Guildford , 1988.

Bolshevism, Germy: *Coping with Tourists: European Reactions to Mass Tourism*, Berghahn Books, Oxford, 1995.

Brunt, Paul: *Market Research in Travel and Tourism*, Butterworth Heinemann, Oxford, 1997.

Chandler, Harry and Carter, John: *Chandler's Travels: A Tour of the Life of Harry Chandler*, Quiller Press, London, 1985.

Clark, Mona: *Interpersonal Skills for Hospitality Managers*, Chapman Hill, London, 1995.

Conlin, M. V.: *Proceedings of the Travel and Tourism Research Association twenty-second annual conference*, Hyatt Regency Hotel, Long Beach, California, 1991.

Cooper, C. and Messenger, S.: *Tourism Education and Training for Tourism in Europe*, Italy, 1991.

Davidson, R and Maitland, R: *Tourism Destinations*, Hodder and Stoughton, London, 1997.

Davidson, Rob: *Travel and Tourism in Europe*, Harlow, Addison Wesley Longman, 1998.

Donald E.: *Public Personnel Management: Contexts and Strategies*, Prentice Hall, Upper Saddle River, NJ, 1998.

Eckel, Peter J.: *College & University Foodservice Management Standards*, AVI Pub. Company, Westport, 1985.

Edgell, David L: *International Tourism Policy*, Van Nostrand and Reinhold, New York, 1990.

Emery, William H.: *The Chef's Guide to Practical Restaurant Cookery*, Van Nostrand Reinhold, New York, 1988.

Fowler, Peter: *Heritage and Tourism: In the Global Village*, Retailed, London, 1993.

Frechtling, Douglas C: *Practical Tourism Forecasting*, Butterworth Heinemann, Oxford, 1996.

Gunn, Clare and Var, Turgut: *Tourism Planning*, Retailed, London, 2002.

Hays, Judi Radice: *Restaurant & Food Graphics*, PBC International, Glen Cove, 1994.

Hinkin, Timothy R.: *Cases in Hospitality Management: A Critical Incident Approach*, Wiley, New York , 1995.

Hoffman, Edward: *Project Management Success Stories: Lessons of Project Leaders*, John Wiley & Son, New York, 2000.

Ireland, Lewis: *Quality Management for Projects and Programs*, Upper Darby, PMI, 1991.

Kharbanda, O. and E. Stallworthy: *Waste Management Towards a Sustainable Society*, Auburn House, New York, 1990.

Laws, E.: *The ATTT Tourism Education Handbook,* Tourism Society, London, 1997.

Lucas, Rosemary E.: *Managing Employee Relations in the Hotel and Catering Industry*, Cassell, London, 1995.

MacCannell, Dean: *Tourist, The: A New Theory of the Leisure Class*, Macmillan, London, 1976.

Nijkamp, Peter: *Sustainable Tourism Development*, Avebury, Aldershot, 1995.

Powers, Thomas F.: *Introduction to the Hospitality Industry*, Wiley, New York, 1995.

Richards, G.: *The Development of Tourism in Central and Eastern Europe*, Tilberg University Press, Tilberg, 1996.

Robert C.: *Cases in Hospitality Marketing and Management*, John Wiley, New York, 1997.

Stear, L.: *Design of a Curriculum for Destination Studies*, Annals of Tourism Research, 1981.

Timothy R.: *Cases in Hospitality Management: A Critical Incident Approach*, Wiley, New York, 1995.

Umbreit, T.: *The Role of Education in the Tourist Industry*, University of Utah, Salt Lake City, 1987.

Weiler, B: *Ethnic Tourism*, Belhaven/Wiley, 1992.

# Index

**M**



**N**



**P**



**Q**



**R**



**S**



**T**



**V**



❑❑❑